THE RESHAPING OF AMERICA'S GAME

THE RESHAPING OF AMERICA'S GAME

Major League Baseball after the Players' Strike

Bryan Soderholm-Difatte

ROWMAN & LITTLEFIELD
Lanham • Boulder • New York • London

Published by Rowman & Littlefield
An imprint of The Rowman & Littlefield Publishing Group, Inc.
4501 Forbes Boulevard, Suite 200, Lanham, Maryland 20706
www.rowman.com

6 Tinworth Street, London SE11 5AL, United Kingdom

British Library Cataloguing in Publication Information Available

Library of Congress Cataloging-in-Publication Data

Names: Soderholm-Difatte, Bryan, author.
Title: The reshaping of America's game : Major League Baseball after the players' strike / Bryan
    Soderholm-Difatte.
Description: Lanham, Maryland : Rowman & Littlefield Publishing Group, 2021. | Includes biblio-
    graphical references and index. | Summary: "The Reshaping of America's Game describes the
    major developments and challenges that took place in Major League Baseball during the 25-plus
    years following the players' strike, including cheating scandals, steroids, analytics, and changing
    demographics"—Provided by publisher.
Identifiers: LCCN 2020043447 (print) | LCCN 2020043448 (ebook) | ISBN 9781538145951 (cloth) |
    ISBN 9781538145968 (epub)
Subjects: LCSH: Baseball—United States—History—20th century. | Baseball—United States—His-
    tory—21st century. | Baseball—Corrupt practices—United States. | Baseball—Statistical meth-
    ods. | Major League Baseball (Organization)—History.
Classification: LCC GV863.A1 S6885 2021 (print) | LCC GV863.A1 (ebook) | DDC 796.3570973—
    dc23
LC record available at https://lccn.loc.gov/2020043447
LC ebook record available at https://lccn.loc.gov/2020043448

To Jodi, to whom I am so grateful for all that she has brought to my life.

CONTENTS

PREFACE

All things considered, the 25 years since the players' strike ended have been arguably the most dynamic quarter century in baseball history. The country and the world, increasingly interdependent, raced into the new millennium. Major League Baseball no longer had the luxury of timeless tradition to fall back on, even if timeless tradition remained its bedrock. Growing the game required appealing to the new generation of millennials operating in a much faster-speed world while continuing to nurture older generations who thrive on the slower pace and respect for the history of the game they grew up with.

As a sport to be watched, Major League Baseball had long been eclipsed by the speed and athleticism, clash and fury, of the NFL and was competing with (if not overtaken by) the speed and quickness of the NBA. For younger baseball watchers, it was about highlights; games that had consequence; never-ending scrutinizing of players, managers, and the front office; and the postseason. Older fans appreciated all that but were also content with the solace and narrative of a long season—for which most younger fans lacked patience—and the nostalgia it brought of their younger years. For Major League Baseball, it has been the balancing act between entertainment and tradition that has reshaped the game.

Throughout its history, the institution of Major League Baseball has had to grapple with an innate "no change is good change" conservative bias masquerading as blessed nostalgia for the traditions of the game (as in baseball forever in the good old days), which threatened to leave the national pastime looking retrograde—on race, on geography, on its size, on labor relations—as America grew and prospered in the twentieth century, particularly after World War II. On race. On geography. On size. On labor relations.

Major League Baseball shamefully excluded Black players until Branch Rickey unilaterally signed Jackie Robinson to play for the Brooklyn Dodgers' top farm team in 1946 and promoted him to the major-league club in 1947, notwithstanding fierce opposition to his move and to the very idea of integration by virtually every other major-league franchise. Although Robinson and other African American and Latino trailblazers in the 1950s certainly put the lie to specious arguments that Black players were not as good as white major leaguers, most franchises were slow to integrate at the major-league level.

And Major League Baseball's "no change is good change" approach was visibly apparent in its franchise geography remaining exactly the same for half a century between 1903 and 1952—16 teams in 10 cities— never mind that America extended from sea to shining sea all those years and that its population had nearly doubled from 76.2 million in 1900 to 151.3 million in 1950, according to the US Census. With no franchises on the West Coast, especially now that air transportation had substantially reduced the time to get there from when the country relied on railroads for cross-country travel, the league was ignoring a rapidly growing part of the country where the Triple-A level of baseball played in the Pacific Coast League was quite popular.

If by midcentury excluding Black players from Major League Baseball had become morally unsustainable in post–World War II America, having so many teams in so few cities had become economically unsustainable. Five franchises moved to new cities in the 1950s, including the Dodgers and Giants, who left New York City (Brooklyn and Manhattan) for California (Los Angeles and San Francisco), finally extending the major leagues' geographic horizon to the West Coast. But it was not until 1961 and 1962 that finally, after 60 years of the same 16 teams, existing franchise owners agreed on the necessity of admitting newcomers to their exclusive club called Major League Baseball: four new teams, two each in the American and National Leagues.

For all the teams that slow-walked integration, with varying not-credible justifications for doing so, Major League Baseball came to embrace integration and basked in the praise of being at the forefront of the civil rights movement. And expansion proved lucrative by growing the indus-

try, especially with the advent of Eastern and Western Division alignments and a championship series in each league leading into the World
Series in the major leagues' second round of expansion in 1969, boosting
fan interest and television revenues. Eight years later, the American
League added two new franchises. The National League did the same in
1993.

Major League Baseball now had 28 teams playing in 26 North
American cities, including two in Canada, and was about to introduce a
three-division alignment—Eastern, Central, and Western—for both
leagues and a new "wild card" dimension to the postseason. Beginning in
1994, the three division winners and the second-place team with the best
record in each league would meet in two league division series, the winners of which would advance to the league championship series, whose
winning teams would play in the World Series. Except there was no
World Series—or any postseason—in 1994, because the one significant
change that franchise owners fought hard against and did not come to
embrace was free agency. The devastating players strike that aborted the
1994 season in August and did not end until April 1995 was to defend the
right to free agency for players with six major-league seasons behind
them—a right extending back less than two decades—against franchise
owners' self-interested imperative to roll it back.

Together with *America's Game in the Wild-Card Era: From Strike to
Pandemic*, this book covers the years from baseball's return from the
strike in 1995 to the COVID-19 pandemic of 2020 that led to a major-
league season unlike any other: only 60 games, with no fans in the stands.

This book focuses on the factors and challenges that have reshaped the
game in the 25 years since the strike, while *America's Game in the Wild-
Card Era* covers the competitive environment. The two books together
complete a history of Major League Baseball that began with *America's
Game: A History of Major League Baseball Through World War II*
(2018), followed up by *Tumultuous Times in America's Game: From
Jackie Robinson's Breakthrough to the War over Free Agency* (2019).

INTRODUCTION

Prelude to Baseball's Great Reckoning

Somewhere in this favored land the sun is shining bright,
Movies are playing somewhere, and somewhere hearts are light;
And somewhere adults are shouting, and somewhere children laugh,
But there is no joy in Baseball—*The Mighty Game's on Strike.*

(Borrowing from Ernest Thayer's 1888 classic ballad "Casey at the
Bat," revised for 1994)

It had come to this: a day of reckoning. On August 12, 1994, exactly 13 years and two days after a devastating two-month shutdown of Major League Baseball by a players' strike in the middle of the 1981 season ended, the players were once again on strike.

This strike would be far more serious and have far more cataclysmic consequences for the national pastime. It ultimately cost Major League Baseball the entire postseason, including the World Series. The last time there was no World Series was way back in 1904, before the annual Fall Classic between Major League Baseball's American League and National League pennant winners had become an institution; the first World Series had been played only the year before, in 1903. When America went "over there" to Europe to fight in World War I, the 1918 minor-league season was abruptly ended in midsummer and the major leagues terminated their season at the beginning of September, one month short of its scheduled end. But the 1918 World Series was played. When America fought three years on multiple fronts in World War II—in the Pacific, in North Africa, in Europe—and the home front endured strict rationing of strategic materials, the major leagues played a full 154-game schedule each season, even though teams were decimated by the loss of players—including major-league headliners—serving their country in wartime. The All-Star Game was cancelled in 1945, but the World Series was played every year. In both world wars, the president of the United States thought it important that Major League Baseball play on, primarily to help keep up morale on the home front and for soldiers in uniform on the front lines.

America was not at war in 1994. There was no national emergency. But Major League Baseball's shutdown that year—and no World Series—was a stark reminder that, while baseball is fundamentally a sport, it is also an industry. And for baseball's franchise owners, there was no issue more fraught with peril, to the point of even being an existential threat, than player relations. The battle lines were over teams' control of their players, explicitly limiting for whom they played and how much they were paid.

The historical legal underpinning for that state of affairs—the reserve clause in player contracts—was as old as Major League Baseball itself. Its original intent was to bring the roster and payroll stability the new industry required to be a viable business enterprise and to grow in the 1880s by precluding players, particularly baseball's best players, from becoming free agents at the end of every season to sign with whichever team offered them the most money. The reserve clause was standard in all player contracts, most of which were for one year at a time. By allowing teams to renew any player's contract for the next year if a new deal could not be reached, it effectively bound players to their teams in perpetuity until their rights were traded or sold to another team, which then assumed the contract, or they were released.

The reserve clause was a poison pill for the players. They could not negotiate their worth on a free market. Teams used it to control their payrolls by limiting the salaries of their best players, who in turn were not paid fair market value. Salary suppression for baseball's highest-paid players had the cascade effect of limiting the baseball earning potential of the much larger number of less-talented players that round out major-league rosters. This did not mean that the best players did not have leverage with the owners to command very handsome salaries. Baseball was a business, after all. Its assets were the players whose exploits brought in the fans and grew the game's popularity. It was not in their interest for owners to alienate their fan base by getting into protracted salary disputes with their best players, no matter how much they played the "greedy ingrate" card against them. And it was not in Major League Baseball's institutional interests for the best players to call their owners' bluff by sitting out a season. Owners sometimes traded (or sold) their best players when their salary demands became exorbitant but were nonetheless within reason.

Babe Ruth frequently used the popularity of his soaring home runs to ensure he had by far the highest salary in baseball, famously saying he had a "better year" than Herbert Hoover (after America plunged into the Great Depression in 1929) when queried about how he felt about being paid more than the president of the United States. In 1947 Bob Feller negotiated a contract with Cleveland that included a bonus provision based on the substantially greater attendance on days he pitched than in the Indians' other games. Because of the reserve clause, however, neither Ruth nor Feller nor any other of the best-paid major leaguers had sufficient leverage to earn their true market value, and lesser players had no leverage at all.

Every effort by the players to improve their lot in combating the reserve clause and negotiating better salaries met with failure. Most famously, the United States Supreme Court ruled unanimously in 1922 that the reserve clause did not violate antitrust statutes because Organized Baseball was not interstate commerce as defined in antitrust legislation. It was a definitive victory for Major League Baseball at the expense of its players, but one the owners knew rested on a thin definitional reed that might at some point be revisited. Fifty years later, in outfielder Curt Flood's legal challenge to the reserve clause, the Supreme Court affirmed the 1922 ruling. But this time it was a split decision, with Justice Thurgood Marshall suggesting that federal labor statutes might be more relevant than antitrust regulations when it came to the legal vulnerability of the reserve clause.

Enter Marvin Miller, the feisty head of the Major League Baseball Players Association. Miller was an aggressive advocate for players' rights in negotiating collective bargaining agreements with Major League Baseball. And, despite the owners' best efforts to warn players away from supporting *his* agenda, his agenda was really the players' agenda, and they had Marvin Miller's back. By 1973, pressured by Miller's relentlessness and having endured the major leagues' first players' strike, which delayed the start of the 1972 season, the owners had agreed to neutral salary arbitration for players with at least two years in the major leagues (since raised to three) and to an independent arbitrator to hear player grievances.

In December 1975, baseball's independent arbitrator ruled that Andy Messersmith, having pitched for the Los Angeles Dodgers that year without signing new contract, was a free agent. The standard contract's reserve clause, said the arbitrator in Messersmith's union-backed case, applied *only* for the one year specified for a player without a new contract, contrary to the owners' contention that the reserve clause could be renewed year after year after year no matter whether the player ever signed a new contract. Henceforth, any players playing a year without a contract would also be free agents. Bowing to the logic of the owners' argument that chaos would ensue if every player could be a free agent nearly every year, Miller negotiated a regimen where players would remain under franchise control in their first six years as major leaguers, subject to binding salary arbitration after three years, after which they would be eligible to sell their services to the highest bidder on the free-agent market.

Free agency did for the players what they wanted. With multiple teams competing to sign the best free agents in any year's off-season market—and particularly since New York Yankees owner George Steinbrenner's enthusiasm for corralling the best players was driving up the bidding—player salaries escalated exponentially. This had the cascade effect of setting a market value baseline for non–free agent players eligible for salary arbitration. All of which made the owners determined to roll back free agency. In the 1981 negotiations for the next collective bargaining agreement, they insisted the union agree that teams signing a "premier" free agent had to compensate his former team with a player off its major-league roster, which made it less a free agent signing than a trade. They dared the players to go on strike. The players did. The strikes lasted two months before the owners backed down. In the mid- and late 1980s, the owners tried a coordinated conspiracy to suppress player salaries—first by refusing to engage with free agents in the marketplace, then by keeping each other informed about which free agents they wanted to keep or go after and what salaries and terms they were offering to players on the market. The owners' comeuppance came when baseball's independent arbitrator ruled against them on the charge of collusion and ordered them to pay $280 million in damages to cover estimated lost salary and years in the contracts signed by free agents during the collusion years.

As devastating as the collusion ruling and associated penalties were to Major League Baseball institutionally, baseball's owners were more determined than ever to neuter free agency and end, once and for all, the escalation in player salaries—not just for free agents, but for all players—despite the fact that their worst-case scenarios for the impact of free agency had not come to pass. Free agency did not ruin competitiveness because the richest teams cornered every year's market on the best players available; the 1980s were the most competitive decade in baseball history, with 20 of the major leagues' 26 teams winning at least one division title, and the high-spending Yankees just one. Free agency did not lead to financial ruin for the national pastime. In large part because of lucrative cable television contracts, exciting division races and compelling postseason series made Major League Baseball more profitable than ever.

The owners nonetheless insisted free agency was economically devastating to Major League Baseball. They claimed that most teams were losing money and that small-market teams in particular were financially struggling and could not compete in an environment without a cap on player salaries. Led by hard-liners with Allan "Bud" Selig, owner of the small-market Milwaukee Brewers, out front, franchise owners prepared for an all-or-nothing showdown with the players' union, now led by Donald Fehr—as dedicated to the cause and pugnacious as Marvin Miller. Their goal was to neutralize free agency by demanding the players accept a salary cap on roster payrolls and a revenue-sharing plan for major-league teams. But first they cleared the deck by ousting Commissioner Fay Vincent, whom they considered an unreliable advocate for the hard-line position he was expected to uphold, and naming Selig "acting" commissioner with full authority to take on the players' union.

It all came to a head in the summer of '94. Adhering to Selig's absolute "no compromise" stand on a salary cap when negotiations with the players stalemated, the owners were prepared to call the union's bluff about going on strike in the absence of a new collective bargaining agreement that protected the totality of free agency. Persuaded by Selig's assurance that major-league players had so much to lose in salary that they would not stay on strike for long, baseball's owners were prepared to sacrifice the rest of the 1994 season, if it came to that.

It did come to that. When major-league players began their open-ended strike on August 12, nobody knew how long the strike might last. But the commitment of both sides to their position suggested it might last a very long time. Baseball's real day of reckoning, therefore, would not come until Major League Baseball returned to the fields of dreams in front of . . . how many fans, and what size TV audience?

Part I

Baseball Back in Business

I

BASEBALL IN RECOVERY

Every gambit Selig tried to end the players' strike on the owners' terms failed. He threatened to cancel the rest of the 1994 season and the World Series unless the players caved. They didn't. There was no World Series. In November, the owners proposed a tax on teams exceeding a certain payroll threshold as an alternative to a salary cap on team payrolls. The players saw that as a salary cap in all but name, which it was. The owners threatened to declare an impasse and implement their salary cap and revenue-sharing plan and take their chances in court. Selig backed down, knowing the owners would lose, when President Bill Clinton offered a mediator to help the two sides reach a settlement. When the National Labor Relations Board (NLRB) warned that an unfair labor practices complaint was about to be issued against Major League Baseball, the owners agreed to revert to the terms of the last collective bargaining agreement, only to have Selig declare that henceforth the owners' player relations committee—and that committee alone, not individual teams—could negotiate player contracts, which would have effectively rendered the free agent market meaningless.

Nothing was resolved by the time spring training 1995 beckoned. The president of the United States himself directly intervened, telling both sides at the White House that if baseball could not resolve its own issues, he would ask Congress to take it up legislatively, which risked threatening baseball's enduring antitrust exemption. Selig announced that Major League Baseball was prepared to play the 1995 season with replacement players, hoping to crack the players' unity. The owners even thought they had a stalking horse in Philadelphia Phillies stars Lenny Dykstra and Darren Daulton. That gambit failed, too. Reading from notes at a well-attended players' union meeting that most likely were crafted by team executives, Dykstra's suggestion that it was time to make a deal with the owners provoked such a backlash that he ended up saying he was fully behind the players' stand. What happened instead was that Detroit's Sparky Anderson, the most highly esteemed manager in baseball, said he would not manage replacement players; Major League Baseball was told that Canadian law prohibited the use of strikebreakers, so Toronto's Blue Jays would need to find a new home in the United States if they played with a team of replacements; Orioles owner Peter Angelos, whose star player Cal Ripken Jr.'s consecutive-games streak was on the line, declared that Baltimore would not use replacement players; and minor-leaguers were warned by the players' union that they would be considered scabs and banned from membership and its privileges if they agreed to be replacements.

In mid-March, the NLRB brought the players' case against baseball's owners before a federal court in the Southern District of New York. The judge to whom the case was assigned was Sonia Sotomayor, on her way to an ultimate appointment as an associate justice on the United States Supreme Court. She grew up in the Bronx, an avid Yankees fan. On the last day of March, with the scheduled Opening Day just days away, Sotomayor ruled that the owners could not impose their own salary cap and revenue-sharing plan on the players, that the terms of the previous collective bargaining agreement prevailed until a new agreement was reached, and that neither side—and this meant specifically the owners—could declare an impasse without her approval. Her ruling did not itself end the strike, but the owners now clearly understood that continuing their hard-line stance would result in financial penalties that were likely to far exceed the $280 million they had been assessed over collusion. 'Twas far better to accept that going for broke trying to neutralize free agency had failed, return to the playing fields in 1995, and come back to the issue with the understanding that free agency was forever and maybe there were other ways to contain rising player salaries.

Major-league players returned to often hostile receptions at ballparks around the country. Union officials were booed. So was the acting commissioner. Attendance was down everywhere. No National League ballclub in 1995 came close to their average attendance per game in 1994 before the strike hit. Only three American League teams drew more people per game to their ballparks in 1995 than the previous year—the Cleveland Indians, dominating the Central Division and playing just their second season in an impressive new downtown ballpark, by less than 1 percent; the California Angels, contending for the Western Division title after having the worst record in the league in the strike-shortened 1994 season, by 1 percent; and the Boston Red Sox, taking early command of the AL East after failing to compete since their 1990 division title, by an appreciable 8 percent. Not even the Baltimore Orioles, with their own brand-new ballpark on the waterfront that had opened in 1992 and Ripken in pursuit of Lou Gehrig's 2,130 consecutive games played, matched their average attendance from before the strike, although they were the only team whose attendance exceeded 3 million.

But Oriole Park at Camden Yards was filled to capacity on September 5, 1995, when Ripken, going 3-for-5 with a home run against the Angels, tied Gehrig. Camden Yards was sold out again the next day as Ripken played his 2,131st game in a streak that started on May 30, 1982. The president of the United States was there. So was Selig. And so was Joe DiMaggio, a teammate of Gehrig's. More than 5 million nationwide watched on TV when, rising to the occasion, Ripken went 2-for-4 with another home run. A few voices, including traditionalists who feared Gehrig's legacy was now somehow diminished, had argued that Ripken should voluntarily have ended his streak at 2,130 to honor Gehrig, whose consecutive-games streak came to an end on April 30, 1939, only because he was suffering from amyotrophic lateral sclerosis—the disease that came to bear his name—and so might have continued on much longer had he been a healthy 36-year-old.

It was, however, a unifying moment for baseball fans across the country—however alienated they may have been because of the strike that canceled the World Series—and, indeed, for all of America. Once the game was official, with the Orioles leading, 3–1, in the middle of the fifth, amid a display of fireworks, Ripken stepped out of the dugout for several curtain calls to acknowledge his hometown fans' celebration of his achievement as a ballplayer and all that he represented as a person. There was no sitting down. There was no quieting down. It almost seemed there was no way the game was going to go on. Finally, in recognition of what the fans meant to him (and to baseball), with prodding from some of his teammates, Cal Ripken began a slow jog around the playing field—along the grandstand railing up the right field line, around the outfield, along the grandstand railing down the left field line, past the Angels dugout where every member of the opposing team applauded the Baltimore shortstop for all that he was, and back to the Orioles dugout. It was a lovefest.

Major League Baseball needed Cal Ripken to do what he did at that moment, in a new stadium built to evoke the classic feel of early twentieth-century ballparks. His jog around the field was not in any way to be confused with a victory lap. Ripken's appeal was not just his baseball skills, his work ethic, his commitment to DiMaggio's principle to always play his best because you never know who might be watching for the first time. It was his commitment to Baltimore rather than seeking to be better paid elsewhere (such as New York), his community engagement, his reserved demeanor and humility, his innate decency. His jog was a *Field of Dreams* moment—a restoration of the mythic purity of the game of baseball, a cleansing of baseball's soul that had been sullied by the strike. The owners' intransigence and the players' strike had betrayed the game. Ripken's lap around the ball field, his reception of the adoration given him, and his appreciation to the fans for being there for baseball, seemed to exorcize the devil in the game. The feeling was mutual between player and fans. It would not be too much of an exaggeration to say that if Babe Ruth saved Major League Baseball from the Black Sox scandal, then Cal Ripken Jr. saved Major League Baseball from the strike that canceled a World Series.

The 1995 season was also rescued by a scintillating five-game division series between the wild-card New York Yankees and the Seattle Mariners, who surged to the AL Western Division title for the first time in franchise history after overcoming a 12½-game deficit with just 38 games remaining. The Mariners lost the first two games in New York, then won the next three in Seattle, coming from behind in all three games and winning the final game in 11 innings, to advance to the American League Championship Series. The drama of that series was an immediate validation of the new three-round postseason format occasioned by Major League Baseball's realignment to three divisions and a wild card in each league.

The next year, with the major leagues back to a full 162-game schedule (the 1995 season had been shortened by 18 games to allow the players a truncated spring training once Sotomayor's end-of-March ruling finally ended the strike), baseball's continuing recovery was facilitated by the arrival of a pair of compelling shortstops, friends and rivals, who played on opposite coasts. They sat on their respective team's benches during the epic 1995 Seattle–New York Division Series, one on the Mariners' active roster, the other as a prospect invited to share in the postseason experience, even if not as a player. The former was Alex Rodriguez, the latter was Derek Jeter. Both were given charge of the all-important shortstop position in 1996, beginning on Opening Day. Both had epic seasons.

Turning 21 on July 27, A-Rod, as Rodriguez would soon enough be universally known, became the major leagues' third-youngest batting champion since the start of the twentieth century after 20-year-olds Al Kaline in 1955 and Ty Cobb in 1907. (Ironically, Cobb and Kaline both played for Detroit and were born within a day of each other, 48 years apart—tyrannical Tyrus on December 18 and "Mr. Tiger" on December 19.) A-Rod's .358 average and 54 doubles led both leagues, and his 141 runs topped the AL. He also had 215 hits, belted 36 home runs, and drove in 123 runs. In his first year as a regular, Rodriguez narrowly missed by four votes being the American League's Most Valuable Player. Derek Jeter, a year older and playing a leadership role in helping the Yankees win the division, the pennant, and their first World Series since 1978, was unanimously voted the AL's Rookie of the Year. And on the first of September, Nomar Garciaparra, another compelling young shortstop, started his first major-league game for the Boston Red Sox.

However much Ripken's come-together-America moment, the exploits of the game's best players and the emergence of new stars like Jeter and A-Rod, and the excitement of division races, the wild card, and an extended postseason helped revive fans' interest in the national pastime, all was not yet forgiven. A profound sense of betrayal was still keeping many faithful away from major-league ballparks. In fact, per-game home attendance in 1996 for 10 of the majors' 28 teams declined from 1995—the first year back from the strike—and only four clubs exceeded their average attendance from the 1994 strike season. Even the Yankees, despite winning their first division title since 1981 with a compelling cast of players, failed to match their attendance from 1993—the last time a full 162-game schedule was played. Overall, 10 million fewer fans—60.2 million in 1996—attended major-league games than the 70.3 million who had attended three years before, in 1993.

And while Major League Baseball was struggling to make headway in winning back the fans, the issues that led to the devastating strike were still not resolved. Negotiations for a new collective bargaining agreement between the Major League Baseball Players Association and Major League Baseball did not begin until November 1995, after a federal appeals court, as expected, affirmed Sotomayor's ruling in March that forced the owners to back down and cleared the way for the 1995 baseball season. It wasn't until a year later that an agreed deal between the players' union and the owners' lead negotiator, Randy Levine, most recently New York City's commissioner of labor, was presented to the owners for approval. There was, of course, no salary cap—a redline the owners knew could not be even broached with any hope of getting a deal. The players, however, chastened by the pox-on-both-your-houses attitude that prevailed among Americans during the 1994–1995 strike, made two significant concessions. They agreed to a modest payroll tax that would contribute to the owners' revenue-sharing plan and, for the first three years of the new five-year agreement, to a trial run of a "luxury tax" on teams exceeding a designated player payroll threshold, provided the threshold was at a level high enough that few clubs would reach it.

Then it all came undone, the first public indication of which was Acting Commissioner Bud Selig and union president Donald Fehr screaming at each other in full view of the cameras during Game Six of the 1996 World Series. Hard-liners among the owners insisted that the deal Levine reached with the union, after Selig had empowered him with full authority to negotiate on their behalf, was unacceptable. Despite being warned by Levine that spurning an agreement he had negotiated in good faith on their behalf would lead to an outcome even more catastrophic than what happened in 1994—the players would go on strike, the owners would lose in court, and the players' union would never again have faith in the owners' integrity—Selig, almost certainly against his better judgment but knowing there was enough hard-line opposition that the supposedly finalized agreement would be rejected, maneuvered for more votes against it to give the owners greater leverage back at the negotiating table. In fact, they had none. As Levine predicted, the union rejected the owners' new demands outright, the most unacceptable of which was there were no limits on how many teams could be assessed a luxury tax—which in effect would be a salary cap.

And then what was undone came undone itself on November 19 when Chicago White Sox owner Jerry Reinsdorf, the hardest of the hard-liners, who many believed had outsized influence with Selig, signed Cleveland's slugging free-agent outfielder Albert Belle to a five-year, $55 million deal. It was the most lucrative contract any major-league player had yet received, and it included a provision that guaranteed he would remain one of the three highest-paid players for the duration of his contract even if Reinsdorf had to throw more money into it. Reinsdorf explained that like any owner, he had to do what was best for his team. If that meant outbidding rival franchises for the services of an exceptional player on the free agent market, so be it; until there were restraints in place, that was the system within which he must operate to give his team the best chance to win. "It doesn't mean I like the system," he said.

It's understandable that Reinsdorf, the owner of a team he wanted to be successful, channeled his inner George Steinbrenner in signing Belle. One of baseball's most fearsome sluggers, Belle had powered Cleveland—the White Sox' rival in the AL Central—to division titles the two previous years, crashing 98 home runs (which almost certainly would have been more than 100 had the 1995 season been the full 162 games instead of 144 because of the strike) and driving in 274 runs while batting .314. And now he was a free agent. Having the financial resources to compete in the bidding for Belle, knowing he would command a hefty contract, Reinsdorf couldn't resist—even knowing full well Belle's reputation for being brash, outspoken, impolitic in his dealings with the media, and a public relations nightmare for his team—especially since pairing Belle in Chicago's batting order with first baseman Frank Thomas, who had 80 homers, 245 runs batted in, a .329 batting average, and a .457 on-base percentage in 1995 and 1996, would give the White Sox baseball's most intimidating power duo.

Unapologetic about signing Belle, Reinsdorf was firm nonetheless that Levine's deal with the players' union was unacceptable and that the owners should once again go to the brink—and beyond, if necessary—to carry the day. As in 1994, he believed the players would not remain unified in a strike for very long. Having taken advantage of the free agent system to improve his ball club, Reinsdorf was, in effect, asking his fellow owners to protect him from himself. A week later, the owners overwhelmingly approved the deal Levine had negotiated—and Reinsdorf most strongly still opposed—without changes. They did so, presumably shamefacedly, it being the lead driver of the owners' hard-line position had just undercut that very position.

For the players and their union, Reinsdorf's Albert Belle signing almost certainly calmed anxieties that the luxury tax might morph into a de facto salary cap that would reduce free agents' leverage and lower salaries across the spectrum of major-league players. What was important was to keep the payroll tax threshold high enough that few teams would exceed it, and those teams that did—franchises like Steinbrenner's Yankees and maybe even Reinsdorf's White Sox—would be willing to pay the tax for the privilege of improving their ball club with the best players available on the free agent market.

Free agency was alive and well, and "super-agent" Scott Boras was more than willing to strongly recommend to his top-tier player clients that they declare for free agency rather than accept a lesser deal than they might otherwise get on the market to stay with their current team. Boras was notorious for leveraging Steinbrenner and the well-heeled Yankees to increase his clients' paydays or to up the ante with other teams. In 1998, after the Yankees had just completed a championship season for the ages—114 wins in the regular season and a record-setting 125 wins including the postseason—Boras played hardball with the Yankees on behalf of Bernie Williams, their star center fielder. Williams had just won a batting title and led the team in both slugging and on-base percentage. Boras and Williams were insisting on at least seven years with an average annual salary of $15 million. Steinbrenner was committed to no more than five years with an average annual salary of $12 million.

The Yankees played their hand by making it known they were going after Albert Belle, who was back on the free-agent market after two years in Chicago. Meanwhile, Williams was set to accept an offer of seven years for more than $90 million from the Yankees' division archrivals in Boston. Belle, however, decided he preferred to be in Baltimore, much less of a pressure-cooker media market than New York. Williams called Steinbrenner to say he preferred to stay in New York, where he had begun his career, but needed "the kind of offer you make to free agents from other teams that have never done anything for the Yankees." Steinbrenner increased the Yankees' offer to seven years and $87.5 million to keep him in New York. Williams's was now the highest free-agent contract ever— until pitcher Kevin Brown, another Boras client, got seven years and $105 million from the Dodgers less than three weeks later.

Two years later, Alex Rodriguez, also represented by Scott Boras, became a free agent. He had just had his third-straight 40-homer season in 2000, with a then-career-high 132 RBIs, and batted better than .300 for the fourth time in his five years as Seattle's shortstop. He was the best shortstop in baseball, not only a force at the plate but excellent defensively. A-Rod's combination of hitting prowess, power, speed, and defense had him already—at the age of 25—being compared with the greatest shortstops of all time. Many there were who thought that by the end of his career Alex Rodriguez would be in the same conversation as Honus Wagner as the best ever to play his position—and one of the best to ever play the game.

It was obvious that very few teams would be able to afford what A-Rod was demanding on the open market. Steinbrenner was not shopping for him—not yet, anyway—in large part because the Yankees had their own stellar shortstop, Derek Jeter. The other team in New York, however—the Mets, who had just lost the 2000 World Series to the Yankees in five games—did romance him, if for no other reason than Rodriguez would immeasurably improve the Mets' prospects for many repeat trips to the World Series. Even more important, A-Rod would be pitch perfect for taking on the Yankees and their shortstop Jeter for the allegiance of New York's millions of baseball fans. Rodriguez's asking price, however, was too much: A-Rod was not willing to give a discount to join the team he grew up rooting for, and the Mets front office claimed to be put off by his extravagant demands for special privileges, apparently including access to a private jet. The Mets' romantic interest did not lead to ardent pursuit.

Instead, it was the Texas Rangers that signed Alex Rodriguez, a team that in 2000 had just plummeted from a franchise-record 95 wins the previous year, and three AL Western Division titles in four years, to 91 losses and last place in the division. A team that had never made it out of the division series round of the postseason. A team with enough weaknesses that, even with the extraordinary A-Rod playing shortstop and batting in the middle of the order, did not figure to be competitive for a championship in the near future, especially not with the jaw-dropping contract—10 years and $252 million, or $25.2 million a year—Rangers owner Tom Hicks gave to the young superstar. In 2001, A-Rod's paycheck alone would account for 25 percent of the Rangers' player pay-

roll—that's for one player in a game in which 10 (including the designated hitter in the American League) must start every day.

Bud Selig, now officially the commissioner, was apoplectic about the
Texas Rangers making Alex Rodriguez a 252 million-dollar man. Major-
league players and their union were amazed but hardly dismayed, both for
the same reason. While A-Rod may have been such an exceptionally
talented ballplayer that nobody was likely to break his record contract in
terms of total value or average annual salary anytime soon, his new
contract set the bottom line much higher than it had been, or otherwise
would be, for highly coveted free agents. As it happened, the luxury tax
on teams exceeding the player payroll threshold that the players had
agreed to in the 1996 collective bargaining agreement expired in the year
2000. Selig was determined to bring it back.

As for A-Rod, he was every bit the A-star he was paid to be the first
three years of his new deal. But while his team finished last each year, his
friend and rival Derek Jeter went to his fifth and sixth World Series.
Rodriguez, wanting to play for a winner; Hicks, finding his expensive
investment was not helping the Rangers win; and Steinbrenner, ever on
the lookout for the best player in baseball, made it perhaps inevitable that
in 2004 A-Rod—and the remainder of his contract—would be traded to
the Yankees.

2

SUPERPOWERS

How the Braves and Yankees Got That Way

In baseball's first year back from the strike in 1995, Atlanta's Braves decisively won their division with the best record in the National League, had an easy time plowing through their division series and the National League Championship Series, and handily won the World Series against Cleveland—the team with the best record in the majors. They picked up where they left off in 1993, not counting 1994 when no division titles were awarded and no postseason played because of the players strike, although in a new division. The Braves had won three division titles in a row in the NL West and went to two World Series, losing both. Now in the geographically more logical NL East, the Braves would win their division eleven straight years before their always-first string ran out in 2006.

In 1996, New York's Yankees won the AL East without much drama, had an easy time plowing through the division and league championship series, and beat the Braves in the World Series. After having to settle for the wild card the next year, in 1998 the Yankees won their first of nine straight division titles. It was their third of 13 consecutive trips to the postseason, beginning with their wild-card entry in 1995, before missing out in 2008. Only the 1991–2005 Braves, with their 14 division titles in a row, have a longer history of consecutive years in the postseason. Atlanta went to five World Series in their 14-year run, the last in 1999, but won just one. The 1996–2007 Yankees played in six World Series, winning four.

They were baseball's new superpowers—parallel decade-long dynasties the likes of which baseball had not seen since the Yankees' dominance of the American League from 1947 to 1964 and the Brooklyn Dodgers' dominance of the National League from 1947 to 1956. Atlanta's dynasty was characterized by exceptional pitching, headlined by a trio of future Hall of Fame pitchers—Greg Maddux (arriving as a free agent in 1993), Tom Glavine, and John Smoltz. The Braves led the majors in fewest runs allowed 11 consecutive years from 1992 to 2002. The latest iteration of the Yankees' "forever" dynasty that dated back to Babe Ruth and their first pennant in 1921 was headlined by a quintet of home-grown stars—Derek Jeter, Mariano Rivera, Andy Pettitte, Jorge Posada, and Bernie Williams.

Nobody could have seen a baseball superpower coming when Braves general manager Bobby Cox took over as manager in June 1990. The Braves finished last that year with the worst record in the major leagues. It was their third straight last-place season, and fourth in five years. Although there were no great expectations for the Braves entering the 1990s, Cox as GM since October 1985 had been building the foundation for a competitive team through player development and astute trades and free agent signings. When he stepped down from the executive suite to the dugout, the Braves already had on their major-league roster pitchers Tom Glavine, John Smoltz, Steve Avery, and Charlie Leibrandt. Glavine and Avery had been signed by Atlanta in baseball's annual amateur draft. Smoltz, a minor-league prospect, and Leibrandt, an established veteran, were acquired in trades. Also on the big-league roster were outfielders David Justice and Ron Gant and middle infielders Mark Lemke and Jeff Blauser, all products of Atlanta's rejuvenated minor-league system. They would be the core players that kick-started Atlanta's Brave dynasty.

In December 1990 John Schuerholz, the Braves' new general manager, signed Cardinals free agent third baseman Terry Pendleton, mostly for the veteran leadership he could provide. Pendleton, at best an average major-league player in his seven St. Louis seasons, gave the Braves much more than that. He was their best position player each of the next two years as the Braves rose to become the National League's team to beat. Leading the league in hits and batting average, and slugging 22 homers (his previous career-high was 13), Pendleton beat out Barry Bonds for the Most Valuable Player Award. With due respect to the Braves' exceptional starting pitching, Pendleton was the player most responsible for them becoming the first team in history to rise from last place and the worst record in the majors to play in the World Series. In 1992 Pendleton had another exceptional year, and the Braves were back in the World Series.

Owned by cable TV magnate Ted Turner, the Braves televised their games nationwide on Turner's cable network, giving his team a national following as well as lucrative broadcast revenues. Marketing the Braves across the country was strong incentive to make and keep the team competitive, and cable revenues provided the means. In 1993 the Braves signed Greg Maddux to the largest free agent contract given a pitcher, and in July traded for high-priced San Diego Padres first baseman Fred McGriff to bolster an unexpectedly anemic offense. Atlanta stormed from 10 games back of the Giants on July 22 to win 104 games and another NL West division title. The Braves went from the third-lowest player payroll in the National League in 1991, when they unexpectedly went from last place to the World Series, to the NL team with the highest payroll every year from 1994 to 1998, exceeded most years only by a handful of American League clubs.

Gone after the 1997 season were first baseman McGriff, second baseman Lemke, shortstop Blauser, and backup shortstop Rafael Belliard. Gant was released in spring training 1994 after breaking his leg driving an all-terrain recreational vehicle; Pendleton left as a free agent in 1995; and Justice was traded in the spring of 1997 after spending nearly the entire 1996 season on the disabled list. In the meantime, the Braves strengthened their roster by promoting homegrown players—catcher Javy Lopez in 1994, third baseman Chipper Jones in 1995, center fielder Andruw Jones in August 1996, and right-hander Kevin Millwood in 1997. The Joneses would be two of baseball's highest-impact position players over the next decade.

A distinguishing characteristic of the franchise after 1997 was the skill and frequency with which Atlanta changed its player roster to take account of free agent losses (real or potential) and the aging-out of core players and still keep winning—division titles, that is. Beyond always finishing first, the Braves were snakebit in the postseason, making it to just one more World Series—in 1999, where they were wiped out in a Yankees sweep. While exercising more deliberate budget mindfulness after the July 1996 merger of Turner's media empire, whose assets included his baseball team, with Time Warner, the world's largest media company, Schuerholz judiciously played the free agent market and made strategic trades to fill out the Braves' roster around their essential core—Atlanta's trio of aces, the two Joneses, and shortstop Rafael Furcal after his impressive Rookie of the Year debut in 2000.

From 1998 to 2005, Atlanta's core regulars included a string of six first basemen, beginning with free agent pickup Andres Galarraga from 1998 to 2000, when he left as a free agent. The Braves changed second basemen four times in five years before Marcus Giles was ready to assume the position full time in 2003. They had seven different starters in left field, including Chipper Jones who played there in 2002 and 2003 to make room at third base for free agent Vinny Castilla; Chipper returned to third when Castilla left in 2004 after a disappointing tour in Atlanta. They had five different starters in right field, including free agent pickup Brian Jordan for three years (1999 to 2001); Gary Sheffield, acquired for Jordan in a trade with the Dodgers, the next two; and in 2004, top-tier outfielder J. D. Drew, for whom they surrendered pitching prospects Jason Marquis and Adam Wainwright to the Cardinals.

However rapid the turnover of core position regulars, Bobby Cox was masterful in integrating new players into the Braves' always-first National League dynasty. He could do so against the backdrop of excellent pitching, even after John Smoltz required Tommy John surgery in 2000, putting him out for the season. Just days before the season began, Schuerholz signed veteran right-hander John Burkett, whose career appeared to be over, to take Smoltz's place in the rotation alongside Maddux, Glavine, and Millwood, whose 18–7 record and 2.68 earned run average the previous year made him the best pitcher on the 1999 Braves. Returning in mid-May 2001, Smoltz struggled through five starts, was back on the injured list in June, and returned in late July to work his way back to form in the bullpen. By mid-August, Smoltz was the Braves' closer, pitching in 19 games with 10 saves and striking out 28 of the 83 batters he faced in 21⅔ innings the rest of the way. The next three years, Smoltz was one of the game's premier closers, notching 144 saves in 210 games between 2002 and 2004, and striking out 243 batters in 226⅓ innings.

After leading the 101-win 2002 Braves with 18 wins apiece, Tom Glavine left as a free agent and Millwood was traded before he would be eligible for free agency the next year. Schuerholz replaced them by trading for San Francisco ace Russ Ortiz and signing former Houston star pitchers Mike Hampton and Shane Reynolds as free agents to back up Maddux in the starting rotation. Ortiz came through with 21 wins as the Braves again won 101 games and their division in 2003. But the Braves' streak of leading the majors in fewest runs allowed 11 years in a row came to an end; Atlanta's pitching staff was just ninth in the National League in earned run average. Greg Maddux left as a free agent after the season.

The beginning of the end for Atlanta's baseball dynasty came in 2003, not just because Glavine was gone and Maddux would soon be, but because Ted Turner no longer owned the franchise. Time Warner's 2001 merger with AOL reduced his clout, ultimately leading him to leave the media empire—and the team—he had built. Time Warner AOL was less willing than Turner had been to spend liberally for the sake of being always first, or than George Steinbrenner was to keep his Yankees a "forever" dynasty. By 2005, when the Braves reached the end of their run of 14 straight division titles, they were no longer in the top tier of major-league teams in player salaries; their payroll was just sixth among the 14 National League teams.

The Braves were willing to let their best players go as free agents: Glavine and Maddux, Lopez and Sheffield after 2003, Drew after 2004, Furcal after 2005, Giles after 2006. Lopez, Sheffield, and Drew capital-ized on having just had the best year of their careers when they were up for free agency. Notwithstanding his 32 home runs, arbitration-eligible first baseman Adam LaRoche was traded after the 2006 season; he was paid just $420,000 as a third-year player in Atlanta that year, but earned $15 million in Pittsburgh over the next three seasons. And the Braves made no effort to keep Andruw Jones when he became a free agent after an uncharacteristically poor season offensively in 2007, notwithstanding his 41 homers the year before and 51 the year before that in 2005, and his relatively young age, at only 31. Tim Hudson, who came to Atlanta as a free agent in 2005 and pitched there for nine years, would be the last significant free agent signed by the Braves for more than a decade to have a long-term tenure with the club.

In the nine years from 1991 to 1999, Atlanta won eight straight divi-sion titles, with an incomplete for 1994 because they were second in the NL East with the second-best record in the National League when base-ball's music stopped. In seven of those nine years, the Braves had the

NL's best record—four times with more than 100 wins—and in four they had the best record in the majors. They went to five World Series, losing four times. The last time the Braves played in the World Series was 1999. Over the next six years, Atlanta won six more NL Eastern Division titles, but only once made it as far as the league championship series. Twice they had the National League's best record—in 2002 and 2003—and failed to make it out of their division series. Yet, for their record 14-straight division titles, coming away with only one championship has left the 1991–2005 Atlanta Braves somewhat diminished in the annals of baseball superpowers—especially in comparison with the contemporaneous New York Yankees.

The Yankees had not been to a World Series or won a division title to compete in the postseason since 1981. Their roster had been in a perpetual state of turnover since then as Steinbrenner kept trying to build a winner by acquiring other teams' star players, either as free agents or in trades. Top-tier players like Dave Winfield and Rickey Henderson were not enough to boost the Yankees to a division title, even though they played well in the crucible of New York City, made all the more fraught by their Boss's intense scrutiny of any and all failures. Other star free agents "spit the bit" in New York, to use Steinbrenner's famous putdown of one of his free agent pitcher acquisitions. First baseman Don Mattingly and southpaw Ron Guidry were the only stars in pinstripes to play for the Yankees in the 1980s to come up through their minor-league system.

And Steinbrenner changed managers so often it was both farcical and cringeworthy. The Yankees went through 19 managerial changes in Steinbrenner's first 19 years as the Boss, including Billy Martin five times. Buck Showalter, the 19th of those managers, was named to take charge of the Yankees following their dismal 91-loss 1991 season, making him number 12 in the 11 years since they had last been to the World Series. The only other team to change managers as often in any 10-year period as Steinbrenner's Yankees between 1981 and 1992 was Chicago's 1957–1966 Cubs—and they, only because they rotated managers as part of their "college of coaches" system in the 1961 and 1962 seasons.

Showalter lasted four years as Yankees manager, setting a record for uninterrupted seasons at the helm thus far in the Steinbrenner era. He survived his first year in 1992 despite a season that ended with 76 wins—just a 5-win improvement from the previous year—perhaps only because the Boss, thanks to his personal vendetta against Winfield, was banished by the commissioner from involvement in any baseball decisions. Notwithstanding his Yankees having the American League's best record when the game was shut down in August 1994 and winning the AL wild card with the third best record in the league in 1995, Showalter's tenure was doomed when the Yankees lost three straight in Seattle after taking a 2–0 lead in their best-of-five series division. He wasn't exactly fired. Steinbrenner's gambit was to force Showalter, whose contract had just expired, into either acquiescing to the diminishment of his authority or quitting. Steinbrenner backed down and offered him a new two-year contract, but Showalter spurned the offer, knowing his career prospects were bright even leaving the Yankees.

As Steinbrenner's famously nicknamed "baseball people" knew, even if the Boss's vision was obscured by his only-now-counts approach, the 1994 and 1995 seasons forecast that New York's Yankees were primed for another run of extended excellence—and perhaps even a new era of dynastic dominance in what was arguably the best division in baseball, the American League's Eastern Division. And rather than relying on signing free agents or trading for expensive stars, the foundation had been patiently laid in the Yankees' farm system. The foundation bricks were five players who would lead the Yankees to five division titles and a wild card, four pennants, and three World Series championships in the next six years: center fielder Bernie Williams, called up in July 1991, whose 1995 season established him as a bona fide star; left-hander Andy Pettitte and righty Mariano Rivera, both rookies in 1995; Derek Jeter, a September call-up in 1995 who took over at shortstop on Opening Day in 1996; and Jorge Posada, still in Triple-A in 1996, but destined to follow Bill Dickey, Yogi Berra, Elston Howard, and Thurman Munson in the line of distinguished Yankees catchers.

In addition to harvesting homegrown talent, which heretofore had not been a hallmark of Steinbrenner's ownership, the Yankees had made a series of astute trades and free agent signings that focused more on filling specific position needs than simply acquiring the brightest stars—transactions that were among the last made while Steinbrenner was still officially banned from having a say in his team's baseball decisions. In 1993 the Yankees added three players, signing as free agents Boston third baseman Wade Boggs and Toronto southpaw Jimmy Key to anchor their starting rotation and trading for right fielder Paul O'Neill, a left-handed hitter whose power played to the dimensions of Yankee Stadium. They were the Yankees' three best players in their dominance of the American League in 1994, before the season came to an abrupt end.

Their future looking bright, the Yankees picked up Expos closer John Wetteland on the cheap just days before the 1995 season got underway, as Montreal, despite having the best record in baseball the previous year only to be denied the postseason because of the strike, gave greater priority to dumping the salaries of star players than trying for a championship. Toward the end of July, struggling with a .500 record, but just 4½ games back of first-place Boston, the Yankees plundered Toronto's last-place Blue Jays for right-hander David Cone, one of the best pitchers in baseball. Cone was 9–2 after the trade. Wetteland saved 31. Carrying a losing 57–59 record into September, the Yankees won 22 of their final 28 games, including 11 of their last 12, to outpace five other teams for the AL wild card.

Not to say that the Yankees wouldn't have been just as successful over the next six years under Buck Showalter, but Steinbrenner's hiring Joe Torre to replace him proved an inspired choice. Like his predecessors in the Steinbrenner era, Showalter chafed at the Boss's incessant criticism and meddling in areas he considered the manager's prerogative. Just 39 years old in 1995 and not having made it to the major leagues as a player, Showalter was still trying to make his mark in the game. He had an ego. He was sensitive to having his authority undermined. No matter how successful the Yankees were, at some point his clash of egos with Steinbrenner would have risked his being summarily dismissed by the Boss or caused him to quit.

Torre, on the other hand, was a decade and a half older, with a distinguished 16-year playing career that included a batting title and Most Valuable Player Award, and already had 14 years' experience as a major-league manager—5 with the Mets, 3 with the Braves, and 6 with the Cardinals. It didn't matter that he was fired from all three jobs. He was comfortable with who he was. His years of baseball experience made him a masterful diplomat, capable of letting his ever-opinionated, quick-to-panic Boss vent without losing his cool, all while maintaining his authority in the dugout. Insulating his players and coaches from any melodrama erupting from the owner's suite, Torre had the respect of both his bosses—Steinbrenner and the general manager—and his players. Torre accomplished the seemingly impossible task of surviving Steinbrenner's outbursts and tirades for 12 years because, as related in his book *The Yankee Years*, "When George said something you just say, 'He's the Boss, blah blah blah,' and do what you want to do. Just don't challenge it with George."

Of course, no one could foresee any of this at the time. What they did see was that Joe Torre did not have the résumé of a winning manager, and Steinbrenner was always about winning. Never mind that the teams Torre had in his 14 years as a manager were almost always either very bad or middle-of-the-pack quality; the Yankees had been down this road before. Just days after losing a tight three-team race for the pennant in 1948, they replaced manager Bucky Harris with Casey Stengel. That decision had scribes scratching their heads because, like Torre nearly half a century later, Stengel's managerial career had little to commend. Burdened with very bad teams in the National League, only once in his nine years as a manager did any Stengel team have a winning record—and then, just barely. Like Casey, Torre would have to contend with the expectations of a franchise accustomed to winning. In Torre's case, he would also have to contend with predictable outbursts of emasculation inflicted by the owner on his manager. The decision to hire Torre was met with widespread skepticism that he could possibly succeed with Steinbrenner hovering over him, along with ridicule of the new hire being naive or a "Clueless Joe," as New York's *Daily News* famously put it, for not understanding what he was getting into working for the Boss.

Almost immediately after going with the recommendation of his "baseball people" that Torre was the best available manager with major-league managing experience, Steinbrenner had buyer's remorse. Unhappy that the New York news media had not jumped on the Torre bandwagon—and especially that there was more than a hint of ridicule over his decision to hire "Clueless Joe"—the Boss tried to make amends with the departed Showalter, inquiring whether he might like to return to Yankee Stadium. By this time fully engrossed in discussions about helping build a competitive team that he would also manage with the Arizona Diamondbacks, a National League expansion team whose first season would not be until 1998, Showalter was not open to the suggestion—especially not with the Boss unwilling to rein in his interventionist impulses. So, Joe Torre it was. Although armed with a two-year contract, Torre had every reason to believe his career with the Yankees would be short-lived if they didn't finish first in 1996—and maybe even if they did but didn't get to the World Series. Stengel surely had a similar concern in his first year as Yankees manager way back in 1949.

Torre's 1998 Yankees joined the pantheon of baseball's greatest single-season teams ever by winning 114 regular-season games—a new American League record—and sailing through their division series, the league championship series, and the World Series with an 11–2 record, their only two losses coming in the ALCS. They won their division by 22 games, led the majors in scoring, and gave up the fewest runs in the American League. All told, the Yankees won five division titles and a wild card in Torre's first six years as manager. They played in five World Series, winning them all until the 2001 Arizona Diamondbacks beat them with a ninth-inning walk-off bloop single beyond shortstop Deter Jeter's reach off incomparable closer Mariano Rivera in the seventh game.

Like the Braves, the Yankees made savvy trades and used the free agent market to complement their homegrown "Core Five." In 1996, they traded for Tino Martinez to replace just-retired Yankees icon Don Mattingly at first base, and re-signed their own elite free agent pitcher, David Cone. In 1997, they signed free-agent lefty David Wells. In 1998, they picked up second baseman Chuck Knoblauch and third baseman Scott Brosius. In 1999, it was the indomitable Roger Clemens (for whom they gave up Wells). In June 2000, outfielder David Justice came by trade. And in 2001, another ace, free-agent Mike Mussina, signed up for pinstripes.

But the retirement of Brosius and Paul O'Neill after the 2001 World Series, along with letting Martinez go to make room for slugging premier free agent first baseman Jason Giambi, was a turning point for Joe Torre's Yankees, even though they remained the team to beat in the American League. In Torre's next six years as manager—before departing in another Steinbrenner-orchestrated maneuver after the 2007 season because their string of nine straight division titles came to an end with only a wild-card berth and no World Series—the Yankees won more games and had a higher winning percentage (.609) than in his first six years (.601). In each six-year period, the Yankees won five division titles and a wild card. Despite making the postseason every year, despite their Core Five staying intact until Bernie Williams retired in 2007, and notwithstanding being fortified by a host of expensive high-profile players like Giambi, Alex Rodriguez, Gary Sheffield, Kevin Brown, and Randy Johnson, they went to only one more World Series in Torre's managerial tenure—in 2003—

and did not win. Derek Jeter said, and many professional baseball observers and most Yankee fans fervently believe, that the New York Yankees were not the same. Buster Olney, covering the Yankees for the *New York Times*, called Game Seven of the 2001 World Series "the last night of the Yankee dynasty."

3

"CHICKS DIG THE LONG BALL"

It was a commercial that probably would not have been made twenty years later because of its stereotypical and sexist depiction of women attracted to male athletes. But in 1999 Nike, one of America's foremost athletic shoe companies, produced "Chicks Dig the Long Ball," in which Atlanta Braves pitching aces Greg Maddux and Tom Glavine—"Hey, a couple of Cy Youngs over here"—envious of the attention St. Louis Cardinals slugger Mark McGwire gets from female fans as he blasts one batting practice pitch after another out of the park, buy a pair of Nikes (of course), hit the gym, and bulk up to enhance, shall we say, their sex appeal. They are more than pleased with themselves—fist bumps—when a female fan recognizes them . . . only to ask "Hey, you guys seen Mark?"

The commercial hits home precisely because, in a historical echo of the 1920s (and 1950s), the home run had become all the rage in Major League Baseball. And just as the driving force behind that rage in the 1920s was Babe Ruth, the Sultan of Swat, whose prodigious blasts over the fence were jaw-droppingly awesome, so now it was Mark McGwire and, to a lesser extent, Sammy Sosa, Ken Griffey Jr., and Barry Bonds. The Nike commercial was made in 1999, the year after McGwire and Sosa both shattered the single-season record for home runs that had stood since Roger Maris hit 61 in '61 to eclipse the Babe's 60 in 1927—no longer the record, but still an iconic number in baseball lore. McGwire finished the 1998 season with 70, Sosa with 66.

Baseball had never seen anything like their assault on one of the game's most sacred records. Their duel to pass both Ruth and Maris was reminiscent of Maris's duel with Mickey Mantle in 1961 to top the Babe's 60, except that Maris and Mantle were on the same team and McGwire and Sosa were on rival teams. Their duel also epitomized a new era in which home runs dominated the game as never before. It would not be too much of a stretch to say that, just as the Babe's blasts both revolutionized the game, putting an end to the Deadball Era, and saved the game from the stain of the 1919 Black Sox scandal that undermined its very foundation, so did McGwire and Sosa complete the rescue of the game from the stain of the 1994–1995 players' strike that turned many Americans away from what had once been called the National Pastime.

Ironically, among the unknowns had there been no strike in 1994 was whether, after 33 years, Maris's record 61 home runs would have fallen. Like Maris taking aim at the Babe's 34-year-old single-season record of 60 homers, the player pursuing the record in 1994 was an unassuming slugger who kind of came out of nowhere. Maris had hit 39 homers in 1960 and 28 the year before, but if anyone was going to pass Ruth, most would have assumed it would be either established superstar Mickey Mantle, the young Harmon Killebrew, or perhaps Rocky Colavito, whose 42 homers two years earlier led the American League. Similarly, Matt Williams, third baseman for the San Francisco Giants, had hit 33 homers in 1990, 34 in 1991, and 38 in 1993 but was not thought to be someone likely to enter Babe Ruth territory. Mark McGwire, whose 49 homers in 1987 set the rookie record, might be. McGwire's fellow Bash Brother on the Oakland A's, Jose Canseco, was also a possibility, as was Barry Bonds, or maybe even that kid in Seattle—Ken Griffey. Matt Williams was probably a consistent 30-homers-a-year guy, but not someone to make the slugging immortals on baseball's Mount Olympus—Ruth and Gehrig and Jimmie Foxx, Hank Greenberg, and Mel Ott—look down and take notice.

On the day the 1994 season came to an abrupt end, Williams was ahead of Ruth's 1927 pace, and his 43 home runs through the Giants' 115 games was exactly where Maris was in 1961. Sixty-one homers were also within reach for Griffey and for Houston's Jeff Bagwell, whose 40 and 39 as of August 11 put both ahead of Ruth's pace. Already there were 10 players with 30 home runs; on the same date a year earlier, only four of the 21 batters who ended up with 30 homers for the season had that many.

McGwire, however, was not one of baseball's 30-homer batsmen on August 12, 1994. Neither was Sosa, whose 33 homers in 1993 signaled his breakthrough as a slugger. Having crashed 220 home runs in his first seven years, McGwire's career took a turn toward the brittle in 1993 when a foot injury caused him to miss nearly the entire season. Back for the start of 1994, McGwire made it through his team's first 23 games, reinjured his foot, missed 43 games, was forced out of action again two weeks before the strike put everyone out of action, and ended up with just 9 home runs for the year. Sosa had 25 homers when the players went on strike, but only one in the previous 19 games.

Babe Ruth's eye-popping 54 homers in 1920, his first year with the Yankees, following his then thought-to-be-beyond-belief 29 for the Red Sox the year before, was the catalyst for the home run revolution that put an end to the Deadball Era. The 1920s and 1930s were a relatively high-scoring hitters' era characterized by some of the greatest names in home run history. Ruth, Gehrig, Ott, Foxx, and Greenberg were pioneers of the long-ball era, and by the beginning of the 1940s, there were also Joe DiMaggio, Ted Williams, and Johnny Mize. And yet, in the 21 years from 1920 to 1940, only 12 players hit as many as 40 homers in any one season. They did so only 33 times, one-third of those by the Babe alone and another third by Gehrig and Foxx. There were only three years— 1929, 1930, and 1936—in which as many as three batters hit 40 in the same season (including four in 1930). Those were three of only four years between 1901 and 1996 that major-league teams averaged more than five runs a game. (The other year, 1925, in which Ruth missed close to half the season, was ironically the only year in the 1920s that nobody reached the 40-homer plateau.) The 50-homer barrier was crossed eight times during those years—exactly half by the Bambino, all in the 1920s, followed by Hack Wilson, Foxx (twice), and Greenberg in the 1930s.

After a slump in baseball's power game in the first half of the 1940s extending through World War II, Greenberg (in 1946) and Mize and Ralph Kiner (both with 51 homers in 1947) kicked off a new home run era that surged to unprecedented levels in the 1950s, even in comparison to when Ruth was king. The percentage of hits that were home runs reached 9 percent for the first time in history in 1950. The long ball accounted for 10 percent of hits for the first time in 1955—a year that six players, all in the National League, hit over 40—and stayed at about 10 percent until the mid-1960s, a pitchers' era. The new generation of compelling sluggers that came of age in the 1950s included Duke Snider,

Mickey Mantle, Willie Mays, Eddie Mathews, Hank Aaron, Ernie Banks, and Frank Robinson. Sixteen different players cracked the 40-homer barrier 37 times in the decade. Each year from 1953 to 1955 there were six batters who did so, and Mantle had yet to have his first 40-homer season. Mays with 51 in 1955 and Mantle with 52 the next year, however, were the only batters to hit more than 50 in the '50s.

Then came 1961. Eight players, paced by Maris's 61 and Mantle's 54, slugged 40 or more homers. Six were in the American League, where the per-team average for home runs increased by 12 percent from the previous year as batters took advantage of the dilution of quality pitching occasioned by Major League Baseball's first expansion. Nine years later, seven batters hit over 40—the anomaly this time being that, after five years of a pitchers' era culminating in the 1968 Year of the Pitcher, sluggers were able to tee off on pitchers throwing for the first time from the lower mound mandated by Major League Baseball to reduce their advantage. Still, with the exception of Boston shortstop Rico Petrocelli, whose career high in homers in his four previous big-league seasons was 18, the names of those crashing 40—Killebrew, Aaron, Frank Howard, Reggie Jackson, Willie McCovey, and Carl Yastrzemski—were not surprising. They were baseball's most renowned power hitters. Going into the 1994 season, 1961 and 1969 were the only two years in which more than six players hit 40 homers in the same season, and the six times that as many as six batters topped 40 were all in an 18-year spread from 1953 to 1970.

Forty-homer seasons declined in the 1970s and 1980s even as Eddie Murray, Mike Schmidt, Dave Parker, George Foster, Dale Murphy, and Darryl Strawberry were name-brand sluggers. There were only two seasons between 1971 and 1992 that as many as four players hit 40 in the same year, and five when none did. But there was also change afoot, exemplified by Oakland's Jose Canseco and Mark McGwire. Power hitters were beginning to bulk up with the twin objectives of driving more baseballs out of the yard and looking physically imposing and intimidating while doing so. If the 1993 season, when runs per team soared from 4.1 a game to 4.6 and five players blasted 40 homers, seemed at first an outlier after two decades of modest slugging performances, it proved to be a harbinger of the power to come. In August 1994, as the Damocles' sword of a players' strike hung over the game, 11 players were on a pace toward 40 home runs, with three—Matt Williams, Griffey, and Bagwell—having a shot at 61. 'Twas a slugfest never seen before in baseball.

When the strike ended and the games resumed on April 25, 1995, it may have seemed that baseball's power surge in 1993 and 1994 *was* an anomaly. The schedule was necessarily shortened from 162 to 144 games because the season began three weeks late to allow a modicum of spring training once a federal court ruled in favor of the players, and only four players reached the 40-homer threshold—Albert Belle with 50, and Frank Thomas, Jay Buhner, and Dante Bichette each with 40. Picking up where he left off in 1994, Matt Williams got off to a fast start with 13 homers in his first 36 games, fouled a ball off his foot, missed more than two months, and ended up with 23 home runs in 76 games. Even had he not broken his foot on that foul ball, Williams was only on pace to hit 52 for the 144-game schedule, and 59 had no games been wiped off the slate. Whether he would have passed Roger Maris in 1994 had the season played out is unknowable, but that turned out to be his only year of possibility, just as 1961 was for Maris.

The next eleven years were an era of unprecedented power baseball. For 35 years, the most players to hit 40 homers in the same year was eight—the record set in 1961. That changed in a big way in 1996 when more than double that number—17 players—crossed the 40-homer threshold. That a healthy Mark McGwire led the majors with 52 long balls was not surprising. That Brady Anderson, primarily a leadoff batter whose home runs in eight prior big-league seasons totaled 72, was second with 50 was not only surprising, it seemed improbable. The 1996 season proved to be no anomaly when it came to 40-homer seasons, because in 1997 there were 12 who did the same thing. Ken Griffey led the American League with 56, the first of two consecutive years he would lead the league with precisely that number; Larry Walker topped the National League with 49; and McGwire's 58—34 of which he sent soaring for Oakland before being traded at the end of July to St. Louis—led the majors. The trend continued. From 1996 to 2006, the number of players hitting 40 homers in the same season was at least eight every year, and in 10 of those years—all except 2002, when four players hit that many in each league—they numbered more than that.

Forty home runs in a season was a milestone. Since Babe Ruth, there had always been elite sluggers capable in any given year of knocking 40 out of the park. What was unusual now was how routine that accomplishment had become. And because so many players were doing it, it was almost to the point of diminishing the significance of the achievement itself. The 40-homer threshold was crossed an astonishing 130 times by 54 players from 1996 to 2006—astonishing because before those 11 years, only 72 players had done so a total of 157 times in the *three-quarters of a century* since Ruth in 1920 was first to crash through the 30-, 40-, and 50-homer barriers, which he did all in one year.

And whereas 50 home runs had been reached 19 times by 12 players—including the Babe four times, and Kiner, Mantle, and Mays twice each—between the Babe's 54 in 1920 and Belle's 50 in 1995, it took just the next 11 years for 12 players to more than double the number of 50-homer seasons with 20 of their own, from Mark McGwire's 52 in 1996 to Ryan Howard's 58 and David Ortiz's 54 in 2006. McGwire and Sosa tied Ruth for the most 50-homer seasons, but while the Babe had a five-year gap between his first two in 1920 and 1921 and next two in 1927 and 1928, McGwire (1996 to 1999) and Sosa (1998 to 2001) did so in four consecutive years. And it's worth remembering that such great all-time sluggers on baseball's Mount Olympus as Aaron, Banks, Killebrew, McCovey, Ott, Frank Robinson, and Ted Williams never crossed the 50-homer barrier—not even once.

It was very clear that no home run records were safe, and that reaching the career milestone of 500 home runs was no longer as rare as it had been in the past. Of the 27 players with more than 500 homers, five crossed that sacred threshold in the space of just six years between 1999 and 2004—McGwire in 1999, Bonds in 2001, Sosa and Rafael Palmeiro in 2003, and Griffey in 2004. Seven others have reached that total since then.

One thing was obvious: The players were bigger, more muscular, and stronger. How they got that way was, to the extent addressed publicly, attributed to hitting the weight room. These guys were buff. There were rumblings of steroid use by some sluggers, including a *Los Angeles Times* exposé in 1995, but it was hard to find anyone particularly concerned. Nobody—not players and their union, not franchise owners, not Major League Baseball authorities, not the sports media—had the inclination to expose performance-enhancing cheating. A convenient rationale for dismissing explanations that broached the possibility of cheating was that batters were swinging ferociously for the fences without regard for the pileup of inevitable strikeouts in pursuit of that quest.

Whatever the reason, baseball's power boost beginning in the mid-1990s kicked off baseball's highest-scoring era since the 1930s. In fact, however, runs-per-game from the mid-1990s to the mid-2000s were actually slightly less than the 4.9 runs averaged by major-league teams in the 1920s and 1930s. But now, a third of all hits went for extra bases, and for the first time in history, the number of hits that cleared the fences was consistently—year after year—more than 10 percent of the total. The only year to date since 1996 in which home runs have not accounted for *at least* 11 percent of all hits was 2014, when scoring dipped to a 22-year low of 4.1 runs a game and only 10 percent of hits went out of the park.

The ubiquity of Dr. Long Ball changed the psychology of the game, and for reasons beyond the obvious potential immediate scoring impact of one swing of the bat, especially with runners on base. Hitting for power, more than hitting for average, became the dominant offensive currency. Batting orders were worked out to ensure a distribution of power up and down the lineup. Playing for one run, except in late innings of tight ballgames, gave way to always trying for a big inning. Position players understood that in the free agent marketplace, the most money and best contracts went to those who could drive the ball a long way, or—as it was said in the 1960s—it was the power hitters who drove Cadillacs. There were few who decried baseball becoming a power-driven game, as John McGraw and Ty Cobb did in the 1920s in both their awe and disdain for Babe Ruth's home run revolution.

And baseball fans loved it. Home runs opened up big leads for their teams. Home runs allowed their teams to overcome big deficits. Home runs were exciting when they capped a rally. They were majestic in flight. They made for high stakes in the showdown between pitcher and batter. And not to be dismissed, choreographing medleys of home runs became a poetic, balletic, enervating staple of sports news programming. Home runs were entertaining. The commercial had it right—as great as pitchers like Greg Maddux and Tom Glavine were, it was the explosive power of Mark McGwire and Sammy Sosa that caused fans to pay attention.

The chasing down and shattering of Roger Maris's home run record in 1998 gave definition to the power hitters' era that straddled the end of the twentieth and beginning of the twenty-first centuries. But as McGwire and Sosa, neck-and-neck, both bore down on 61 homers, there was none of the drama of a race against an ever-diminishing number of games, as there was for Maris—whose 61st home run did not come till the final game of the season—closing in on Ruth and would have been for Matt Williams, whose pace was not ahead of Maris, but exactly even, in 1994. McGwire and Sosa both had already blasted 55 home runs by the end of August. That put them six home runs from Maris with 24 games yet to play.

By the time Sosa's Cubs arrived in St. Louis for two games against McGwire's Cardinals on September 7 and 8, "Big Mac" had 60 home runs—one away from Maris—and "Slammin' Sammy" had 58. Nearly 43,000 were on hand at Busch Stadium on September 7, Labor Day, to see if history might be made. They didn't have to wait long; McGwire hit number 61 off Mike Morgan in the very first inning. He did not break the record that day, but he did the next with a fourth-inning blast off Steve Trachsel for number 62. Sosa got two hits in the two games, both singles. Six days later, Sosa hit numbers 61 and 62 in the same game in front of his home fans at Wrigley Field against Milwaukee, tying him with McGwire, for whom number 63 still awaited. There were still two weeks to go when Sosa caught up to McGwire. Big Mac hit number 63 the next day; Sosa did the same the day after. McGwire belted his 64th on September 18 and 65th on the 20th. Another two-homer game for Sosa on September 23 again evened him up with McGwire, and both hit their 66th home run of the season on September 25. There were now just two games left on the schedule. St. Louis was at home against Montreal. Chicago was in Houston, fighting for the wild card.

McGwire went deep twice in both his games to finish the year with 70 home runs. How many more he might have hit had he not missed eight games to deal with various aches and pains is another unknowable—but also relevant, given that his record lasted just three years until Barry Bonds smashed 73 in 2001. Sosa did not homer in either of his games, nor did he clear the fence in a 163rd game his team was forced to play against the Giants for the National League wild card. Sammy Sosa ended the year with 66 home runs. Thanks to his league-leading 158 runs batted in (and the Cubs making the postseason), Sosa swamped McGwire, whose 147 RBIs were second, in the MVP voting. McGwire, however, was baseball's most impactful hitter based on offensive wins above replacement.

They were at it again the next year. Both once again soared past the 61-homer marker. This time trailing Sosa 55 homers to 51 at the end of

August, Big Mac crashed 14 to Sammy's eight in September to edge out Sosa, 65 home runs to 63. Of the 13 batters to hit 40 in 1999, they were the only ones to crush more than 50. (In 1998, Griffey with 56 and San Diego's Greg Vaughn with 50 joined them in the 50-and-over club.) That turned out to be Big Mac's last epic season. At 36 years old with a history of injuries, McGwire struggled through spring training in 2000 with hurt knees. He nonetheless got off to a good start with 30 homers, 69 RBIs, and a .303 batting average in 70 games before landing on the injured list before the All-Star break with a serious limp and patella tendinitis. Returning to the roster two months later only because rosters had expanded for September and the Cardinals were headed to the postseason, McGwire had only 18 at-bats in 18 games, ending the with 32 home runs—far behind the nine National Leaguers who belted more than 40 that year. Sosa led the majors with 50 homers.

In 2001, Sammy Sosa cruised past 60 homers for the third time in four years and once again had to settle for runner-up. This time his 64 homers paled in comparison to the record-shattering 73 crushed by Barry Bonds. McGwire, dealing with a persistently bad knee, played only 97 games, in which he knocked out 29 homers but batted just .187 while striking out 118 times in 299 at-bats. Mark McGwire retired after the season, 17 home runs shy of 600—a threshold previously reached by only Babe Ruth, Willie Mays, and Hank Aaron—and which might now be the new hard-to-reach career milestone for sluggers to aim for.

If the feel-good story that brought the baseball world together when Ripken broke Gehrig's iconic consecutive-games record was the singularity of an achievement by a player whose work ethic was above reproach and who was as upstanding a person as one could imagine a true American hero being, McGwire's surpassing Maris was a virtual lovefest uniting the nation in celebration. Competing to be the first to 62, McGwire and Sosa played on teams that were not only division rivals, but historical rivals dating back to the 1920s and 1930s. But theirs was a friendly competition. Each wanted the record for himself yet rooted for the other's success, using that in part to drive his own quest forward. As he rounded the bases after his record-setting home run, McGwire was congratulated by every opposing player on the infield. He lifted the Cubs catcher off the ground in a bear-hug. Sosa saluted McGwire from right field, then joined the scrum on the field to congratulate his rival in the great race to 62. Big Mac lifted him off the ground too. McGwire hopped the railing adjacent to the Cardinals' dugout and hugged all of Maris's children, whose father passed away 13 years before his record was broken. Watching him whisper something to each of them was the ultimate feel-good moment.

Amid the summerlong giddiness that two players—not one—were chasing Maris and with fans of both genders "digging the long ball," it was easy not to pay attention to the canary in the coal mine: the bottle of androstenedione spotted in Big Mac's locker by an eagle-eyed reporter. Nobody was willing to question why it was that home runs were flying out of ballparks at unprecedented rates—as though baseball's power game was on steroids.

4

SELIG'S GROWTH LEGACY

After nearly six years as acting commissioner, Bud Selig was finally officially named commissioner of baseball by unanimous vote of the league's owners in July 1998. Even as Selig insisted, in all modesty (of course), that he did not necessarily *want* to be commissioner, and while the owners conducted a perfunctory search for the next commissioner, the owners all knew he wanted the job, loved the job, and was consolidating his position as "acting" in the job. And the owners were united behind him—even George Steinbrenner, whose free-spending ways on free agents and opposition to revenue-sharing ran counter to Selig's agenda. "This search for a commissioner is a charade," Steinbrenner told the *New York Times* in February 1998. "Selig's a great consensus builder. I grow impatient with him at times, but he's the ideal guy."

Fixing the game's ailments and making Major League Baseball— which by now was clearly second fiddle in American sports to the National Football League, and probably third fiddle to the National Basketball Association—great again was the role Selig believed he was destined to play. Making it official, the owners gave Selig carte blanche as commissioner. There was no reason not to. Major League Baseball's $2.5 billion in revenues in 1997 was more than twice what they were when Selig engineered the coup against Fay Vincent that made him acting commissioner in 1992. And Selig was presiding over a baseball renaissance in America, not least of which, in the summer of 1998, was Mark McGwire and Sammy Sosa both chasing Roger Maris's record 61 homers in a single season. Selig had to give up ownership of the small-market

Milwaukee Brewers to avoid the appearance of a conflict of interest, but that was a small price to pay to become commissioner de jure, especially since the Brewers' new owner was his daughter.

Selig had his conditions. Specifically, he wanted to centralize all Major League Baseball operations in the Office of the Commissioner. He had set the stage when he was still "acting" in July 1997 by establishing a president and chief operating officer for Major League Baseball. In September 1999, after Selig had officially held the office for more than a year, a century of the American and National Leagues being run independently by a league president came to an end when he took control of both leagues' executive and administrative functions. Schedules, assigning umpires (there would be no separate cadres of umpires whose styles were peculiar to each league), disciplinary actions, and policies and procedures would all be in the hands of Major League Baseball. Bowing to tradition and baseball history, however, Selig assured baseball fans that the two leagues would remain separate competitive entities and that the National League, at least for the foreseeable future, would not be forced to accept the American League's designated-hitter rule, thereby keeping its distinctive style of play where pitchers had to bat for themselves.

And in January 2000, the owners granted Selig the power to take from the rich (think: Steinbrenner's Yankees) to give to the poor (perhaps his daughter's Brewers). His discretion here concerned reallocating the distribution of each franchise's share of Major League Baseball's ballooning national television revenues, in the "best interest of baseball," to ensure competitive balance in the canyon-size revenue disparity between big and small market teams that existed in baseball's world. The commissioner's power was absolute, but only over the owners. He still had to contend with the players' union, which—having "won" the war over free agency by going on strike in 1994 and subsequently negotiating a collective bargaining agreement to their liking in 1996—had arguably become if not complacent, at least less confrontational.

Selig's was the biggest power grab by a commissioner since the first commissioner, Judge Kenesaw Mountain Landis, demanded that his authority to make decisions in the "best interests of the national game of baseball" be absolute and not subject to override by franchise owners or the two league presidents acting in concert. As Major League Baseball's immediate priority then was restoring credibility in the wake of the 1919 Black Sox scandal, the highly esteemed sitting federal judge whose very demeanor epitomized "integrity" knew he had baseball's owners and both league presidents over a barrel. They needed him more than he needed them. His becoming baseball's czar, whose decisions would be final with no avenue for appeal, immeasurably weakened the authority of the league presidents. Landis's quick and decisive actions to deal with the Black Sox fallout made him synonymous with the integrity of Major League Baseball. The owners dared not try to dismiss him; there was in fact no provision for firing him in the Major League Agreement that made him commissioner. Nor did they dare refuse him one seven-year term after another, even though some were at times unhappy with the breadth of his jurisdiction. Landis became, in effect, commissioner for life, holding the position until his death in November 1944.

Once the Judge (also jury and executioner, especially since there was no players' union during his tenure) took his place among baseball's immortals on Mount Olympus, baseball's owners acted immediately to reassert themselves in Major League Baseball's power equation with amendments to limit the commissioner's authority. Subsequent amendments over the years had the effect of increasing the commissioner's responsibilities while simultaneously preventing him from acting independently on any issue of fundamental importance to the leagues and franchise owners. Leveraging his position as baseball's first commissioner to come from the ownership clique, even if "acting" at first, Selig upended the convention of neutralizing the power of the office by centralizing all authority in his hands—first to take charge of negotiations with the players' union that led to the 1994 strike and then to assume a leading role in boosting major-league revenues.

Up till now, the business of baseball had been baseball. Early on in Selig's reign, however, the horizons of baseball's business expanded to include savvy marketing, with its all-important subsets of merchandise and media. Following the precedent set by the NBA, marketing the game became as important as pennant races. The revenues generated from national media rights and products licensed by Major League Baseball were a significant source of the revenue sharing Selig had been advocating as the owner of a small-market franchise since before the strike and was now implementing as the commissioner.

Selig retired in 2015 after 23 years serving as the commissioner of baseball. Turning the reins over to Rob Manfred, his longtime deputy groomed to succeed him, Selig left having presided over 13 consecutive years of record-setting earnings for Major League Baseball. Sales of MLB merchandise accounted for about a third of Major League Baseball's $9.5 billion in revenues; MLB Advanced Media had more than 3.5 million digital subscribers, including on cellphone apps; MLB Network was a year-round mainstay sports channel that included comprehensive coverage of off-season deals and free agent signings. Major League Baseball had lucrative contracts with ESPN and Fox Sports for regular-season and postseason games. Money coming from corporate sponsors of Major League Baseball increased dramatically. Individual franchises profited handsomely from their own media deals and sponsorships. Exactly half of baseball's 30 major-league teams were valued at over $1 billion by *Forbes*; four were over $2 billion. This was the Selig legacy that made baseball's owners proud.

Selig's legacy included implementing initiatives to goose fans' interest in the game. The most important of these was adding interleague games to the regular-season schedule in 1997, which led ultimately to a second wild card in league pennant races. Selig had little problem persuading franchise owners and the players' union on the merits of interleague games, which included marketing regional and especially city rivalries for teams in different leagues, not to mention national television revenues for broadcasting those games.

It wasn't as though the concept hadn't been thought about before, however much it bucked the tradition of teams playing regular-season games only against clubs in their own league. During the Great Depression in 1933, Chicago Cubs president Bill Veeck Sr., one of the baseball's most innovative executives, proposed regular-season interleague games as a way to entice people to the ballpark in troubled economic times. While his proposal was not taken up for consideration, Veeck's idea found expression that very year—one in which only three of baseball's 16 major-league teams averaged as many as 7,000 fans a game—in a special exhibition game between the best players in each league before a crowd of more than 47,000 at Comiskey Park in Chicago. It was such a success that the American League versus National League All-Star Game has been a much-ballyhooed annual event in the middle of the baseball season every year since, except the World War II year of 1945 and 2020 because of the COVID-19 pandemic.

The idea of regular-season interleague play resurfaced from time to time in the intervening years, never gaining traction until Selig pushed the issue in the mid-1990s. It didn't help that three of interleague play's strongest advocates—St. Louis Browns owner Bill Veeck Jr. (the even more innovative son of the older Bill Veeck, with an eye to incessant entertaining) and Cleveland Indians general manager (and former Detroit Tigers star) Hank Greenberg in the 1950s, and Oakland A's owner Charlie Finley in the 1970s—were disliked, if not despised, by their fellow franchise executives. Scheduling interleague games during the regular season had the most salience when Major League Baseball was grappling with expansion scenarios in 1960 and the mid-1970s that included adding just one new team to each league, making for an odd number that necessarily meant a team from one league would have to play a team from the other virtually every day of the season. In the first instance, Major League Baseball settled on a two-team expansion in the American League in 1961, followed by the National League in 1962, making both 10-team leagues. In the second, rather than put Seattle in one league and Toronto in the other in 1977, both new franchises were placed in the American League.

The appeal of interleague play, proven by the popularity of the All-Star Game, was that baseball fans in one league would be able to watch star players they had been hearing so much about from the other league play in games against their team. And because historically most baseball fans in cities with two teams were fiercely aligned with one in their personal allegiance and typically disdained the other, even though they were in different leagues, matching them up for interleague games that counted in the standings would fuel competitive rivalries that heretofore had no outlet for resolution absent their meeting in the postseason.

In the past, cities with teams in each league—Boston, Chicago, Philadelphia, St. Louis, and New York—frequently played exhibition series between them for city bragging rights. At first, before there was radio to broadcast World Series games, "city championship series" were an alternative to the World Series for those cities whose teams weren't in it. City series mostly came to an end by the 1920s, except in Chicago, where the Cubs and White Sox kept at it until 1943, when the United States was fighting World War II. Once the war ended, the major league cities with two teams resumed city series for bragging rights, but now they took place in the week just before Opening Day rather than in the postseason.

Before long, those games became more of a final tune-up for the regular season—which they would have been in any case—than any meaningful competition for city bragging rights. In New York, however, the Yankees and the Giants or Dodgers from 1946 until both NL teams left town for the West Coast in 1958, and the Yankees and the expansion Mets from 1963 to 1984, competed annually in an *in-season* game (and sometimes two) for the Mayor's Trophy to raise funds for sandlot baseball. That ended when both franchises—especially the one in the Bronx owned by Steinbrenner—lost interest in playing a meaningless game in the middle of the season.

Interleague play was a smashing success when it was introduced in 1997 with teams in the two leagues playing only against clubs in their corresponding geographic division. In 2002, the major leagues' interleague schedule began rotating opposing divisions so that in every three-year cycle each team would have played every other club in the other league. To keep local bragging rights in play, however, Major League Baseball made sure that city and regional rivals in different leagues played six games against each other. The most important interleague rivalries were the Mets and Yankees in New York and the Cubs and White Sox in Chicago, each of whose fans had no love lost for the other team in town. Rivalries between the Angels and Dodgers in the Los Angeles area and the Giants and Athletics in the Bay Area, where team loyalties were less fiercely mutually exclusive—perhaps because of the traffic congestion between Anaheim and Los Angeles and chilly San Francisco Bay between the cities of San Francisco and Oakland, or maybe just because Californians are more "chill." Manufactured interleague cross-state rivalries between Miami and Tampa Bay in Florida, St. Louis and Kansas City in Missouri, Houston and Dallas (the Rangers) in Texas, Cincinnati and Cleveland in Ohio, and promoting a Canadian rivalry between teams in Montreal and Toronto were not as compelling. The number of interleague games for each team ranged from as few as 12 to as many as 18, depending on the division.

The impact on division races was that the symmetry in scheduling that had been a hallmark of Major League Baseball—each team in a division playing the same number of games against the same teams their division rivals played—was no longer possible. In 2007, when the Mets lost the NL East to the Phillies by a single game, their identical 8-7 records in interleague games obscured the fact that the only American League opponent they had in common was Detroit, against whom both won one of three. The Mets had to play the formidable Yankees six times because of their city affiliation; the Phillies didn't have to play them at all. Although the Yankees were a wild card in 2007, only two teams—both in the American League—won more than their 94 games. Philadelphia did play 96-win AL Central–winning Cleveland three times, while the Mets did not, but facing the Indians three times—the Phillies lost twice—was not the same as having to play the Yankees six times. The Mets split their six games with the Yankees. All told, the four American League teams the Mets played in 2007 combined for a .520 winning percentage, while the five AL teams the Phillies faced—none more than three times—combined for a winning percentage just a shade over .500.

An ironic consequence of the interleague schedule was to diminish the stature of the All-Star Game. The longtime showcase for the best players in the two leagues facing off against each other had already devolved into more of an entertaining exhibition game with no real competitive stakes, unlike in the first five decades of annual All-Star Games, when winning meant league bragging rights that were mightily important. Now that actual teams from the two leagues played midsummer games that counted in the standings, interleague games had the effect of making the All-Star Game a lovefest to appreciate baseball's best and most popular players— not always one and the same—and for them to appreciate each other.

The All-Star break, with a Home Run Derby and other festivities preceding the ame itself, had become an entertainment bonanza. With team broadcasters lobbying fans to vote for their team's players, the voting for starting position players was more a popularity contest than a recognition of the league's best players. Each league's pennant-winning manager from the year before tried to get nearly every All-Star into the game, meaning starting position players were usually out of the game by the late innings (and, increasingly, even earlier). Contrast that with the 1967 All-Star Game that went 15 innings before the National League finally won, 2–1, in which 9 of the 16 starting position players—then chosen by players, managers, and coaches—played the entire game.

As a counterpoint to the 1967 game, both managers in the 2002 All-Star Game, played in Selig's home town of Milwaukee at the new stadium—Miller Park—he had lobbied hard for public money to fund, ran out of players with the score tied 7–7 after 11 innings, forcing the commissioner to call an end to the proceedings. Chafing from that embarrassment and acknowledging the increasing irrelevance of All-Star Games as competitive games, Major League Baseball determined that in 2003, the All-Star Game would have consequential stakes. "This time it counts," was the promotional lead, the gimmick being that the pennant-winning team from whichever league won the All-Star Game would henceforth have home-field advantage in the World Series. Up till then, home-field advantage in the World Series alternated every year between the AL and NL. "This time it counts" counted until 2017, when home-field advantage in the World Series was given to the pennant-winning team with the better regular-season record, unless that team was a wild card.

Selig's most significant—and popular—legacy was raising the stakes in division races by instituting in 2012 a single-elimination game between two wild cards to determine which would advance to the league's five-game division series round. The decision was a masterstroke in that it gave competitive teams a compelling reason to finish first in their division rather than settle for second place and the opportunity to better prepare for an extended postseason run, as had sometimes been the case when two teams competing for the division title played much of the final month with the near-certainty that both would make the division series round, whether as the division winner or the wild card.

With a one-game wild-card game in which there is zero margin for error, winning the division now mattered greatly. The three teams with the best record in the National League in 2015—St. Louis with 100 wins, Pittsburgh with 98, and Chicago with 97—were all in the Central Division. St. Louis led the division every day since mid-April, but rather than coasting to the finish line with assurance that they'd be in the division series even if they slipped into second place, as had been the case since 1995, the Cardinals were forced to play hard to ensure they finished on top to avoid the wild-card playoff, in which anything could happen. The Pirates and Cubs both battled for the division title to do the same, as well as for home-field advantage if they were wild-card teams—which both, in the end, were. The Pirates played at home. The Cubs won. Pittsburgh's season was done.

The year after expanding the wild-card format, Major League Baseball's next step was to transfer the Houston Astros from the National to the American League, creating two 15-team leagues with three divisions of five teams each. The equivalent odd number of teams in both leagues required that interleague games now be played from opening day to closing day all season long rather than in "interleague schedule" weeks during the summer months. Each team plays 20 interleague games, including four every year against their opposite-league division rival and the other 16 against all the teams in a specific division in the other league on a rotating basis. Every third year, when the two leagues matched up by geographic division in interleague play, teams play six games against their opposite-league division rival. As for within their own league, each team plays its division rivals 19 times for 76 games and 33 games against the five teams in each of the two other divisions, with an asterisk. The asterisk is that one team in each division—different each year—plays 34 games against one of the outside divisions in their league and 32 in the other. Schedules are still unbalanced in that no team plays the same number of games against all the same teams as their division rivals.

Major League Baseball's going global with overseas games—literally across the oceans—is another legacy of Selig's reign. As globalization was taking hold as the end of the twentieth century, and 2001—perhaps not a space odyssey but certainly an interconnected world—approached, it was inevitable that the major leagues would soon play an official it-counts-in-the-standings game in a country not the United States or Canada (with franchises in Montreal and Toronto). The logical place to start was south of the border. Baseball is enormously popular around the Caribbean Basin, and close proximity to the United States—as well as Puerto Rico, the Dominican Republic, and Venezuela having become major sources of top-tier talent for the major leagues—contributed to Major League Baseball's having an avid following in the region.

It wasn't until August 16, 1996, however, that the first official major-league game to be played in a foreign country took place—in Monterrey, Mexico, between the NL Western Division's first-place San Diego Padres, the home team, and the New York Mets. Appropriate for the circumstances, San Diego's starting pitcher was none other than Fernando Valenzuela, 16 years after "Fernando-mania" swept Los Angeles during his sensational 1981 rookie season, which was a catalyst for the Dodgers winning the World Series. Valenzuela was the winning pitcher in the first major-league game played in his birth country. The Padres took two of the three games. Three years later, the first game of the 1999 major-league season was also played in Monterrey, the "visiting" Colorado Rockies beating the home team Padres on April 4. Also appropriate for the circumstances, Colorado's Mexican-born third baseman Vinny Castilla went 4-for-5. Opening day for most of the other 28 major-league teams was the next day.

The NBA, meanwhile, capitalizing on the popularity of basketball worldwide and its standing as the preeminent team sport in the Summer Olympics, had made itself a global phenomenon by selling itself outside of North America as the world's elite basketball league. In 1990, the NBA became the first of the four major North American sports leagues to play regular-season games across an ocean by opening the season with back-to-back games in Tokyo, Japan. Two years later, some of the NBA's biggest stars came together as the Dream Team representing the United States in the 1992 Barcelona Olympics, captivating basketball fans around the world and giving superstars like Michael Jordan, Magic Johnson, Larry Bird, and Karl Malone an enduring global following. That fall, the NBA opened its season in Yokohama, Japan, and in 1993 the NBA played an official game in London. The payoff for the NBA included opening the door to talented players from elsewhere playing and starring on NBA teams.

Major League Baseball was no doubt the world's elite baseball league. But baseball was still a niche sport whose center of gravity was the northern Western Hemisphere and Japan, with most of the rest of the world—including England and countries of the British Commonwealth, where cricket was the bat-and-ball passion—offering a collective shrug. Unlike in the Caribbean, the major leagues did not have an intense following in Asia, despite baseball's being the long-standing national pastime in Japan, and that Korea and Taiwan had recently established their own professional leagues. Asia's baseball universe being historically more insular and nearly halfway around the world did not help Major League Baseball become more relevant on the other side of the Pacific. Neither was the perception there that Asian ballplayers, even those in Japan's major leagues, were unlikely to be successful in Major League Baseball.

It wasn't as though major leaguers hadn't already traveled the world to showcase their game. In the 1888–1889 off-season, baseball pioneer Albert Spalding—instrumental in founding the National League in 1876 and president of the Chicago White Stockings (today's Cubs), as well as founder and owner of America's premier sporting goods business—organized a world tour featuring exhibition games between his club, second in the National League in the season just ended, and a team made up of players from other teams around the league. They circled the globe going west, with stops in New Zealand and Australia in the Pacific, the British colony of Ceylon (now the island nation of Sri Lanka) in South Asia, Egypt in the Middle East, Italy and France, and London and other cities in the British Isles. Prominent major leaguers making the trip included White Stockings manager and premier first baseman Cap Anson and New York Giants star shortstop John Montgomery Ward, as well as a pitcher named John Healy whose nickname was "Egyptian" because he was born in Cairo, Illinois. This tour is perhaps most famous for the iconic photograph of the two teams playing baseball against the backdrop of the ancient pyramids.

A similar world tour was organized by Giants manager John McGraw and Chicago White Sox owner Charles Comiskey in the winter of 1913–1914. Supplemented by players from other major-league teams, the Giants and White Sox played each other in Japan, China, Australia, Ceylon, Egypt, and several European countries. If spectators in the countries they visited wondered who these guys were, they didn't have to ask about world-famous athlete Jim Thorpe, star of the 1912 Summer Olympics and now a reserve outfielder on McGraw's Giants. This tour included a photo of big-leaguers posed in front of the Great Sphinx and the pyramids in Egypt, an audience with the pope for McGraw, and the United Kingdom's King George V among 35,000 "baffled English spectators," as described by one McGraw biographer, who watched them play baseball in London in February 1914. "Your game is very interesting," said the king. "I would like to know more about it." Four months later, following the assassination of Archduke Franz Ferdinand of the Austro-Hungarian Empire, King George had other priorities. By the end of July, Europe had plunged into the first of the twentieth century's world wars. Three years later, the United States was also at war.

The major leagues' next overseas forays focused on Japan's growing love for baseball. With the blessing of Commissioner Landis, players from the minor leagues and a handful of major leaguers journeyed to Japan in the 1920s to not only play games but run coaching clinics. In 1931, Lou Gehrig; cornerstone star players Mickey Cochrane, Al Simmons, and Lefty Grove of the Philadelphia Athletics team that had just won its third-straight pennant; and Brooklyn's Lefty O'Doul—one of baseball's best hitters at the time—were among the big-leaguers who barnstormed in Japan. Presumably of no concern to them, Japan was at war in China, having invaded Manchuria in September, which some historians consider to have been the starting gun for the second of the twentieth century's world wars. The next year, after winning his second National League batting title, O'Doul returned to Japan specifically to give baseball instruction to players in the Japanese collegiate league.

If there was such a thing as baseball diplomacy, it was a monthlong tour of 12 Japanese cities by major-league all-stars led by manager Connie Mack in November and December 1934 that led directly to the founding of professional baseball in Japan. If Olympian Jim Thorpe was the high-profile celebrity athlete on the round-the-world tour organized by McGraw and Comiskey 20 years before, this time it was Babe Ruth, whose spectacular home runs and fame preceded him across the ocean. Other all-stars included Gehrig, Jimmie Foxx, Charlie Gehringer, and Lefty Gomez. O'Doul, having just played his last year in the big leagues, was also on the trip, as was a journeyman second-string catcher named Moe Berg. While Ruth was always the center of attention in his comings, goings, and performance on Japanese ball fields, Berg was relishing his role as a tourist with a moving-picture camera, inconspicuously taking in the sites in Tokyo, including capturing the cityscape from rooftops that, in the mythology of "the catcher was a spy," were ostensibly used—they were dated, after all—to help orient American pilots on bombing missions over Japan during World War II.

Unlike the 1888–1889 and 1913–1914 tours pitting two teams of major leaguers against each other for foreign audiences, the 1934 excursion to Japan was the American all-stars playing a team of Japan's best players, most of whom had benefited from the instruction of American ballplayers like O'Doul. Although the Japanese team was thoroughly outplayed, the Japanese game's exposure to major-league players only deepened Japan's love for baseball. Two years later, Japan had its first professional baseball league. Seven years after Ruth and his fellow Americans took Japan by baseball storm—and they were loved for it—the Japanese attacked Pearl Harbor. Babe Ruth became a Japanese curse word. But it wasn't personal.

After the war, O'Doul organized several postseason barnstorming tours of Japan by major-league players. Following the 1953 season, New York's Giants as a team accepted an invitation from Tokyo's Yomiuri Giants to play a series of exhibition games in Japan. Two years later, the

Yankees went, and in 1956 it was the Dodgers. Although it was not an annual occurrence, major-league teams frequently traveled to Japan in the 1960s and 1970s after the regular season ended to play Japanese teams. At any time during these years, Major League Baseball *could have* played regular-season games in Japan. It was the jet age, after all; unlike Spalding, McGraw and Comiskey, and Ruth and O'Doul, they didn't need to clamber aboard ocean liners for a leisurely sail to get there. But given the distance involved, and the jet lag, and the fact that a 162-game schedule requires every team to play virtually every day, such games could not realistically be played during the season. It was just not practical. A regular-season option would be practical only if the games were played while spring training was winding down, allowing for a few days of recovery upon return before Opening Day on the schedule. That is what the NBA had done, and its teams' schedules had the advantage of frequent days off and few games on back-to-back days.

And that is what Major League Baseball finally did on March 29 and 30, 2000, when New York's Mets and Chicago's Cubs, alternating as the home team, played the first two games of their season schedules against each other in baseball-mad Japan four days before Opening Day on April 3. Mets catcher Mike Piazza, in a losing cause, became the first player to hit a home run in an official major-league game played outside the North American continent. The next day, Mets outfielder Benny Agbayani, pinch-hitting with the bases loaded in the 11th inning of a tie game, smashed a grand slam in the Tokyo Dome to give his team from the East Coast a split in their season-opening series against a team from the Midwest on the other side of the vast Pacific Ocean. Born in Hawaii, of mixed Pacific Island inheritance, Agbayani was the perfect American multicultural hero for a game played in the Far East.

Major-league teams returned to the Tokyo Dome to play their first two games on the schedule before baseball's official Opening Day in 2004 (Yankees against "home team" Tampa Bay), 2008 (Red Sox against the "home" Athletics), and 2012 and 2019 (both years the A's "hosting" the Mariners). All four of those two-game sets featured a prominent Japanese-born player as a core regular on his major-league team, all of whom had starred for at least seven years on Japanese teams. Outfielder Hideki Matsui, in his second year with the Yankees after 10 years playing for Tokyo's Yomiuri Giants, went 3-for-9 with a home run and three runs batted in to open his 2004 season in his two-game return to the Tokyo

Dome. Right-hander Daisuke Matsuzaka, in his second year in Boston after seven pitching for the Seibu Lions, was the Red Sox' starting pitcher in their first game of the 2008 season. He gave up two runs in five innings, but it was another Japanese pitcher who got the win in relief—lefty Hideki Okajima, a 12-year veteran of baseball in Japan also in his second year with the Red Sox.

Finally, in 2012, Japanese fans got to see the return of their prodigal son in a major-league game. His name was Ichiro Suzuki, a superb craftsman with the bat and terrific outfielder, identifiable as simply "Ichiro" in both countries. He had been Major League Baseball's most prominent Japanese player since signing with Seattle in 2001 after nine outstanding seasons in the Japanese leagues. He did not disappoint in his much anticipated 12-years-later return to Japan, going 4-for-5 in the Mariners' first game of the 2012 season; Suzuki's 11th-inning RBI single capped a two-run rally to beat Oakland, 3–1. In 2019, Ichiro played the last two games of his career for the Mariners in Japan, going hitless in five at-bats against the Athletics. In the second of those season-opening games, on March 21, 2019, Seattle southpaw Yusei Kikuchi, after eight years pitching for the Seibu Lions, made his big-league debut—the first of his 32 rookie season starts—giving up a run on four hits in 4⅔ innings.

An ambition to enhance the international exposure of the major-league game and promote baseball in a country with a nascent interest in the sport led the Dodgers and the Arizona Diamondbacks, as the home team, to Sydney, Australia, for their first two games of the 2014 season, a week before Opening Day. While baseball had been played Down Under since Spalding's 1898–1899 global tour touched there, it had never attracted more than a handful of adherents. There was, however, a long history of amateur and semipro leagues that had sent 27 Australians to the major leagues by the time reigning National League Cy Young Award winner Clayton Kershaw took the mound for Los Angeles at the Sydney Cricket Grounds on March 22, 2014. The Diamondbacks had a lefty reliever from Sydney on their staff—Ryan Rowland-Smith, who had not pitched in the major leagues since 2010—but he did not appear in either game in Australia and was released after six appearances in April.

Commissioner Rob Manfred pushed the foreign-games envelope further in 2019. Major League Baseball began its regular-season schedule with Seattle and Oakland playing two games in Tokyo in March, a week before Opening day; Cincinnati and St. Louis squared off for two mid-

April games in Monterrey; Houston and the Los Angeles Angels played two games in Monterrey in early May; and the Yankees and Red Sox took their world-renowned rivalry to London for two games at the end of June. Despite having to cross the Atlantic and a five-hour time difference between the eastern United States and England, the Yankees and Red Sox got just two days to fly to London and acclimate to the time change and one day to return home and recover. The nearly 119,000 who filed into London Stadium for the two games were not "baffled English spectators," as they had been in 1914; many were Americans who traveled to London specifically to watch the Yankees play the Red Sox, and baseball—while certainly not a mainstream sport in the United Kingdom—was not as "baffling" a proposition as it had been a century before.

'Twas not Yankees versus Redcoats in the colonies back in 1776, but the Yankees did trounce the Red Sox in England—twice—by scores of 17–13 and 12–8—not so much your typical major-league games.

5

BASEBALL'S ASIAN-PACIFIC TIDE

Ichiro Suzuki was a phenomenon in his "rookie" year of 2001. His slashing batting style, where he was already running hard out of the left-handed batter's box as he made contact, became instantly recognizable. His 242 hits were the most since Bill Terry smacked 254 in 1930, a year when major-league hitters collectively batted .296. His .350 batting average led the league. He struck out only 53 times in 738 plate appearances—just 7 percent of the times he came up, when the major-league average was 17 percent. He led the majors in stolen bases with 56 and was caught just 14 times. When he was in the on-deck circle waiting his turn to bat, many eyes in the ballpark would turn to watch him, not the batter, as he went through a precise and graceful series of stretches that were mesmerizing. Playing right field in Seattle for the Mariners, he had a huge media entourage covering his first year and reporting ad nauseam on it across the Pacific to a very interested audience in Japan. He was called by his first name, Ichiro, not his last, Suzuki.

Ichiro won both the American League's Rookie of the Year and Most Valuable Player Awards in 2001. The only previous time that had happened was for Boston outfielder Fred Lynn in 1975. But while Lynn was a 23-year-old *actual* rookie, Ichiro was 27 years old with nine years, 951 games, 1,278 hits, 118 home runs, and 119 stolen bases in 132 attempts behind him playing for Kobe city's Orix Blue Wave in the Japan Pacific League in Nippon Professional Baseball. Yep, Ichiro Suzuki was from Japan. He was only the eleventh Japanese player in the major leagues, and the first position player. The first ten were all pitchers, all but one of whom made their big-league debut in 1995 or later. Only one of them, the Dodgers' Hideo Nomo, was an established star.

It was a long time coming, Japanese players in the major leagues, given that baseball was Japan's national pastime, too—even more so than in America, since Major League Baseball's popularity by now paled in comparison to that of the NFL and NBA. Professional baseball in Japan was still in its formative stages when World War II intervened. When the war was over, US occupying forces encouraged the Japanese love affair with baseball as a cultural tool for facilitating systemic reforms to put an end to militarism and promote democratic and free market institutions in Japan, and to align Japan with the United States in the rapidly escalating Cold War with the Soviet Union. Nippon Professional Baseball, divided into two leagues—the Japan Pacific League and Japan Central League—with franchises owned by large business and industrial corporations whose names identified the teams, had been thriving since the 1950s.

Frequent postseason tours by major-league teams beginning in the mid-1950s built bridges between Major League Baseball and Nippon Professional Baseball. If cross-fertilization of both countries' major-league-level players was in the future, it was for decades decidedly one-way. Beginning in the 1960s, Japan became a destination for a very few major leaguers at the end of their careers wanting to continue playing longer or in midcareer but struggling to hang on as major leaguers. Given the much smaller physical stature of most players in postwar Japan and the absence of an extensive and layered minor-league system to feed Nippon Professional Baseball, the assumption was that Japanese "major leaguers" could not compete in Major League Baseball. For one thing, the quality of competition and play in the Japanese leagues were considered inferior not only to the major leagues, but to Triple-A as well. The Japanese style of play was more small ball, a throwback to the Deadball Era, than the power game then prevailing in Major League Baseball. Japanese players had speed and agility and were well practiced and disciplined. But it was thought that Japanese hitters would be overpowered by major-league pitchers, that long flies belted by Japanese sluggers would fall short of the bigger dimensions of major-league ballparks, and that while some might get by on craftiness and pinpoint control, Japanese pitchers would be shredded by big-league hitters and clobbered by major-league sluggers.

In a groundbreaking act of international baseball diplomacy, blessed by the major league commissioners in both countries, the San Francisco Giants and Osaka's Nankai Hawks in the Japan Pacific League reached a player-exchange agreement that allowed a trio of the Hawks' young prospects to play in the Giants' farm system in 1964. For the Hawks (and Japanese baseball), it was an opportunity for their young players to gain experience and hone their skills in the proving, grooming grounds of a top-tier major-league team. For the Giants (and Major League Baseball) it was a chance to check out just how good young Japanese prospects were relative to American ballplayers their age just getting started in their professional careers. The Japanese prospects had to sign a Giants contract, complete with the reserve clause, that included an option clause for San Francisco to pay Nankei $10,000 should any of them be promoted to the majors. Both franchises assumed the Giants would release the Japanese players at the end of the season to return to Nankei, because none of them was expected to be remotely ready for the major leagues, especially with only a year of seasoning in the low minors.

But in the realm of unintended consequences, one of them was ready. Excelling as a reliever for San Francisco's Single-A affiliate in Fresno, 20-year-old right-hander Masanori Murakami was an unexpected September call-up, making him the first Japanese player ever to play in the major leagues. Murakami pitched 11 innings in his first eight games, all out of the bullpen, without allowing a run before surrendering three in four innings to blemish his perfect ERA on the last day of the season. Sufficiently impressed, the Giants offered Murakami a major-league contract for 1965, and sent the necessary $10,000 to Nankei, rather than release him from his contract so he could return to Japan and pitch for the Hawks. This provoked baseball's equivalent of a major diplomatic row between Major League Baseball and Nippon Professional Baseball involving both leagues' commissioners. Murakami was caught in the middle, with both the Giants and the Hawks claiming his rights. Nankei finally agreed to allow Murakami to honor his Giants contract and pitch for them in 1965, after which San Francisco would let him return to Japan if that's what he wanted. Torn between two poles, Murakami returned to San Francisco in 1965 with mixed results. In nine of the 45 games he pitched in relief, Murakami gave up more runs (21) than innings pitched (11⅔) for an earned run average in those games of 16.20. In his other 34 appearances, totaling 62⅔ innings, Murakami's ERA was an excellent 1.44.

Murakami, who had difficulty with the language and culture, was subjected to demeaning ethnic stereotypes. Murakami did not, however, face the racist bigotry that Black and Latino players had. It helped that he played in San Francisco—a city with a large Asian population—and for the Giants, a franchise at the forefront of diversifying its major-league roster. Ironically, the greatest resistance to Japanese players in Major League Baseball came from Japan. Rather than rooting for their native son to show that a Japanese player could effectively compete in the major leagues, there was widespread sentiment in his home country that Murakami should return to pitch for Nankei. His family wanted him home, not across the vast Pacific in America, reinforcing that sentiment. He was castigated in some circles as a traitor to his country. Masanori Murakami returned to Japan and the Nankai Hawks in 1966. It would not be until 30 years later that another Japanese player—also a pitcher—would play in the major leagues, leaving unanswered the question of how well some of the elite players in Nippon Professional Baseball in those years would have fared had they had the opportunity to play in the major leagues—foremost among them the great Japanese slugger Sadaharu Oh.

The 26-year-old Oh was entering his prime when Murakami went back to Osaka in 1966. Oh's 48 home runs that year for Tokyo's Yomiuri Giants gave him 260 in his first seven years. He was Japan's Babe Ruth. He was Japan's Josh Gibson. He was a contemporary of Hank Aaron and Willie Mays, albeit on the far side of the Pacific. Although Sadaharu Oh was undersized compared to most major-league sluggers, he was the same height and weight as Mays and an inch taller and slightly heavier than former New York Giants slugger Mel Ott, owner of 511 big-league homers. Oh finished the 1976 season with 716 home runs—two more than the Babe for worldwide bragging rights. His 50 home runs in 1977 at the age of 37 put him 11 ahead of Aaron for the most on the worldwide all-time list.

Oh finished his career in 1980 with 868 home runs. His 30 that year were the fewest he had hit since his third season in the Japanese leagues in 1961. There was much debate during his career, and after, about how many home runs Sadaharu Oh would have hit playing in the majors. The presumption was that having to bat in bigger major-league stadiums against better, harder-throwing major-league pitchers, he surely would not have topped Ruth or Aaron or Mays, and perhaps not even Ott. But since there was not a chance of that happening after Murakami's one full season in 1965—at least not for several decades—we'll never know for sure.

While no Nippon Professional Baseball players gave up home and country to play Major League Baseball in the 1970s and 1980s, a handful of major leaguers crossed the Pacific to extend their careers in Japan, as did a handful of young players hoping for a career breakthrough. Former major leaguers playing in Japan believed that any number of Japanese players had the skills and ability to play Major League Baseball. Following both leagues' 1990 season, a Japanese all-star team stunned visiting major-league all-stars (both teams including many young players at the beginning of their careers) by beating them four times in seven games. It was no longer unthinkable for Japanese players to believe they could compete very successfully in the major leagues. Seattle Mariners stars Ken Griffey Jr. and Randy Johnson said so specifically to Hideo Nomo, outstanding rookie pitcher for Osaka's Kintetsu Buffaloes, after the right-hander throttled the major leaguers in one of the games. Nomo, it should be noted, had the physical build of many American pitchers—he was 6-foot-2 and 210 pounds. (Murakami, at 6-feet and 180 pounds, was also on the big side for a Japanese player.)

Nomo liked hearing that. He was Kintetsu's ace the next four years, with more strikeouts than innings pitched every season. He also made the acquaintance of Tokyo-born, LA-based talent agent Don Nomura, whose professional ambition was to represent Japanese baseball players wanting to play in the major leagues. After Japan's 1994 season ended, Nomo unexpectedly announced his voluntary retirement from Nippon Professional Baseball, despite having just turned 26. Nomura brokered meetings with three West Coast teams, and in February 1995 Hideo Nomo signed with the Los Angeles Dodgers. After a short stint in the minor leagues, Nomo made his first big-league start on May 2 in San Francisco. He walked the bases loaded in the first inning, survived a one-out double in the third—the only hit he allowed—and threw five shutout innings.

The controversy surrounding Nomo's being the first Japanese to play in the major leagues since Murakami was in Japan, not the United States. Nomo's voluntary retirement was perceived as a selfish subterfuge of Japanese cultural norms to clear the way for a major-league career in

America. As in Major League Baseball, the reserve clause in Nippon Professional Baseball contracts bound a player to his former team if he voluntarily retired but then unretired—a measure intended to prevent players from doing just that so they could, in effect, be free agents—unless, that is, he unretired to play professional baseball in another country, which was the strategy Nomura worked out with Nomo. Making himself a trailblazer, Nomo's LA sojourn was widely covered by the Japanese media. Many fans back home rooted for him to fail, not necessarily because they did not want a Japanese player to succeed in the crucible of Major League Baseball, but because of how he engineered becoming a Dodger.

Nomo was anything but a failure. His forkball flummoxed National League batters. As the city had been with "Fernando-mania" when Valenzuela burst on the scene in 1981, Los Angeles was caught up in "Nomo-mania." Nomo made 28 starts, was 13–6 with three shutouts to tie Greg Maddux (arguably the best pitcher in baseball), had a 2.54 earned-run average (second in the league to Maddux), and led National League pitchers in strikeouts and strikeout ratio with 236 K's in 191⅓ innings. He easily outpaced Atlanta's Chipper Jones to win Rookie of the Year honors. Nomo won three of his last four starts, including the game that clinched at least a tie for the division title, in the next-to-last game of the season. By the end of the year Hideo Nomo was being celebrated in Japan for his terrific first year in the majors. His success was a long-awaited vindication of Nippon Professional Baseball, and Japan's unique baseball culture, as measuring up to major-league standards.

Perhaps even more important, Nomo was no one-year major-league wonder. He won 16 in 1996; his 16th win was a no-hitter against the Rockies in Colorado's Coors Field, a hitters' paradise because of the altitude. In 1997, Nomo reached his 500th career strikeout in fewer innings than any major-league pitcher before him. Traded to the Mets in June 1998, Nomo returned for a Hollywood encore as a free agent in 2002, going 16–6 that year and 16–13 in 2003. Shoulder problems in 2004, after he had thrown 1,787 innings in the major leagues following 1,051 in the Japanese leagues since beginning his professional career 14 years earlier, marked the near end horizon for Hideo Nomo. He was the first Japanese player with an extended major-league career, and it was a very successful one. Nomo won 123 major-league games while losing 109.

There was no longer a question that Nippon Professional Baseball players—or at least the best Japanese *pitchers*—were capable of competing successfully in the major leagues. Many Japanese players wanted to test their abilities in the majors—the best competition in the baseball world, with all due respect to the Japanese leagues. Major-league teams were well aware of who the best Japanese players were, followed their fortunes, and were even willing to pay a small fortune to those who came to play for them. The reserve clause in Japanese contracts, however, bound players to their teams for nine years before they became eligible for free agency, after which they could pursue offers from major-league teams—unless, of course, a player took up Nomo's "voluntarily retiring in Japan" gambit. To shut down that option but allow Japanese players the opportunity to sign with major-league teams before they became free agents, while protecting the Japanese leagues from the effects of being preyed upon by Major League Baseball's much better-capitalized clubs, Nippon Professional Baseball in December 1998 negotiated a multistep "posting" system to systematize the process.

The bottom line of this system was to ensure Japanese clubs received lucrative (some would say unreasonably lucrative) compensation for any of their players signed by a major-league team before they became free agents. Any major-league team could bid on a Japanese player posted by his team by informing the commissioner of Major League Baseball how much it would pay to the team for exclusive rights to negotiate a contract with the player. Because all bids to the commissioner were confidential, each team was in effect bidding against itself; no team had any idea which other clubs were interested in the same Japanese player or how much they were willing to pay his Japanese team to get him. The commissioner would forward the highest bid—and *only* the highest bid, without naming any of the teams with lesser bids—to the Japanese club, which could withdraw the player if it considered the offer too low. Should the Japanese club approve the bid, the major-league team had 30 days to negotiate a contract acceptable to the player. Failure to reach agreement would mean the player was off the table until the next year, preventing him from trying to choose his preferred destination.

As a historical aside, until Jackie Robinson and Larry Doby proved Black players could compete with the best in the heretofore all-white major leagues, the Negro Leagues were the only avenue for Black players to have professional baseball careers. It was major-league teams' signing large numbers of young Black players in the 1950s, at first from the Negro League teams they played on and then as amateur prospects, that effectively killed off the Negro Leagues. It didn't matter that nearly all were sent first to the minor leagues, as was true for white players, where many failed to make the grade for promotion to the big leagues, opening the door to Black players for a chance to play in the majors put an end to the Negro Leagues' reason to be. While the major-league door was now open for Japanese players, the requirement that major-league teams pay twice for a Japanese player not yet a free agent in Japan—first the posting fee to buy exclusive negotiating rights to the player, and then his contract—meant that, even if some of its best players left to play Major League Baseball, few would leave in any given season, guaranteeing that the competitive integrity of Nippon Professional Baseball would remain intact.

By the conclusion of the 2000 season, seven Japanese players had followed Hideo Nomo from Nippon Professional Baseball to the major leagues, all of them pitchers. Japanese pitchers had shown they could be successful against major-league hitters. That Japanese position players had yet to prove they would not be overmatched batting against hard-throwing major-league pitchers was only because none had crossed over to Major League Baseball. That changed in 2001.

Ichiro Suzuki had hit .359 since becoming an everyday regular for the Orix Blue Wave in 1994, never once failing to win the Japan Pacific League batting title. New York Mets manager Bobby Valentine called Suzuki one of the five best baseball players in the world, based on his experience managing Chiba's Lotte Marines in the Japan Pacific League in 1995 when he was between major-league managerial jobs. He had won seven straight batting championships, and there was every reason to believe Ichiro would make it eight in a row in 2001—except he desperately wanted to test his skills in the major leagues, especially having proven to be a tough out in postseason exhibition all-star games against visiting major-league pitchers.

Although Suzuki was still a year away from free agency, Orix agreed to make their superstar player available to major-league teams. And the Seattle Mariners, whose majority owner was the president of Nintendo, the global Japanese consumer electronics and digital-gaming corporation based in Kobe—the Blue Wave's home city—were very interested in him. Seattle had an influential ethnic Japanese community that would help him feel at home. The Mariners already had a high-profile Japanese player to welcome him aboard—closer Kazuhiro Sasaki, signed as a free agent after 10 years pitching for Yokohama, who had just won the AL's 2000 Rookie of the Year Award with 37 saves. And the Mariners had just gone to the postseason for the third time in six years. Seattle was the perfect destination for Ichiro. The Mariners' secret $13 million posting fee was the high bid for Suzuki.

Agreeing to a three-year contract worth $14 million, Suzuki joined a 2001 Mariners team that many in baseball assumed would not be nearly as formidable as the year before because they no longer had the services of two of Major League Baseball's best players—superstar shortstop Alex Rodriguez, the recipient of a 10-year, $252 million free agent contract that sent him to Texas, and superstar center fielder Ken Griffey Jr., traded to Cincinnati in 1999 to accommodate his desire to play closer to his home in Florida. Seattle ended up not missing them.

Ichiro made for a compelling superstar in his own right. He went 2-for-5 in his first game. Going hitless in four at-bats the next day made his second game the only time in his big-league career, which spanned 2,653 games and 9,934 at-bats, that Ichiro Suzuki went to sleep with a career batting average less than .300. Quick out of the box and fast, Ichiro was hard for infielders to defend. Played at normal depth, he was a threat to beat out infield hits on balls not hit directly to an infielder; played in, he'd rip the pitch through the infield. Playing in 157 games, Ichiro failed to get a hit in only 21 of them. His only slump was when he went four games in mid-July without a hit. The Mariners won 116 regular-season games, setting a new American League record. Suzuki went 12-for-20 as Seattle beat Cleveland in their division series, but was stymied in the ALCS, which the Mariners lost to the Yankees in five games.

Two years later, another batting star in Nippon Professional Baseball—perhaps even bigger, because he played for Tokyo's Yomiuri Giants, Japan's analogue to the New York Yankees' "forever" dynasty—made his major-league debut—with the Yankees, who signed him for three years and $21 million as a Japanese free agent. Solidly built at 6-foot-2 and 210 pounds (versus Ichiro's lithe 5-foot-11 and 165 pounds), Hideki Matsui was affectionately known in Japan—and henceforth in America, too—as "Godzilla" for his bad complexion and power-hitting stroke that terrorized pitchers. In 10 years for Yomiuri from 1993 to

2002, Matsui crashed 332 homers, had 889 runs batted in, and batted .304. He was a three-time MVP in Japan's Central League. Godzilla had just enjoyed the best year of his career with 50 home runs, 107 RBIs, and a .334 batting average. He had not missed a game since his rookie year in 1993, having played in 1,250 consecutive games by the close of Japan's 2002 season.

The Yankees didn't have to pay a posting fee to acquire his rights, but George Steinbrenner pulled out all the stops to sign Matsui by negotiating a partnership agreement with the Yomiuri Giants during the summer of 2002 that, in the end, had little practical effect. Breaking his rule against such participation, he also sent Yankees stars Jason Giambi and Bernie Williams on a postseason tour of Japan by major-league players to sell Matsui on the merits of playing for baseball's Greatest Team on Earth. Although he was legally a free agent, Matsui sought the blessing of his team's politically powerful owner, which he got, with the bonus of the owner telling him that if he wanted to play in America's major leagues, it should be with the Yankees—the only major-league team with as storied a history as the Yomiuri Giants. That sealed the deal.

Given the historical prominence of both the Yomiuri Giants and New York Yankees, and that Matsui was the first Japanese power hitter to try his craft in Major League Baseball, the Japanese media coverage of Godzilla's first year in New York was even more intense than it had been for Ichiro. More than 500 reporters were present in New York City when Matsui was introduced as the newest Yankee. Matsui got a hit in each of the Yankees first six games in 2003 but waited till his first game at Yankee Stadium, the seventh of the season, to hit his first major-league home run. It was a grand slam on April 8 that proved the difference in the Yankees' 7–3 win against the Twins. Godzilla ended up with only 16 homers, but his 106 RBIs were the most by a Yankees rookie since Joe DiMaggio's 125 in 1936. He was second in the AL Rookie of the Year voting. The Yankees won their division and went to the World Series, with Matsui getting a critical double off Red Sox ace Pedro Martinez and scoring the tying run in a three-run eighth-inning rally that staved off defeat in Game Seven of the ALCS, allowing his team the chance to win in 11 innings. Matsui's three-run first-inning homer led the Yankees to victory in Game Two of the World Series against Florida's Marlins.

Both Ichiro and Godzilla went on to have very successful major-league careers. Suzuki virtually guaranteed his place in Cooperstown in his first 10 years with Seattle, never once with fewer than 200 hits or a batting average less than .300. In 2004, on his way to his second batting title with a .372 average, Suzuki broke George Sisler's single-season record of 257 hits set in 1920 with 262; his 225 hits in 2009 gave him nine consecutive years with at least 200, breaking Willie Keeler's prior record of eight straight years from 1894 to 1901; and his 214 hits in 2010—the fifth year in a row he led the league, and the seventh time in his career—equaled Pete Rose's 10 years with 200 hits, except Ichiro's were all in a row. Only Ty Cobb led his league in hits more often than Ichiro, and Cobb did so twice with fewer than 200 hits.

Suzuki finished his career with 3,089 hits in the major leagues, which came after his 1,278 hits in Japan's major-league equivalent. His 4,367 hits in the two "major" leagues are the most of anyone to ever play the game, surpassing Rose's 4,256. While there is merit to the argument that the quality of baseball, including the pitching, is better in the major leagues, the proposition that Rose's 427 minor-league hits should be counted in a career-hits faceoff between the two players, giving Rose 4,683 (316 more than Ichiro), on the grounds that Nippon Professional Baseball is more Triple-A than major-league level is misplaced on two counts. First, Rose never played a game at any minor-league level higher than Single-A, which was not as high-quality as the Japanese leagues during Ichiro's career, and second, the 162-game major-league schedule that Rose played was nearly 25 percent longer each year than the schedule Suzuki played in Japan.

Hideki Matsui followed up his "rookie" major-league season with 31 homers (his career high) and 108 RBIs in 2004, and 23 homers and a career high 116 RBIs in 2005, while playing every Yankees game. That earned him a new four-year, $52 million contract to continue playing for the Yankees. Matsui ran his consecutive-games streak, including in Japan, to 1,769—519 of them as a Yankee—before breaking his wrist trying for a diving catch 32 games into the 2006 season. By 2009, Matsui was primarily a designated hitter, and it was in that role that Godzilla excelled as his 28 home runs in 2009 helped the Yankees return to the top of the AL East for the first time since 2006 and to their first World Series since 2003. Starting just three games as the DH in the Yankees' six-game takedown of Philadelphia's Phillies in the World Series and pinch-hitting in the three others, Matsui was the series MVP with 8 hits and 8 RBIs, including 3 home runs, in 13 at-bats. He was a one-man wrecking crew in the Yankees' Game Six victory to clinch the series, driving in six of their seven runs. That was his last game as a Yankee. Playing for the Angels in 2010, the Athletics in 2011, and Rays in 2012 on separate free-agent deals, Godzilla retired with 175 major-league home runs, giving him a career total of 507 between the major leagues and Nippon Professional Baseball.

In contrast to the big-league success stories of Nomo, Ichiro, and Matsui were the cautionary tales of Hideki Irabu and Kazuo Matsui that not all Japanese stars testing their skills in Major League Baseball would live up to their hype. Irabu was a big, heavyset, 6-foot-4, 240-pound hard-throwing right-hander whose ambition was to pitch for the Yankees. Matsui, 5-foot-10 with excellent speed and a golden glove to match his spiky orange-tinted hair, was the first prominent Japanese infielder to cross the Pacific.

A nine-year veteran in Japan whose career began as a 19-year-old in 1988, Irabu was a power-pitcher whose 46–34 record, 2.76 ERA, and 10.2 strikeouts per 9 innings in 710 innings pitching for Chiba's Lotte Marines between 1993 and 1996 attracted the attention of both the Yankees and San Diego Padres. Notwithstanding the Yankees' interest, the Padres made the better offer, and so it was to San Diego that Chiba sold Irabu in January 1997. Except Irabu refused to pitch for the Padres. It had to be the Yankees. And so, in late May, San Diego finally traded him to the Bronx. Even though he had yet to throw a single pitch, even in the minor leagues, the Yankees signed him to a four-year deal worth $12.8 million. (Nomo earned just half that in his first four years with the Dodgers, and that included his $2 million signing bonus.)

Matsui was signed by the Mets seven years later, in 2004, after nine years starring at shortstop for Tokorozawa's Seibu Lions, in which he had a .309 career batting average and 305 stolen bases. Just as Steinbrenner, envious of Ichiro's success and high profile in Seattle, went after Godzilla to have his own Japanese star—Irabu *not* having measured up—the Mets went all out to bring a Japanese star of their own to their New York rivalry with the Yankees by offering him $23 million for four years and persuading Jose Reyes, their impressive 20-year-old rookie shortstop, to play second base to make room for "Little" Matsui, as Kazuo became known to distinguish him from the Yankees' Hideki.

Both players had auspicious big-league debuts. When Irabu started his first major-league game in New York on July 10, 1997, there were nearly 52,000 fans jammed into Yankee Stadium, not to mention 300 reporters, most of them from Japan. Just 16,100 fans, by contrast, were in the stands at San Francisco's Candlestick Park on May 2, 1995, when Nomo became the first Japanese pitcher to step on a major-league mound since Murakami, and 34,159 were at Dodger Stadium for his home debut on May 12. Irabu rose to the occasion in his first big-league start, striking out nine and giving up two runs on five hits in 6⅔ innings to beat Detroit. He struggled the rest of the season, however, with a 5–4 record and 7.09 earned run average. Matsui, batting lead-off for the Mets on Opening Day 2004 in Atlanta, hit a home run on the first major-league pitch he saw, doubled in his next at bat to drive in a run, walked with the bases loaded his third time up to bring home another run, had another double, and was intentionally walked in his fifth plate appearance. He was batting 1.000. Matsui finished with a .272 batting average in 114 games, missing most of August and September with a severe ankle injury.

Irabu's preferred destination proved disastrous for his career. Perhaps because of the media pressure in both New York (which bedeviled many major-league stars whose careers began in other cities) and Tokyo, he failed to live up to expectations. Ineffective his first year, Irabu had a credible 13–9 record for the 114-win 1998 Yankees but struggled the last three months of the season and did not pitch in any postseason games for the unstoppable World Series–winning team. Meanwhile, Irabu's arrogant behavior and indulgent lifestyle—for cigarettes, alcohol, and food— violated the Yankees' professional ethics and got him on the wrong side of both his teammates and owner George Steinbrenner. His being late to cover first base in a spring training game in 1999 prompted the Boss to call Irabu "a fat pussy toad," which was the beginning of his end in New York. Irabu was 11–7 with an unsightly 4.84 ERA in 1999 and again made no starts as the Yankees won another World Series. After a 29–20 record in three years with the Yankees, Irabu was traded to Montreal. He pitched his last major-league season in 2002 for the Texas Rangers. Nine years later he was dead—a suicide.

Kazuo Matsui's was a cautionary tale less tragic than Hideki Irabu's, but was also likely influenced by the hype he was given. The Mets' signing of Kazuo was heralded by his being the cover story for *ESPN The Magazine*, in which he was described as having "as much speed as Ichiro and nearly as much power as Godzilla" and called one of the five best shortstops on the planet alongside Alex Rodriguez, Nomar Garciaparra, Derek Jeter, and Miguel Tejada. And, as the cover photo made clear, Kazuo Matsui was not like the inscrutable Ichiro, nor like the formal and polite Hideki Matsui; Little Matsui was very much an outgoing, hip-hop personality. Proving inadequate defensively at shortstop—in 2005, he and Jose Reyes swapped positions, so Kazuo was now a second baseman—hamstrung by injuries, and finding major-league pitchers much tougher on him than those in Japan, Matsui became an itinerant. He was traded to Colorado in 2006, went to Houston in 2008, and was back in Japan by 2011. Playing in 630 major-league games, of which he started 565, Matsui was only marginally better than a replacement player from Triple-A.

Sixty-three Japanese players have left Nippon Professional Baseball to play in the major leagues since Hideo Nomo voluntarily retired to do so in 1995. With the exception of Ichiro and Hideki Matsui, those most coveted by major-league teams were elite starting pitchers in Japan. Daisuke Matsuzaka's first two years with Boston were close to expectations—15–12 in his 2007 "rookie" year, helping the Red Sox win the World Series, and 18–3 record in 2008. Hiroki Kuroda's 211 starts in seven big-league seasons from 2008 to 2014 are the second most by a Japanese pitcher in the major leagues after Nomo's 318 starts. Yu Darvish, in his second start of his third year in the majors in 2014, reached his 500th strikeout in fewer innings than Nomo, and Darvish's 11.1 K's per 9 innings is the best all-time career ratio by a starting pitcher. Masahiro Tanaka has proved a reliable and occasionally exceptional pitcher, winning 63 percent of his decisions since coming to the Yankees in 2014. Like Nomo and Irabu, they were all six feet or taller and over 200 pounds. While Kuroda was eligible as a free agent in Japan to negotiate unencumbered with any major-league team, Boston paid a $51 million posting fee for negotiating rights to Matsuzaka; Texas, $51.7 million for Darvish; and the Yankees, $20 million for Tanaka.

In addition to language and culture, Japanese starting pitchers, used to pitching once a week in Japan, have had to acclimate to the rigors of starting every fifth day in the major leagues. Most of the elite starting pitchers coming from Japan have spent all or nearly all of at least one season on the injured list with arm problems. Matsuzaka's big-league career came to an end at age 33 because of arm injuries. Tommy John surgery and later recurring elbow problems cost Darvish the 2015 season and most of 2018. Shohei Ohtani, a superb hitter as well as a top-tier starting pitcher in Japan, started just 10 games for the Angels in his 2018 "rookie" season before needing Tommy John surgery and did not pitch at all in 2019; he did, however, continue to be effective in his other role as a designated hitter. Since his first year with the Yankees, Tanaka's frequent elbow issues have raised the specter of the Tommy John operating table that he so far has been able to avoid.

Major League Baseball is also drawing players from South Korea and Taiwan. Both countries' passion for baseball was seeded by their imperial overlords when they were ruled by the Japanese for half a century before World War II put an end to Japan's Asia-Pacific empire. Their professional leagues were just getting off the ground floor in the 1980s—1982 was the inaugural season for the Korea Baseball Organization, and 1989 for the Chinese Professional Baseball League in Taiwan—but both countries were noted for the quality of their youth, high-school, and college baseball programs. One could say Japan created a youth league monster in Taiwan, whose Little League teams captured 17 Little League World Series in 28 years from 1969 to 1996 before temporarily withdrawing from its affiliation with Little League Baseball until the early 2000s. South Korea in 1982 was the only country to interrupt Cuba's run of 12 championships in the 13 Baseball World Cup series played between 1976 and 2005, and was runner-up five times. Taiwan's national team finished second or third four times in those 13 series. (Amateur US and Japanese national teams, by contrast, both won five second- and third-place medals in Baseball World Cup competition those years.)

Twenty-three South Koreans and 16 born in Taiwan have played in the major leagues, nearly all signed as amateur free agents in their teens and very early twenties. Top high school and college players in South Korea and Taiwan, however, did not have the advantage of a professional baseball superstructure as well developed and competitive as Nippon Professional Baseball, although the Korea Baseball Organization is catching up. But drawing the attention of big-league scouts in international competition and occasionally in collegiate championship series in their home countries, their baseball career options were not limited to the professional leagues of their home countries. Whereas major-league teams could assess the development of Japanese players by how well they did their first years in the Japanese leagues—widely considered to be akin to at least Double-A, if not Triple-A—before considering whether to invest in them, the prospects they signed in South Korea and Taiwan had to prove themselves in the minor leagues.

In order of appearance, the first Asian ballplayer from across the Pacific to play in the major leagues after Masanori Murakami in 1965 was not Hideo Nomo (or anyone else) from Japan, but a solidly built 6-foot-2, 200-pound right-hander from South Korea named Chan Ho Park. The Dodgers signed Park, who had just turned 20, in January 1994, considering him to be one of the best amateur pitchers in the world based on having seen him pitch in international competition. Destined for the Dodgers' Double-A affiliate, Park began the season in Los Angeles, pitching twice in relief before being sent down. By 1996, Park was in Los Angeles to stay. The next year, he was a regular in the Dodgers' starting rotation alongside Nomo. LA's Korean community celebrated him as much as the city's Japanese community celebrated Nomo, and Dodgers fans celebrated both. Park outlasted Nomo with the Dodgers. From 1997 to 2001, after which he left LA as a free agent for Texas, Chan Ho Park averaged 33 starts and 213 innings a year, winning 75 while losing 49. Park left Major League Baseball in 2010 with 124 career wins and 98 losses; Nomo was 123–109 in his big-league career, after having already compiled a 78–46 record in Japan.

Outfielder Shin-Soo Choo and left-hander Hyun-Jin Ryu are the two most prominent Koreans to play in the major leagues since Park. Originally signed out of a South Korean high school by Seattle, Choo reached the big leagues in 2005 but made his mark playing seven years in Cleveland and one in Cincinnati before signing as a major-league free agent with Texas in 2014. His 218 major-league home runs are the most by an Asian-born player. Unlike Park and Choo, Ryu's seven outstanding seasons in the Korean league was what drew the Dodgers' attention. In a posting system similar to Major League Baseball's agreement with Nippon Professional Baseball, the Dodgers were able to sign Ryu for six years and $36 million only after paying his Korean team nearly $26 million for negotiating rights. After going 14–8 and 14–7 his first two seasons with the Dodgers, Ryu missed the next two years with shoulder and elbow problems and more than three months in 2018 with a groin injury in a year he finished with a 10–5 record and 1.97 ERA in 15 starts. Ryu's 14–5 record and league-leading 2.32 earned run average in 2019 set him up for a seven-year $130 million free agent contract with Toronto, for whom he was the second-best pitcher in Major League Baseball the first year of his contract in 2020, according to the pitching wins above replacement metric.

None of the players from Taiwan who've made it to the major leagues were on any of Taiwan's Little League World Series championship teams, nor did any play in Taiwan's professional league, which has not lived up to the reputation of the island nation's little league organization and whose integrity has been compromised by corruption and scandals involving professional gamblers betting on baseball. They attracted the attention of big-league scouts mostly in collegiate-level international competition. Except for lefty Wei-Yin Chen, who proved himself pitching five years in Japan for Nagoya's Chunichi Dragons, all were schooled as prospects in the minor leagues. The first to make it to the majors was outfielder Chin-Feng Chen, a September call-up by the Dodgers in 2002, who played just 19 games in the majors in parts of five seasons.

Only three players from Taiwan—all pitchers and all six feet or taller—had appreciable big-league careers. Right-hander Chien-Ming Wang with the Yankees and lefty reliever Hung-Chih Kuo with the Dodgers both debuted in 2005 after four years in the minor leagues; Wei-Yin Chen got his first start with the Orioles in 2012 after being signed as a Japanese-league free agent. (An opt-out clause in Chen's Chunichi contract allowed Baltimore to avoid having to post a bid for his rights.) Chen was 46–32 in 117 starts for Baltimore from 2012 to 2015, including 16–6 in 2014 to help the Orioles to a runaway division title. He finished his career with the Miami Marlins in 2019. Kuo pitched for the Dodgers his entire seven years in the majors, mostly as a reliever, averaging 10.6 strikeouts per 9 innings. Wang appeared headed for a long and productive career, 19–6 and 19–7 in 2006 and 2007, until he tore a ligament in his right foot in June 2008 while running the bases in Houston—the Astros were still in the National League, which meant the Yankees could not use a DH—that cost him the rest of the year and from which he never recovered his effectiveness. He finished his career in 2016 in Kansas City with twice as many major-league wins (68) as loses (34).

6

BASEBALL'S FINEST HOURS

Governments, tech industries, and technophobes feared a breakdown of the digital world—and what the consequences might be for the real world—as the year 2000, or Y2K, beckoned. Far from any of the worst-case scenarios of what might happen, nothing untoward actually did. But somewhere in the isolated, rugged environs of Afghanistan, Osama bin Laden was plotting. Something very untoward happened that fundamentally *did* change the world as we knew it in the first year of the new millennium—on September 11, 2001, a Tuesday that began much like every other day in the United States of America.

On that morning, operatives from bin Laden's terrorist group al-Qaeda who had infiltrated the United States boarded four commercial flights in New York and Boston, took command of the planes after killing their cockpit crews, and flew two of them into the Twin Towers of the World Trade Center in New York City and one into the Pentagon in Washington, DC. The fourth plane was also aiming for a target in Washington until the passengers on board, having learned what was happening in New York, stormed the cockpit; in the ensuing struggle for control of the aircraft, the plane crashed in the Pennsylvania countryside. Both towers of the World Trade Center came down. Nearly 3,000 people died that day, including 343 New York City firefighters and 60 police officers engaged in rescue efforts. It was the largest loss of civilian life in a single day in American history.

All 30 major-league teams were scheduled to play that night. New York's Yankees, atop the AL East by a comfortable 13 games, were to host the AL Central third-place Chicago White Sox. New York's Mets, third place in the NL East, having a disappointing season after playing in the 2000 World Series, were in Pittsburgh to face the team with the second-worst record in baseball. Washington, DC, had not had a team since the 1961-expansion Senators moved to Texas in 1972 to become the Rangers. All commercial and general aviation was grounded for three days. The US intelligence community identified who was responsible. The president of the United States grappled with the national emergency and what to do next. The Pentagon began military planning to deal with al-Qaeda's safe haven in Afghanistan. There was no baseball for six days.

In New York, Shea Stadium became a staging ground for equipment and supplies for rescue workers and victims. It also served as a place for them to rest and sleep. Mets players were extensively involved in helping load food and clothing onto trucks and visiting victims in city hospitals. Perhaps the feel-good moment of that wretched week came when Mayor Rudy Giuliani, whose crisis management on 9/11 and the weeks afterward propelled him into the ranks of herodom, called the Yankees—his favorite team—to ask if they could "help with morale" by visiting central locations where volunteers were hard at work, where injured first responders were being treated, and where families were searching for missing love ones. The mayor was right about the impact Brooklyn-born Joe Torre; star players Derek Jeter, Mariano Rivera, and Bernie Williams; coaches Lee Mazzilli (New York–born) and Willie Randolph (raised in Brooklyn); and the other Yankees would have on New Yorkers. Those they visited were touched by their presence. "You needed to be reminded that life goes on," said America's mayor, "and baseball reminds you of that."

While Americans' worldview had changed in an instant, the president was determined that America's future would not "be one of fear," as he told a joint session of Congress, broadcast nationwide, on September 20. "Life will return almost to normal," he said. "We'll go back to our lives and routines, and that is good." For America, baseball was part of that routine. Commissioner Selig decreed that in addition to the "Star-Spangled Banner," Irving Berlin's "God Bless America" would be played at games for the remainder of the season. The song became a staple of the seventh-inning stretch.

The major-league schedule picked up from September 17. The games that had been missed would be made up in the first week of October, except for one change involving New York City. Rather than hosting the Pirates for a three-game series beginning on September 17, as the schedule had it, the Mets resumed in Pittsburgh—where they were supposed to be on September 11—and took on the Pirates in New York for three games beginning October 1. The Yankees, meanwhile, picked up their season where they were supposed to on September 18—in Chicago. In their first games after 9/11 in cities other than New York, both the Yankees and the Mets were cheered precisely because they represented New York. The Mets took the field wearing FDNY and NYPD baseball caps to honor firefighters and police for their exemplary service to their city in the horrific chaos of the attacks. "We're not playing for ourselves," said Mets reliever John Franco, born in Brooklyn. "We're playing for the whole city of New York."

The first game played in New York after 9/11 was at Shea Stadium on September 21, the day after the president's address to the nation before Congress. The visiting team was the Atlanta Braves, the Mets' archenemy. But this was a time for coming together. The Braves player Mets fans most loved to hate, Chipper Jones, had to admit that if he wasn't playing for Atlanta, he'd be "rooting for the Mets," who were still wearing their first-responder hats. Perhaps his heart wasn't in it, but Chipper did his usual thing at Shea, going 2-for-4 and being in the middle of an eighth-inning rally that gave the Braves a 2–1 lead. In the bottom of the inning, with a runner on base, the Mets' best player, Mike Piazza, hit arguably the most important home run of his career deep over the left-center field fence to win this one—the first game played in New York since that awful day—for the city. It was cathartic. The fans rising in unison to cheer were not just celebrating the home team, they were celebrating each other, they were celebrating community, they were celebrating the resilience of their wounded city, they were celebrating the greatness of their country and the values and freedom for which it stood. "USA! USA!"

Nearly six weeks later, on October 30, President George W. Bush took the mound at Yankee Stadium just before the start of Game Three of the 2001 World Series, the Yankees against the Arizona Diamondbacks, to throw out the ceremonial first pitch. With reports continuing that another terrorist attack might be imminent, the security for this game was the most intense there had ever been for any game anywhere. A lifelong baseball fan and a former owner of the Texas Rangers, the president came through by throwing a strike, notwithstanding his being weighed down by a bulking bulletproof vest under his FDNY warmup jacket. It was another necessary cohering moment to bring Americans together, particularly since the United States was now at war to rid Afghanistan of al-Qaeda and the Taliban regime that had given Osama bin Laden's terrorist group sanctuary.

Ten years later, on a Sunday night, the 1st of May in 2011, New York's Mets were visiting Philadelphia's Phillies at Citizen's Bank Park. The game was ESPN's *Sunday Night Baseball* broadcast, the only game still in progress. The score was tied, 1–1, in the top of the ninth with one out. Daniel Murphy was batting for the Mets, pinch-hitting for Justin Turner. Phillies closer Ryan Madson was on the mound. As Murphy fouled off a 1–1 pitch, the crowd in excess of 45,000 rose to their feet chanting, "USA! USA! USA!" Murphy stepped out of the left-handed batter's box and looked around, perplexed. Neither he, nor Madson, nor their teammates on the field or in the dugouts knew what exactly was going on. But they did know something truly significant and unifying had happened.

"I'll tell you what's going on," Mets radio play-by-play announcer Howie Rose informed his New York–based audience. "There are reports circulating—I'm not sure if they have yet been confirmed by the White House—that Osama bin Laden is dead. How that's happened, we don't know." President Barack Obama was in fact about to address the nation to say that a covert heliborne special forces raid by US Navy SEALs, staging out of Afghanistan against a walled-in residence in a garrison city in Pakistan, had killed the al-Qaeda leader who plotted the 9/11 attacks. Rose proceeded to put it all into perspective: "It's amazing how things seem so important for the moment, like they did when Ryan Howard batted with the bases loaded." That was in the Phillies eighth inning, and Howard was actually batting with two runners—not three—on base; he singled to tie the score. It was Raul Ibanez, two batters later, who batted with the bases loaded; he grounded out to end the inning. "It just takes you back to that awful, awful day, and you wonder why you get upset or worked up about a baseball game in the first place."

It was an electrifying moment, a unifying moment for the country. It was similar, though far less emotionally fraught, to July 20, 1969, also a Sunday, when play in every major-league game was stopped when Apollo 11's lunar module, with astronauts Neil Armstrong and Buzz Aldrin aboard, was moments away from touching down on the moon. Unlike 42 years later, when Americans did not even know the bin Laden mission was taking place, the entire country—the entire world—knew a person was about to land on the moon for the first time. What nobody knew was whether it would be a successful landing or a catastrophic end to a bold, visionary mission whose purpose was as much about Cold War–era patriotism as scientific exploration. At Yankee Stadium, public address announcer Bob Sheppard—whose voice was "as synonymous with Yankee Stadium as its copper façade and Monument Park," in the words of Walter Cronkite, a noteworthy voice himself to whom millions listened during the entirety of the Apollo 11 mission—told the 33,000 in attendance, "Ladies and gentlemen, your attention please. You will be happy to know that Apollo 11 has landed safely on the moon." There was sustained cheering, followed by a moment of silence for the safe return of the astronauts, followed by a recording of "America the Beautiful" to which baseball fans sang along, and then more sustained cheering.

But even with bin Laden dead, America was still at war, in Afghanistan and in Iraq, which the United States invaded in 2003 on the controversial pretext of putting an end to Saddam Hussein's weapons of mass destruction programs. As the 2010s advanced, American troops—mostly special forces—were deployed to Syria and far-flung places elsewhere to train and assist regional allies in combating international terrorist groups to defend America's national interest in global stability and to keep America (and our allies) safe so that the rest of us could go about our lives in comparative peace, comfort, and security.

Other than the week of 9/11, however, Major League Baseball was unaffected by what had come to be called, in fatalistic weariness, America's "forever war." No major-league players, or minor leaguers whose big-league ambitions hadn't been washed out, volunteered or were forced to sacrifice any part of their baseball careers to serve their country in America's response to the 9/11 attacks or the invasion of Iraq. That was very different from all the previous multiyear wars fought by the United States.

In World War I, in which the United States officially became a combatant nation with Congress's declaration of war in April 1917, Major League Baseball's lobbying for an exemption for players from wartime service proved unsuccessful. Faced with the War Department's "work or fight" order for all draft-eligible men, big-league rosters were hit hard in

1918—the first full year the United States fought in the war—when players left their teams to work in shipbuilding and other defense industries or to serve in the armed forces. Many volunteered to fight for their country rather than waiting to be drafted. Some took part in fierce battles on the front lines in France. With the United States in full war footing and the war seemingly mired in stalemate in the summer of 1918, the major leagues cancelled the final month of games, moved the World Series up to the beginning of September, and preemptively cut the 1919 schedule from 154 to 140 games. Had the war continued on, there might not have been a 1919 season.

There were no curtailed seasons during World War II because President Franklin D. Roosevelt thought continuing the national pastime through the war years was "thoroughly worthwhile" for morale on the home front. Major-league rosters, however, were even more decimated than in World War I by players being drafted into the war effort or, to a much lesser extent, volunteering to serve. Few of baseball's established stars, however, were sent to the front lines. Most spent the war years stateside or at relatively secure rear bases engaged in administrative and logistical military roles while also playing on service ball teams. Minor leaguers and players with limited big-league experience—some of whom became major-league stars after having survived fierce fighting on World War II battlefields—got no such consideration. Many players, even those kept far from the fighting, lost three years of their prime baseball-playing years serving their country in wartime, and some lost four.

Major leaguers were also drafted during the Korean War, although they were typically kept far from the action. One notable exception was Red Sox star Ted Williams, called to duty as a reservist despite already having served three years in World War II. Williams's wartime exploits in Korea, including surviving a crash landing after the fighter jet he was flying was hit by enemy fire, earned him accolades as an American war hero, which helped change perspectives of him as baseball's particularly spoiled superstar brat.

No active major leaguers fought in the Vietnam War. To the extent major-league rosters were affected by the war, it was players serving their commitments during the baseball season in the reserves or National Guard, whose units were not sent to Vietnam, for which they signed up to avoid being drafted. Teams also assured that their top minor-league prospects signed up for the reserves or National Guard. The future major leaguers who were Vietnam combat veterans were drafted by the Selective Service before their careers in professional baseball gained minor-league traction. By the time of the 1991 Persian Gulf War, in which the United States led an international coalition in an intensive six-week military offensive to oust the Iraqi forces that had invaded Kuwait, America's was an all-volunteer military. No ballplayers volunteered.

As in all of America's previous wars, individual teams and Major League Baseball as an institution fully embraced a patriotic ethos in support of US soldiers fighting in Afghanistan and Iraq after what happened on 9/11. Renditions of "God Bless America," recognition of US service members at ballparks around the country, and games where players wore camouflage baseball caps and uniforms were heartfelt and sincere—if arguably jingoistic—salutes to the men and women voluntarily willing to put their lives on the line in America's "forever war." It was all very patriotic and well-meaning. It was also somewhat disingenuous. Ballpark tributes carried with them not only gratitude on our part for the service and sacrifices of American soldiers in Afghanistan, Iraq, and elsewhere, but an undercurrent of guilt for not fully understanding, still less having to carry, the burdens they did on our behalf.

The fault, if we want to call it that, was not specific to Major League Baseball, but to America itself. America may have been at war, but the overwhelming majority of Americans were not, at least not in the sense of having a personal stake in any of it. Less than 1 percent of Americans served in the US armed forces at any one time after 9/11. There was no shared sacrifice on the home front, like food or gasoline rationing and buying war bonds, as there had been during World Wars I and II. Nor was there a call to arms—and the risk of injury or death that came with that—for the cross-section of all Americans, as there was in both world wars, Korea, and Vietnam. Americans had not been subject to conscription since 1973. Serving the country in a time of war—the global war on terrorism—was a choice, not an obligation of citizenship. There was no longer a sense of Americans being all in it together, even if it was well understood that fellow Americans voluntarily serving their country in the armed forces were enduring the hardships and casualties, not to mention the traumas that many returned home with, to protect America's strategic interests abroad—including threats to the "homeland" from foreign terrorist groups.

As American politics became increasingly polarized during the Bush, Obama, and Donald Trump presidencies, there was also the not inconsiderable risk of pregame salutes to patriotism taking on a politicized cast, especially given the rise of prominent voices engaged in no-holds-barred partisan political warfare co-opting symbols of American patriotism like the flag or military service. On Memorial Day 2019, a Triple-A affiliate of the Washington Nationals stepped out of bounds in pregame ceremonies honoring US veterans by including a progressive member of the Democratic Party recently elected to the United States Congress in a montage of photographs of notorious world leaders voiced over by President Ronald Reagan's warning to "the enemies of freedom" in his 1981 Inaugural Address. That unauthorized incident aside, Major League Baseball has avoided falling into that trap, even while continuing with beautiful pregame singings of the "Star-Spangled Banner," moving seventh-inning-stretch renditions of "God Bless America," honoring US soldiers and veterans at ballparks, and eventually players wearing "patriotic" uniform caps and jerseys on Memorial and Independence Days. It should be noted that foreign-born players, mostly from Latin American countries, have accounted for about 28 percent of all major leaguers since 2000.

That baseball was ingrained as a patriotic cultural touchstone in America was indisputable, even if the NFL and perhaps the NBA and (in some cities) the NHL commanded more attention. Both the pace of individual games, not dictated by any clock, and the very length of the baseball season—games nearly every day for six months—had their own life cycle. For every team and its fans, there were good times and bad, sometimes calamitous setbacks and miraculous comebacks—just as in life. Much is made of fathers and sons bonding over baseball. The same is true of cities. Just as the Mets and Yankees helped New York City to get through the traumatic events of 9/11, so did the Red Sox in Boston, twelve years later, in the worst terrorist attack in the United States since September 11, 2001.

It was April 15, 2013—Patriots' Day in Boston, celebrated annually by the running of the Boston Marathon and the Red Sox playing at home in a game with a late-morning start time. Even as the Red Sox beat the Tampa Bay Rays, 3–2, on a bottom-of-the-ninth walk-off double by Mike Napoli to improve their record to 8–4 and boost their division lead to 1½ games in the early days of a much anticipated new season, especially after their dreadful last-place ending in 2012, about a mile away from Fenway Park gaggles of runners—not the elite, who had already finished—were crossing the finish line of the grueling Boston Marathon, cheered on by a crowd of spectators. In the throng were two brothers born in Kyrgyzstan (bordering China in Central Asia), whose family had settled in the United States in 2002, carrying backpacks with pressure-cooker bombs stuffed with shrapnel. Suicide bombers, they were not. Putting their packs down 210 yards apart near the finish line, both walked away. They became targets of an intense manhunt after their homemade bombs exploded at 2:49—about 40 minutes after the end of the Red Sox game—killing three and injuring more than 260 others, some very seriously. One brother was killed in a shootout three days later; the other was captured the next day. While their terrorist attack was neither directed by nor coordinated with al-Qaeda or any other foreign extremist group, they were radicalized online by an influential Yemen-based al-Qaeda propagandist whose instruction included bomb making.

The Red Sox were in Cleveland the next three days. They hung a team sweatshirt in their dugout with the words "Boston Strong." They swept the Indians, then returned to Boston for a 10-game homestand that was supposed to start on Friday, April 19. That day's game was canceled because the manhunt for the second bomber was still on. They played the next day, April 20. Wearing their home uniforms with "Boston" across the chest, the Red Sox henceforth that season added the adornment of the Boston "B" that is the insignia on their baseball caps and the word "strong" underneath.

Addressing the Fenway crowd before the game, Red Sox designated hitter, team leader, and fan favorite David Ortiz, affectionately known as "Big Papi," said: "This jersey that we wear today, it doesn't say 'Red Sox.' It says 'Boston.'" Then, after thanking the mayor, the governor of Massachusetts, and police agencies for their purposeful response to the terrorist attack, Big Papi said: "This is our f—ing city. And nobody gonna dictate our freedom. Stay strong." The expletive was a perfect exclamation point to drive home the reassurance that Boston and its citizens—like New York after 9/11, and the whole United States, for that matter—was resilient in the face of adversity and unwavering in defense of American ideals. Those few words by Ortiz, a Dominican-born player who pledged allegiance to the United States when he became a citizen in 2008, were as memorable for their resonance as Lou Gehrig's short "luckiest man" speech in the face of his impending death at Yankee Stadium on July 4, 1939.

The Red Sox dedicated the rest of the season to their wounded city. There were multiple tributes at Fenway to the victims of the marathon bombings, including survivors. First responders were honored at the ballpark. Red Sox players were active all summer visiting bombing victims in hospitals, donating money, engaging in community fund-raising efforts to benefit survivors. And they played great baseball, winning their division handily and tying the St. Louis Cardinals for the best record in the major leagues. They played the postseason with the "Boston Strong" logo from their uniforms cut into the grass in a huge swath of center field at Fenway Park. In their division series, along with the starting lineups and playoff rosters of the wild-card Rays and Red Sox, the team introduced marathon runners, volunteers, police officers, first responders, and others who played heroic roles in the immediate chaos surrounding the bombing. In the league championship series, bombing survivors figured prominently in pregame ceremonies at Fenway, leading the stadium in singing the national anthem or calling out, "Play ball!" They won the World Series—their third since 2004, and their first won at home in Boston since 1918.

David Ortiz was in the middle of it all. In the six games it took to beat St. Louis in the World Series, Ortiz put a personal exclamation point on Boston Strong: 11 hits in 16 at-bats—including two doubles and two home runs—for a .688 batting average and 1.188 slugging percentage, not to mention eight walks, contributing to a .760 on-base percentage.

Part II

Baseball's Battles in the New Century

7

SMALL MARKETS ON THE BRINK

Major League Baseball and the Major League Baseball Players Association began squaring off in the year 2000 on the terms of a collective bargaining agreement to replace the one they agreed to in November 1996, which was set to expire in 2001. In the interest of moving beyond the damage done to both sides and the game of baseball itself, the owners had backed off limiting free agency, and the players had accepted revenue sharing and a test-run of a "luxury tax" on teams exceeding a player payroll set high to get the union's buy-in. Commissioner Selig and the owners knew that specifically targeting free agency was the third rail that, if pushed, could send the game into another existential crisis. Instead, they were determined to substantially increase revenue sharing from 20 percent of teams' local revenues to as much as 50 percent and make permanent a "competitive balance tax," as they preferred the luxury tax be called, of 50 percent on payrolls above $84 million. The Yankees, Dodgers, and Braves all exceeded that threshold in 2000, and four other teams—the Orioles, Diamondbacks, Red Sox, and Mets—were close.

Those were the recommendations of the Blue Ribbon Panel on Baseball Economics that Selig commissioned in 1999 to study the implications of payroll disparity between large- and small-market teams and what could be done about it. The panel was chaired by the commissioner. The study, presented to the commissioner in July 2000, was led by four esteemed Americans, the three most notable being former United States Senator George Mitchell, whose defining political legacy was negotiating an end to the troubles in Northern Ireland; former Federal Reserve Chairman Paul Volcker; and conservative columnist George Will, as big a fan of baseball as he was an observer of American politics. The "independent members," as they were called, were carefully chosen by Selig, who did not include any of the many highly regarded sports columnists covering Major League Baseball. And while the panel had nobody representing the players, it also included a dozen franchise owners and team executives appointed by the commissioner.

Predictably, the panel validated the owners' contention that "large and growing revenue disparities exist and are causing problems of chronic competitive imbalance," and that "these problems have become substantially worse during the five complete seasons since the strike-shortened season of 1994, and seem likely to remain severe unless Major League Baseball undertakes remedial action proportional to the problem." While acknowledging that Major League Baseball as a collective entity was "prospering," given that gross revenues had nearly doubled since the strike, the report stressed that franchise payroll disparities had only gotten worse, making it nearly impossible for low-revenue teams to compete for division titles unless "ownership is willing to incur staggering operating losses to subsidize a competitive player payroll." The seven teams in 2000 paying the least for their Opening Day rosters each had a payroll less than the combined salaries of the three highest-paid players on both the Yankees and Dodgers, according to the report. As it turned out, two of those teams—Chicago's White Sox (not really a small-market team but acting like one with the fifth-lowest payroll) and Oakland's Athletics (seventh from the bottom)—won division titles that year.

Also predictably, the union saw the owners' demands on revenue sharing and the competitive balance tax as a way to rein in player earnings through free agency. Since the end of the 2000 season, the record for lucrative free agent contracts had been shattered three times—when the Rockies offered pitcher Mike Hampton $121 million over 8 years, the Red Sox gave outfielder Manny Ramirez an 8-year deal worth $160 million, and the Texas Rangers committed a staggering—staggering!—$252 million over 10 years to Alex Rodriguez. While A-Rod's contract was too outlandish to be the model, the players' union loved the Hampton and Ramirez deals because they set new baselines for free agency, contract extensions, and even arbitration hearings. Selig and the owners were horrified at their cost. But it must be remembered that three of their fellow owners gave them out, none of whom was George Steinbrenner—

and the Boss could surely be counted on to spend what he could going forward to sign the best players available on the free agent market.

As time expired in November 2001 on baseball's existing collective bargaining agreement, and with the union standing fast against any recommendation whose effect would be to limit players' earning potential, Selig played another recommendation the panel had suggested to deal with the "large and growing revenue disparities" between high-revenue and low-revenue clubs that "are causing problems of chronic competitive imbalance." Franchise owners voted 28-to-2 to eliminate two clubs in 2002, the commissioner announced. In fact, the "possible need to contract by two or more franchises" had only briefly been mentioned in the panel's report, and it was dismissed with the loaded sentence, "If the recommendations in this report are implemented, there should be no immediate need for contraction." For Selig, the threat of contraction—the loss of 50 major-league roster spots if two teams were eliminated—was a cudgel to get the players to agree to the owners' demands on revenue sharing and the competitive balance tax to rein in expenses.

Coming as it did three months before the start of spring training, and with the union filing a grievance the very next day and fans and politicians overwhelmingly skewering the idea, contraction had no chance of being implemented in 2002. But it was now on the table. As spring training got underway, Selig doubled down on contraction, saying baseball's economic state made the elimination of at least two teams "absolutely inevitable" and that 2003 would be the year, pending the outcome of the union's legal challenges. He went on to be quoted by the *New York Times* as saying that many owners favored getting rid of four teams and that, in any case, Major League Baseball "will continue to evaluate our weakest franchises to determine how much contraction is warranted and in the overall best interests of baseball and its fans."

The two teams targeted for contraction were the Montreal Expos and Minnesota Twins. According to the panel, the Expos and Twins were at the very bottom in terms of local revenue derived primarily from gate receipts and local television and radio broadcasting rights in 1999, the last year of data for its July 2000 report. Montreal earned less than 10 percent and Minnesota only 14 percent of the $132.3 million pulled in by the Yankees. The Pittsburgh Pirates were third from the bottom. In the five years of data (1995 to 1999) examined by the commissioner's panel, those three teams had the lowest annual average revenue in Major League

Baseball. Pittsburgh, however, was never in consideration for contraction, despite its being identified in the report as a small-market team with no hope of competing because of its weak take in local revenue. The difference was that in 2001 the Pirates opened a new stadium, mostly financed by public money. So did another small-market team listed in the report as near the bottom in local revenues: the Selig family–owned Milwaukee Brewers. Unlike the Pirates and Brewers, the Twins and Expos failed to persuade their local or state governments to finance new ballparks to replace their worn-out stadiums—the Metrodome in Minneapolis and Olympic Stadium in Montreal.

Montreal's Expos became a ward of Major League Baseball in 2002, after years of financial neglect. Those years began in 1991, when the franchise was sold by original owner Charles Bronfman, one of Canada's wealthiest because his family had (since 1923) owned Seagram's distillery. The Expos, on the edge of insolvency even at the time they were approved as an expansion team in 1969, had been dealt a debilitating body blow to their local revenues by the AL's 1977 expansion that put a team in Toronto, a far larger media market into which Expos baseball broadcasts were now limited to very few by order of Major League Baseball. Bronfman sold the Expos, complaining that free agency was making it impossible for small-market teams like his to compete.

If Bronfman had difficulty raising money, the conglomerate of corporate investors that now owned the Expos was not willing to actually put money into Canada's first major-league baseball team—even though they inherited an organization whose young and very talented players were poised to capitalize on the small-market Pirates' 1993 collapse, occasioned by star players like Barry Bonds leaving as free agents or being traded before they became too expensive to keep. The Expos set the stage in 1993 by winning 94 games to finish second in their division. In 1994, with a $19.1 million player payroll that was second-lowest in the majors, Montreal was ahead of Atlanta's heavily favored Braves by six games in the realigned NL East, had by far the best record in baseball, and were heading for a near-certain postseason when everything came to an end with the players' strike. Montreal's three best players were their outfield, left to right, of Moises Alou, whose .339 batting average was third in the league when the strike hit; Marquis Grissom, second in the league in runs and third in stolen bases; and rising superstar Larry Walker. Right-hander

Ken Hill's 16 wins tied Greg Maddux for the most in the National League, and John Wetteland emerged as one of baseball's most dominant closers. The Expos also had a rising star in right-hander Pedro Martinez, 11–5 in 23 starts.

The year 1994 turned out to be Montreal's last best hope for a pennant-winning team and a chance for a World Series championship. The federal court ruling that ended the strike in April 1995 in favor of the players meant that free agency stood as before. Keeping intact an outstanding young team with a chance to compete for a championship would have increased revenue and bolstered the case for public funding for a modern baseball stadium. Instead, committed to running the team entirely off locally generated revenues, the Expos' new owners made no effort to re-sign Walker, their best player (who also happened to be Canadian), as a free agent for 1995. Within days after major-league teams began an abbreviated spring training to get ready for the season, Wetteland, Hill, and Grissom—all nearing free agency—were traded for marginal players and unproven prospects. Montreal's player payroll in 1995 was reduced to $12.5 million—by far the lowest in baseball. They got what they paid for. After the best record in the game in 1994, the Expos dropped to last place in the NL East in 1995 with the third-worst record in the league.

In 1996, with a major-league-low $16.3 million player payroll (no other team was below $20 million, not even the cash-strapped Pirates), the Expos nonetheless managed 88 wins to finish eight games behind the Braves in their division—after which they allowed outfielder Moises Alou, a rising star and the son of Expos manager Felipe Alou, and new closer Mel Rojas, a cousin of Moises and the manager's nephew, to leave as free agents, and traded Jeff Fassero, their left-handed ace, for nobody of consequence. They dropped to fourth place and a losing record in 1997 on a $19.3 million payroll that was third lowest in the majors. Pedro Martinez broke out with a 17–8 record for a club that went 78–84, had a major-league-best 1.90 earned run average, fanned 305 batters in 241⅓ innings to lead the league in strikeouts per nine innings, and then was traded to the Boston Red Sox.

Wealthy New York–based art dealer Jeffrey Loria came to Montreal's rescue in December 1999 by buying a controlling share of the Expos, following their 97 losses in 1998 and 94 in the season just ended. Both years they were spared from last place in the NL East only because the Florida Marlins cut payroll by getting rid of all the players who'd given

Miami a World Series championship in 1997. The Marlins, like the Pirates and Expos, concluded they could not afford to compete in baseball's free-agency-driven economy. Unlike the Expos' previous owners, Loria was willing to invest in improving the team. Montreal's player payroll rose from the bottom of all major-league clubs at $17.9 million in 1999 to $33 million in 2000—fifth lowest—to $35.2 million in 2001. Despite Loria's cash infusion, however, the Expos ran their string of 90-loss seasons to four in a row.

By now the Expos had some good ballplayers. Right fielder Vladimir Guerrero had become a superstar. "Vladi" was such a talent that after just 258 major-league games, he was signed by Loria's frugal predecessors to a five-year deal in 1999 that would pay him $30 million through the 2003 season. Right-hander Javier Vazquez emerged as one of the best young pitchers in baseball in 2001, and Montreal had an enviable middle infield with shortstop Orlando Cabrera, praised for his defense, and second baseman Jose Vidro, whose 24 homers, 97 RBIs, and .330 batting average in 2000 caused Loria to reward him with a four-year, $19 million contract. All four were Caribbean-born players originally signed by Montreal. But averaging barely over 10,000 fans a game at cavernous Olympic Stadium in 2001, the Expos had the lowest attendance in the major leagues for the fifth straight year, in all of which they fell well short of 1 million.

Loria perceived Montreal's situation as hopeless. Few in Montreal were paying attention to the Expos. They certainly weren't coming to the ballpark, and the local and provincial governments were unwilling to fund a new stadium. He wanted out. In a three-way ownership shuffle brokered by the commissioner, Major League Baseball took the Expos off Loria's hands for $120 million so that he could buy Florida's Marlins for $158.5 million and Marlins owner John Henry could buy the Red Sox. Loria took Expos manager Jeff Torborg, the team's general manager, and most of the front office staff with him to Miami. Major League Baseball appointed Omar Minaya as general manager and named Frank Robinson manager. Now 66 years old and working in the commissioner's office, Robinson had not managed since being fired by the Orioles in 1991. Although the team was now a ward of Major League Baseball, the Expos front office had the authority to make whatever player transactions they wanted, but only within the budget they were given.

Minnesota's Twins, meanwhile, had been consumed since winning the World Series in 1991 with pressuring both the city and the state for funding to build a new ballpark. Public money was not to be had, however, especially when close scrutiny of what the Twins were willing to contribute to help finance the new stadium revealed franchise owner Carl Pohlad had been misleading and disingenuous in his negotiations with the state. Pohlad, one of baseball's wealthiest owners, was already scorned for being unwilling to spend on the Twins' roster (let alone put much money into a new ballpark) and for cashing in the money his franchise received from revenue sharing rather than investing it to improve his ballclub, which endured eight losing seasons in a row from 1993 to 2000. Pohlad was not alone among owners of small-market, low-revenue franchises in not using revenue-sharing dollars for the good of their team.

Despite the smallest player payroll in the major leagues in 2001, the Twins unexpectedly climbed from the depths of the league's worst record the previous year to compete for the division title for half the season. In mid-July the Twins led their division by five games, and the Seattle Mariners—on their way to 116 wins—were the only major-league team with a better record. After that, however, the Twins lost 42 of their last 70 games. While that was still good enough to finish second in their division, winning only 40 percent from mid-July till the end of the season with by far the lowest player payroll in the major leagues did not help their cause in Major League Baseball's contraction plan.

What did help was an injunction by a Minnesota court against the Twins being one of those teams, because Pohlad—undoubtedly knowing what was coming—had signed a one-year contract extension with Minnesota's stadium board, rent free, to play the 2002 season in the Metrodome, and contracts must be honored. Perhaps incentivized by the commissioner's threat to eliminate the Twins, the state legislature in May approved funding for a new baseball stadium in Minneapolis, causing Selig to announce that Minnesota was no longer one of the clubs at risk of being eliminated. The commissioner suggested that Tampa Bay might be on the chopping block instead.

Ironically, the two teams Major League Baseball condemned to be contracted out of existence both shone brightly in 2002. After having finished the previous season with the third-worst record in the American League following the All-Star Game, and despite having the second-lowest payroll in the American League and fourth-lowest in the majors, the 2002 Twins held a 7½-game division lead at the break and finished a commanding 13½ games in front of the AL Central. The Twins benefited from a weak division in which they were the only team with a winning record and the baseball maturation of center fielder Torii Hunter and third baseman Corey Koskie, both in their fourth year as core regulars, and catcher A. J. Pierzynski in his third year. The Twins barely survived their five-game division series with Oakland, a matchup of the two American League teams that paid their players the least, before being wiped out by the wild-card Angels—a team with a better record—in the ALCS.

The Expos won 16 of their first 26 games to finish the month of April tied for first atop the NL East. Toward the end of June, with an eye to competing for the wild card even as the Braves were running away with the division, the Expos traded three highly regarded prospects to Cleveland—Cliff Lee, Brandon Phillips, and Grady Sizemore, all of whom would star for other teams—for right-handed ace Bartolo Colón, already 10-4 for the year. Colón came through with exactly the same record in 17 starts for Montreal. By the end of July, the Expos had slipped out of contention for the wild card, but they finished in second place, with a winning record for the first time since 1996. The Expos accomplished this while paying their players $38.7 million. Only Tampa Bay's Devil Rays had a lower payroll.

At the end of August, Major League Baseball and the players' union reached agreement on a new collective bargaining agreement for 2003 through 2006. The agreement included a competitive balance tax of $117 million in 2003 that would increase by 3 percent the next year and by 6 percent each of the next two years—figures sufficiently high to be acceptable to the union since Steinbrenner's Yankees were the only team to exceed that threshold in 2002. Not surprisingly, Steinbrenner was the only owner to vote against the agreement. Rather than the 40 percent revenue-sharing that the Blue Ribbon Panel recommended and that Selig took to the table, each club would contribute 34 percent of its net local revenue to the pool, which would then be divided equally among all clubs, proportionally benefiting those with the lowest revenue base. As for contraction, that was off the table for the duration of the new agreement, but not necessarily beyond.

As a ward of Major League Baseball, the Expos were living on borrowed time in Montreal. Selig was looking to sell the franchise to an owner in a city or state that would appropriate money for a new baseball stadium. Montreal fans would have just two more years to attend Expos home games, 22 of which in both 2003 and 2004 would be played not in Canada but in San Juan, Puerto Rico. With the writing on the wall, Bartolo Colón was traded before spring training started in 2003. Vladimir Guerrero left as a free agent after the season to continue his Hall of Fame career in Anaheim. He left Montreal with a .323 batting average—still the best in franchise history—and 234 home runs, the most ever hit by a Montreal Expo. Javier Vazquez was traded to the Yankees after the 2003 season to get rid of a pitcher increasingly frustrated by his salary prospects in Montreal. Orlando Cabrera was traded to Boston at the trade deadline in 2004 to replace disaffected superstar shortstop Nomar Garciaparra, who was sent to the Chicago Cubs.

In 2003 the Expos matched their 83–79 record of 2002. They were in borderline contention for the wild card going into September 2003, but Major League Baseball's refusal to allow the club to bring in September reinforcements (as every other team did) handicapped their pursuit of that prize. They ended up fourth. The next year, the Expos finished last in the NL East. And the year after that, they were Washington's Nationals, with Major League Baseball still entertaining offers from several would-be ownership groups. The Expos' best player moving to Washington was Cuban defector Livan Hernandez, whom they had acquired on the cheap from the Giants because he was nearing free agency and to whom they gave a three-year, $21 million contract extension after his 15–10 record and league-leading 233⅓ innings his first year with Montreal in 2003.

While the Expos were doomed in Montreal, the Twins began to thrive in the small-market Minneapolis–St. Paul metropolitan area. Beginning in 2002—the year they were on Selig's chopping block—they won three division titles in a row, another in 2006, and two more in 2009 and 2010. Only in 2002, however, did they make it beyond the division series round of the postseason. They had a compelling homegrown star in Minnesota-born Joe Mauer, whose .347 batting average in 2006, only his second full season in the majors, made him the first catcher since Ernie Lombardi in 1942 to win a batting title. Lombardi won two; Mauer outdid him with three, claiming the crown again in both 2008 and 2009. And in 2010, the Twins moved into their new ballpark.

8

FROM THE A'S TO THE RAYS AND BEYOND

Baseball's Analytics Revolution

In the five years between 2000 and 2004, Oakland's Athletics had the second-best record in the major leagues behind New York's Yankees, averaging 97 wins a year to the Yankees' 98. They and San Francisco's Giants, averaging 94 wins a year, were the only major-league teams to win at least 90 games all five of those years. Not even the Yankees did that, even though they won their division all five years and went to the World Series three times. The Athletics won three division titles and the wild card once, but lost all four of their division series in the maximum five games—the first two times to those damn Yankees.

The A's nearly matched the Yankees win-for-win those five years with less than one-third of Steinbrenner's player payroll. In fact, as a small-market franchise, the Athletics could hardly afford player salaries anywhere near what the Yankees paid their stars. Given that their payroll was consistently among the lowest in the American League, the A's got the best dollar value per win of any team in the major leagues. They did so by value engineering player acquisitions, including making trades and scouting collegiate and high school players, through extensive use of data-driven analytics to identify affordable talent with particular skills.

At first, to the mystification and opposition of their scouts and coaches, practiced in evaluating players by long-standing traditional methods, the A's were not looking for perfect players with the five cardi-

nal baseball "tools"—speed, hitting for power, hitting for average, fielding, and throwing—identified long ago by the likes of Branch Rickey.
They were interested in subtle skills that were often overlooked in their
importance and that might not even be athletic attributes. Foremost for
hitters, Oakland's criteria were the ability to discern the strike zone,
discipline at the plate, and willingness to draw a walk. For pitchers, there
was a greater emphasis on the particulars of past performance rather than
physical size and velocity. With limited financial resources, Oakland's
philosophy in trades, in the free agent market, and in scouting amateur
prospects was, what were players very good at that could help the A's
win ballgames. The A's were after the kinds of players who would come
cheap, at least initially, precisely because they did not rate highly on the
traditional parameters teams used for player evaluation.

The brains behind this innovative, and at first heretical, approach was
Billy Beane, a former first-round amateur draft pick himself whose professional playing career ended in failure. Beane went from that failure to
scouting for the Athletics to becoming a valued assistant to Oakland
general manager Sandy Alderson—architect of the Oakland powerhouse
that went to three consecutive World Series with the best record in baseball each year from 1988 to 1990—to being named GM in October 1997
when Alderson was promoted to team president. Beane took charge of a
team whose 65–97 record in 1997 was the worst in the majors and whose
player payroll was one of the smallest. In July, Alderson had traded Mark
McGwire, by far the A's best and highest-paid player, and the 34 home
runs he had hit in 105 games to St. Louis, allowing power-hitting rising
star Jason Giambi, earning nearly $7 million less than Big Mac, to move
from the outfield, where he was a defensive liability, to first base, where
he wasn't much better.

Beane was soon presiding over a championship-caliber low-budget
team. Joining the scraggly, rambunctious Giambi in the infield full-time
were shortstop Miguel Tejada in 1998 and third baseman Eric Chavez in
1999. All three were dangerous power hitters. And Beane was assembling
a core of dynamic young starting pitchers. Right-hander Tim Hudson was
promoted to Oakland in 1999 and southpaws Mark Mulder and Barry
Zito, first-round picks the two previous years, in 2000. In a telling move
that would come to define Beane's approach to his job, he went with Zito
over the objections of his scouts, whose years of experience told them

Zito, a college pitcher, didn't throw hard enough to justify wasting a first-round pick on him.

After a seven-year hiatus in recovery, the Athletics reclaimed the top spot in the AL West in 2000 on the back of a red-hot 22–7 record in the final month that overcame the 2½-game lead Seattle held going into September. Giambi's 43 homers, 137 RBIs, and .333 batting average earned him Most Valuable Player honors. Hudson's 20–6 record was the best in the majors. In 2001, the Athletics had a dominant 102-win season, only to be swamped by Seattle's 116-win Mariners in the AL West. They had to settle for the wild card. Both years the A's had a better record than the Yankees. Both years the Yankees were their opponents in the division series. And both years the A's lost to the Yankees in five games. Their 2001 division series turned on Derek Jeter's seventh-inning play of the century (it was still early in the twenty-first century) that preserved a 1–0 lead in Game Three for the Yankees when he raced into foul territory on the first base side in the near vicinity of home plate to relay an offline throw from right field to nab the slow-footed Jeremy Giambi, Jason's younger brother. Jason Giambi, whose 38 homers, .342 batting average, and 1.137 on-base plus slugging percentage set him up as the most coveted free agent in the offseason, left Oakland after signing a lucrative multiyear contract with the Yankees (although he did have to tame his straggly mane, per Steinbrenner's mandate).

Giambi's singular impact at the plate could not be replaced by any one player—at least not one Oakland could afford. Rather than try, Beane traded for an aging long-ago star, outfielder David Justice, and signed oft-injured Boston reserve catcher Scott Hatteberg as a free agent. Both came cheap because neither player was much wanted by any other team. While neither was an impact player, Beane's unorthodox approach to player evaluation—specifically prioritizing on-base percentage over more traditional batting statistics like batting average, home runs, and runs batted in—valued their plate discipline. Both were tough outs for pitchers to navigate, requiring opposing pitchers to invest more effort and pitches on them than they would for many higher-profile hitters.

The A's shrugged off Giambi's departure, as well as those of center fielder Johnny Damon and closer Jason Isringhausen, both also free agents, as no big deal. Oakland's 103 wins in 2002 tied the Yankees for the most in the majors. The highlight of their season was a 30–5 stretch from the end of July into early September that included a 20-game winning streak to break the American League record of 19 set by the 1906 White Sox and matched by the 1947 Yankees. (The major league record is 26 by the 1916 Giants.) This time they lost their division series in five games to Minnesota, another low-budget team. Justice and Hatteberg led the club in on-base percentage. Tejada and Chavez, the A's two best position players, were still several years from free agent eligibility; Hudson, Zito, and Mulder were a trio of aces. Zito's 23–5 record allowed him to outpoll Pedro Martinez (20–4) for the Cy Young Award, even though his earned run average and walks and hits per inning were not as stingy and his strikeout ratio was just 7.1 per 9 innings compared to Pedro's league-leading 10.8.

Prior to the 2003 season, Beane picked up Diamondbacks first baseman Erubiel Durazo in a four-team trade for his .390 on-base percentage in four seasons with Arizona to be Oakland's designated hitter. He led the team in walks. The A's won 96 games and another division title in 2003 before losing another five-game division series, and Beane found himself facing the inevitable breakup of his low-budget team. Miguel Tejada left as a free agent, and catcher Ramon Hernandez and center fielder Terrence Long were traded after the 2003 season. But Beane was able to sign Eric Chavez, his own free agency beckoning at the end of the season, to a six-year, $66 million contract extension to stay in Oakland. Given that he was the best all-around third baseman in the league at the time, that deal was a bargain too good for Billy Beane not to make. It certainly helped that Chavez had become more disciplined at the plate after having annoyed Beane and his staff of data analysts with his propensity to swing at bad pitches.

Despite 91 wins, the 2004 A's missed the postseason for the first time in five years, falling a game short after leading the division for most of the final two months. Tim Hudson and Mark Mulder, both a year away from free agency, were traded after the 2004 season. The A's did win another division title in 2006 and finally won a division series in a three-game sweep over Minnesota before being swept by Detroit in the ALCS, after which remaining ace Barry Zito left as a free agent. Third baseman Eric Chavez, injured in midseason 2007, played only 154 games in the four remaining years of his contract.

The ability of Oakland's A's to make the postseason four straight years with the lowest player payroll of any of their fellow postseason travelers—except the 2003 eventual World Series champion Florida Marlins, whose payroll was just $800 less than the A's—did not go unnoticed. Beane's philosophy was memorialized and popularized in the 2003 book *Moneyball*, written by financial journalist Michael Lewis, which in turn became a movie starring Brad Pitt (some might say that Billy Beane never looked so good). And, though it didn't change Selig's narrative, small-market Oakland's counterintuitively extraordinary success undermined Major League Baseball's long-standing argument that the significant revenue disparities overwhelmingly favoring the competitive prospects of big-market teams could be corrected only by measures like revenue sharing and competitive balance taxes to which the players' union must agree.

Even before *Moneyball* hit the bookstores, what the Athletics were doing was an open secret in Major League Baseball. Front office skepticism about the approach was widespread, if for no other reason than it represented a fundamental departure from how business had always been done. But rather than a radical departure, Billy Beane's star turn was more a dramatic leap forward in an evolutionary process that began in the 1980s and 1990s as the industry absorbed modern business practices brought in by new ownership groups buying major-league teams—groups whose principal investors were increasingly from well-heeled corporate America. A handful of other teams had already begun factoring data analysis into player evaluation deliberations. Beane himself had been mentored by Sandy Alderson, who began pushing the importance of on-base percentage over all other statistical categories for position players when Oakland's new owners gave him tight budgets to work within in the mid-1990s. Beane's radical departure was making computer-based data analysis the centerpiece of player evaluations, including identifying, arraying, and manipulating critical data sets that went beyond bubblegum-card stats.

It was inevitable that other teams would follow Oakland's lead in using and developing data-based models to guide their decision-making process in the makeup of their rosters, not only to compete but to be more cost-efficient doing so. It was inevitable that those teams would include the high-revenue big spenders. One of the first of those teams to do so was Boston's Red Sox, which had fallen into the habit of always finishing second to the Yankees in the AL East. Boston finished second to the Yankees for the fifth consecutive season in 2002, the year wealthy financier John Henry bought the Red Sox. They earned the postseason wild card only the first two of those years and were struggling to get back in.

Having relied on data-based analytics to make his fortune as a commodities trader on Wall Street, Henry hired Bill James, the godfather of advanced statistical analysis, as an adviser and tried to entice Beane to come to Boston. When his Billy Beane gambit failed, Henry chose Theo Epstein to be general manager. It was an unconventional choice because, unlike nearly every other GM, including Beane, Epstein had no baseball background as a player. A Yale graduate with a liberal arts degree, his love for baseball had gotten him front office jobs with the Orioles and Padres before coming home to the Red Sox—he grew up in the Boston suburbs—after Henry bought the team. Not yet 29, Epstein already had a reputation as a front office prodigy given to using data-driven analysis of players' performance, even as Beane was doing the same in Oakland.

Among Epstein's first moves was signing a trio of low-profile free agents: Bill Mueller, a competent but hardly standout third baseman with seven years behind him; Mike Timlin, a 37-year-old journeyman reliever with 12 years and 664 games on his pitching résumé; and 27-year-old designated hitter David Ortiz, just released by Minnesota after four years failing to convince them he had much of a future in the big leagues. Epstein also refused to part with Kevin Youkilis, their unheralded eighth-round amateur draft pick two years earlier, whom Beane was angling to get via a deal Montreal had in train with Boston. Beane and Epstein both saw great potential in Youkilis being the "Greek god of walks" for his .457 on-base percentage in 199 minor-league games, including 44 in Double-A. The Red Sox finished second once again to the Yankees in 2003, beat Billy Beane's A's in their division series as the wild-card team, then lost the ALCS to the Yankees in seven games. After which they traded for Arizona's Curt Schilling. Epstein expected Schilling to team up with Pedro Martinez to give Boston a dynamic starting duo that rivaled what the Diamondbacks had with Schilling and Randy Johnson when they took down the Yankees in the 2001 World Series.

Schilling and Ortiz became lifelong heroes to Red Sox Nation for their roles in finally putting an end to Boston's 86 years without a World Series championship in 2004. So, too, did reserve outfielder Dave Roberts, acquired by Epstein from the Dodgers at the end of July, whose stolen base as a pinch-runner in the ninth inning of Game Four of the ALCS with Boston three outs away from being swept by the Yankees was a pivotal ignition moment in the greatest postseason-series comeback in baseball history; the Red Sox went on to beat the Yankees in that game and the next three besides.

Epstein was intent on building a powerhouse team to rival the Yankees. He emphasized player development of prospects to secure the future and trades to improve his team's pennant chances in any given year. Although the Red Sox were a big-market team able to afford star players, Epstein was not as aggressive in pursuing high-priced free agents as Steinbrenner was for his Yankees. His strategy for building a consistent winner paid off in 2007 when the Red Sox finally displaced the Yankees atop the AL East and went on to win their second World Series in four years. Ortiz was still in his prime, Youkilis had become an impact offensive player (which was why Beane wanted him), and Schilling was still a frontline starter. Boston's success at the expense of New York convinced Yankees general manager Brian Cashman of the necessity of having data-analysis capability to rival Theo Epstein's. "We realized there was a lot more going on in this game than met the eye," Yankees historian Marty Appel quotes Cashman as saying.

Meanwhile, unbeknownst to the baseball world, the team with the worst record in the major leagues in 2007—Tampa Bay's Rays—had laid the foundation for beating out both the Red Sox and the Yankees to win the AL East and make it to the World Series the very next year by adopting Moneyball principles of their own. Where Tampa Bay ended up in 2007 was nothing new to the expansion franchise born in 1998 as the Devil Rays, nicknamed after the nom de guerre given to a genus of ocean-swimming rays that looked more devilish—as in dangerous—than they actually were. In their first ten years, the Devil Rays won only 40 percent of the games they played and never lost fewer than 91. Lou Piniella, hired to take over the D-Rays in 2003 after 10 years managing Seattle to four postseason appearances, wanted out of Tampa Bay after three years on the job, despite being a Tampa native, because of frustration about his team owner's lack of commitment to spending enough to improve his roster. In 2004, however, Piniella presided over the first time the Devil Rays did not finish last in their division; they were three games better than Toronto.

Not learning the lesson from earlier expansion teams, Tampa Bay's original owner gave priority to acquiring well-paid aging veterans such as closer Roberto Hernandez and five-time batting champion Wade Boggs, signed as free agents, and power-hitting first baseman Fred McGriff, whose contract was purchased from Atlanta. Two years later, perhaps envious that their fellow expansion franchise in Arizona won 100 games and the NL West in only their second year of existence, the Devil Rays doubled down on that strategy by signing free agent sluggers Greg Vaughn and Vinny Castilla. The club also boosted its player payroll from $38.9 million in 1999 to $63.3 million in 2000. The result was the same—last in the AL East. Billy Beane's A's, meanwhile, won the AL West with a payroll of $33.2 million, just over half Tampa Bay's.

Particularly since Tampa Bay was at best at the upper end of small-market teams, not to mention that indoor Tropicana Field was one of the worst ballparks in baseball, the D-Rays' strategy for building a winner around high-profile veterans was doomed to fail. By 2002, their player payroll was the lowest in Major League Baseball. It still was in 2004 when Stuart Sternberg, who made his fortune as a private equity trader on Wall Street, bought a controlling interest in the franchise. He brought with him two other highly successful Wall Street investors to run the club—one of whom, Andrew Friedman, would take over as general manager after the 2005 season and become *nearly* as well known, and certainly as highly regarded in the industry, as Beane and Epstein. The approach of Tampa Bay's new executive team, related in *The Extra 2%*, a book by financial journalist Jonah Keri, was to apply strategies used by Wall Street investors and traders to build and sustain a contending team.

That "extra 2%" referred to the ways businesses and investors are able to gain a competitive edge, however small, over their rivals to become a profitable venture. It was as much process-oriented as data-based analysis, which was what Beane's Moneyball emphasized. Tampa Bay's Wall Street veterans were rigorous in dissecting and improving every aspect of the D-Rays' operations. And they did so in the context of small budgets that could never approach what the AL's beasts of the East—the Yankees and Red Sox—were capable of spending. On the player roster front, the Devil Rays developed data sets and proprietary analytical methodologies for every facet of the game—hitting, baserunning, infield defense, outfield defense, starting pitching, relief pitching—to identify what improvements were needed, where and why, and whom they had available to fill the need. They studied the market to understand what other teams were doing and where their focus was. Based on this analysis, Tampa Bay targeted players whose attributes were important to their needs but under-valued by most other teams, allowing them to be acquired at a bargain price. At the same time, they determined which of their own players' attributes were highly prized by other teams, but not necessarily what Tampa Bay needed, allowing the Devil Rays to trade or sell them for more than they were worth to their team.

Tampa Bay already had a young core of dynamic players on hand when the front office changed hands—left fielder Carl Crawford, center fielder Melvin Upton Jr. (then known as B. J. Upton), and left-hander Scott Kazmir, all three first- or second-round picks by the D-Rays. Fried-man considered all three to be indispensable for a winning future, howev-er implausible that might have seemed for a team that had won as many as 70 games only once in franchise history. In April 2005, knowing Crawford was eligible for arbitration at the end of the season, Friedman gave him a six-year contract extension worth $33.5 million through the 2010 season. That proved to be money very well spent; a financial analy-sis showed that Crawford's actual value to Tampa Bay during those six years, based on his on-field performance, was nearly $110 million. When he left as a free agent following the 2010 season, Crawford had stolen 409 bases in his nine years with the Rays (including leading the league four times in five years between 2003 and 2007), ran out 105 triples (leading the league four times), hit 104 homers, and batted .296.

Friedman also made a series of trades that did not make much in the way of headlines but were very much in keeping with Tampa Bay's Wall Street–inspired sell-high, buy-low approach to improving the ballclub. In mid-July 2006, he sent longtime D-Rays slugger Aubrey Huff, whose 128 home runs since his 2000 rookie season constituted the franchise record, to Houston for middle-infielder Ben Zobrist, still in the low minors. After winning the National League pennant the year before, the Astros, in their ultimately failing bid to return to the World Series, were willing to part with their promising prospect for a proven power hitter who did not fit in Tampa Bay's future as envisioned by Friedman. Playing all over the infield and in the outfield for the Rays between 2009 and 2015, Zobrist went on to become baseball's best multiposition regular.

In November 2007, Friedman traded rookie outfielder Delmon Young, who played in all 162 D-Rays games that year, and starting shortstop Brendan Harris, also a rookie in 2007, to Minnesota for right-hander Matt Garza and shortstop Jason Bartlett. Young was the first overall pick of the

2003 amateur draft and Garza was a first-round pick by Minnesota in 2005. Both had temperament issues that raised concerns about their ability to succeed. The Twins, however, coming off a year in which they had the second-lowest slugging percentage in the league, placed high value on Young's power potential (which was of much lesser importance to the Rays), and the Rays were impressed by Garza's potential as a starting pitcher alongside Kazmir and right-hander James Shields, coming up on his third big-league season.

Perhaps the devil in the name caused all that losing, because prior to the 2008 season the new ownership group announced that the Devil was coming out of the Rays, and henceforth they would be simply the Tampa Bay Rays. Moreover, instead of a manta ray, the team's new logo would feature the sunshine for which the west coast of Florida was famous. Or maybe all that was needed was some magic performed by Joe Maddon, the Rays' "who-he?" choice in 2006 to replace Lou Piniella as manager, to turn losing into winning. Or maybe it was both.

Whatever it was, Tropicana Field was a happening place in 2008, complete with the cacophony of cowbells (more cowbell!) to incite Rays rallies. Maddon's magic derived from his willingness to use computer-generated data provided by the front office to inform his in-game decisions. The effect was most profound on defense, with the Rays going from the worst team in the majors in making outs on ball in play in 2007 to the best. The upshot of that was that the Rays improved from giving up the most runs in the majors to surrendering the third fewest in 2008. Kazmir, Shields, and Garza were three-fifths of a rotation that started 151 of the Rays' 162 games. Lefty J. P. Howell and Australian-born Grant Balfour, both picked up in low-visibility trades, were exceptional in the bullpen. First baseman Carlos Peña, whose 46 homers and 121 RBIs in 2007—after making the club as a nonroster spring training invitee desperate to keep his six-year career alive—earned him a three-year $24 million contract from Friedman, had another outstanding season. But the star of the Rays' 2008 show was Rookie of the Year third baseman Evan Longoria, whom Friedman regarded so highly, he was signed to a six-year, $17.5 million contract just six days into his big-league career.

The Tampa Bay Rays improved by a phenomenal 31 wins to finish with 97, two games ahead of the Red Sox to win the AL East. Garza beat Boston twice in the league championship series, including Game Seven, to send Tampa Bay's improbable Rays to the World Series. The improbable star of the ALCS was left-hander David Price, the first pick of the previous year's amateur draft, called up in September after winning 12 or 13 decisions in the minor leagues in his first year of professional baseball. With two outs and the tying runs on base in the eighth inning of the seventh game, Price got the final out, then pitched a scoreless ninth for the pennant-winning save. Only after that, in five games, did Maddon's magic fail, perhaps overpowered by freezing rain in Philadelphia that forced a suspension of Game Five after the Rays tied the score in the sixth inning—a suspension that lasted two days before the game continued to its ultimate 4–3 Phillies win. The indoor Tropicana Field, ugly as it was, probably never looked so appealing.

It wasn't long before every major-league team had a cadre of whiz kids—the term here evoking Robert McNamara's team who used economic analysis, computer modeling, and new business management tools to revolutionize problem solving and decision making in the Pentagon in the 1960s—analyzing data for use in player evaluations, player acquisitions, and even managers' decisions in the dugout. And just as McNamara's whiz kids were outsiders brought into the military establishment, few of baseball's twenty-first-century whiz kids were good enough ballplayers, if they played at all in high school and college, to ever consider a playing career. They were typically young, all highly educated (many graduated from elite universities), and obsessed with data analysis—*and* they loved the game. In the new world of baseball analytics, while they didn't exactly replace scouts and front office baseball professionals, their skills allowed them entrée to baseball's inner sanctums, where they played a significant role in shaping the direction and fortunes of the teams that employed them. Some, in the manner of Theo Epstein, were promoted to general manager or even a step above as presidents (or vice presidents) in charge of baseball operations. A few teams filled such senior front office positions by recruiting experts in data analysis and database development from the business world, like Andrew Friedman, with no professional baseball background.

Data analysts in front offices began advising managers on starting lineups, what substitutions—pinch-hitting, pitching, or double-switches—to make and when, tactics in various game situations, defensive alignments, and virtually everything else that took place in preparation for and during games. Managers were expected to comply. Setting the example, Billy Beane had made this quite clear to Art Howe, the A's old-school manager he inherited when he became GM. Hired by Sandy Alderson "to implement the ideas of the front office," as quoted in *Moneyball*, "not his own," Howe may have been the manager, but he was a peripheral figure in the Beane regime, never adapting to the idea that data analysis could, let alone *should*, inform dugout decisions. After the A's lost their division series for the third straight year in 2002, Beane unceremoniously facilitated Howe's departure from Oakland to manage in New York for the Mets.

In Boston and Tampa Bay, however, managers Terry Francona and Joe Maddon, despite having been groomed in old-school baseball before computers became front office accessories, were both open to factoring data analysis into their decisions. That was a big reason why Francona was hired to take over the Red Sox in 2004—never mind that his previous managerial experience was four years at the helm of the Phillies, never once finishing with a winning record—and why Maddon was hired to guide the Devil Rays in 2006 at the age of 52, even though his only major-league managerial experience was twice as an interim manager with the Anaheim Angels in the 1990s. Neither allowed the front office to tell them what to do, but both "wanted the information," as Francona put it in his book *The Red Sox Years*, to use or not.

The most conspicuous display of Maddon's magic with data was that his Tampa Bay Rays revolutionized defensive alignments by their widespread use of infield shifts "precision-engineered" for each hitter according to detailed data analysis of his tendencies. Shading infielders a few feet or even yards from their normal positions based on where individual hitters were known to generally hit the ball was nothing new. Neither was the use of infield shifts—overloading one side of the infield with three defensive players and leaving the other side widely exposed—but that was limited mostly to left-handed power hitters with an extreme propensity to pull the ball, and shifts mostly positioned infielders on the outfield grass just off the infield dirt. What data analysis made clear was that nearly *every* hitter, not just classic pull hitters, tended to hit the ball in a specific direction. What Maddon's Rays did—and soon so did all other major-league teams—was play the percentages by positioning infielders for each batter where he was most likely, or more likely than not, to hit the ball. "None of it," said Maddon, "is done by the seat of our pants."

By 2013, the Rays lost their monopoly on using infield shifts more often than any other team. Where once they were rare and seen by few batters, shifts have become ubiquitous in major-league games. And they have become increasingly sophisticated, taking account of not only the batter but runners on base, the number of outs, and even the ball-and-strike count. The logic behind shifting is that batters rarely deliberately try to hit against it, concerned that would mess up their swing and make them less effective as hitters. What has happened instead to mitigate its effectiveness is that batters deliberately try to drive more balls in the air over infield shifts into the outfield gaps or over the wall. Shifts increased from about 3 percent of balls in play in 2010 to nearly 26 percent of all plate appearances in 2019, according to game data from MLB Advanced Media. The Los Angeles Dodgers, whose 106 wins in 2019 were the most in the National League, employed a shift in just over half the plate appearances against them. The Houston Astros, whose 107 wins were the most in baseball, shifted in just under half of opposing plate appearances. It must have worked, because Houston was first and Los Angeles second in the majors on making outs on balls put into play. In recent years, no team has used shifts as often as the Astros.

While veteran managers like Maddon and Francona, San Francisco's Bruce Bochy, and the Yankees' Joe Girardi made extensive use of the data available to them, they nonetheless managed games with instincts honed from long careers in professional baseball. That said, by 2020 the exponential proliferation of baseball data available to front offices had fundamentally changed the role of managers from real-time strategists to executing moves based on specific situations for which the relative probabilities of success had been quantitatively predetermined from up-to-date information on player performances taking into account any number of variables. Quantitative analyses provide managers more than a menu of options. They offer a singular answer to any given situation. The only limitations are roster size, player availability, and whether a particular player had already been used. Controversially, data to *inform* managerial decisions morphed into data to *dictate* what those decisions should be. Managers are no longer expected to be—and are even discouraged from being—grand strategists in the mold of a John McGraw or Earl Weaver.

With front office data-geek squads driving so much of game preparation and how to handle in-game contingencies, managers increasingly are being hired less for their baseball savvy than for their willingness to work with, and take direction from, the front office to make dugout decisions based on the comprehensive data they are given, as well as their ability to handle the media. How much coaching and managerial experience they have, including in the minor leagues, has become much less relevant— except when franchises want to reassure their fan base about the team's prospects by hiring a veteran manager with a record of major-league success, as Philadelphia's Phillies did when they chose Girardi to replace Gabe Kapler as manager in 2020 after the Phillies failed to meet the competitive expectations of ownership in Kapler's two years as manager. Girardi's résumé included three division titles, two wild-card berths, and a World Series championship in his 10 years as Yankees manager from 2008 to 2017. As a counterpoint, rookie managers Kevin Cash, Maddon's replacement in Tampa Bay; Alex Cora, who led the Red Sox to a World Series championship in his first year as manager in 2018; and Rocco Baldelli, whose 2019 Twins won 101 games and the AL Central Division in his first year (for which he earned Manager of the Year honors) had not managed at any level before being given charge of a major-league team.

The expectation that managers have *played* professionally is no longer even a given. Baseball history is replete with great managers who were mediocre players at best. Some, like Joe McCarthy and Earl Weaver, never made it to the majors; others, like Sparky Anderson and Tommy Lasorda, spent just one year or a handful of games over several seasons in the major leagues. They may have failed at their playing careers, but while failing they gained exemplary baseball IQ, leadership, and mentoring skills that all four honed by managing multiple years in the minors. Mike Shildt, the 2019 NL Manager of the Year for leading the St. Louis Cardinals to a division title after finishing third the previous year, was not good enough as a college player to play at any level of professional baseball; he earned his job by working his way up the Cardinals chain from scout to minor-league manager. Shildt was the first manager in the 121 years since Hall of Fame manager Frank Selee managed Boston's 1898 Beaneaters to the National League pennant to have had that kind of success without having had even a minimal professional playing career.

Baseball's information revolution was manifest not only in player evaluations—as an indispensable tool for trades, free agent signings, and roster construction, and for managers' in-game decision making—but also to improve players' performance. Franchises at the cutting edge in their use of data began hiring trainers and even uniformed coaches with little or no professional baseball background because of their expertise in biomechanics and interpreting data from advanced motion-capture video technology to break down, correct, and fine-tune the pitching and hitting forms of their players. Pitchers in particular have benefited from video technology that allows for precise measurements of pitch speed, movement, and location. At the start of the 2019 season, the pitching coaches for four of baseball's 30 major-league teams had never thrown a pitch in a professional baseball game. Every earlier generation of players would have found that unfathomable. Modern players, however, understand the value of absorbing that information, including about their opponent on the mound or at the plate. Many turned to private tutors for personalized training, taking advantage of biometric feedback to work on their hitting or pitching mechanics.

Michael Lewis made clear in *Moneyball* that Billy Beane and his staff understood that the comparative advantage the A's gained from their data-driven approach to building and sustaining a winning ballclub on a small budget would be short-lived. As other teams followed their example, data-based analysis to drive decision making had the perverse effect of magnifying the big-market/small-market divide. Teams with substantially greater financial resources, like the Red Sox and Yankees, were now using methodological approaches and data-based analysis to value-engineer their rosters while also spending big on free agents and making trades for players with expensive contracts to construct dominant teams at a lower cost than before. Neither the A's nor the Rays, or any other small-market club, could do that.

The Tampa Bay Rays arguably had the worst of it, being in a division with two powerhouse franchises—New York and Boston—committed to competing every year in the World Series. After being the team that nobody saw coming to win the division in 2008, the Rays dropped to third in 2009, won the division again in 2010, and made the playoffs as a wild card in two of the next three years before sliding back to four straight losing seasons from 2014 to 2017. Along the way, the Rays parted ways with free agents Carl Crawford, Melvin Upton, and Ben Zobrist; traded starting pitchers Scott Kazmir, James Shields, and David Price (less than two years after he won the 2012 Cy Young Award), all when they were on the cusp of free agency; and traded coveted young reliever Wade Davis and outfielder Wil Myers (a year after he was 2013

Rookie of the Year). Manager Joe Maddon took his magic to the Chicago Cubs after his Rays fell from 92 wins and the wild card in 2013 to 85 losses and fourth place in 2014. All the while, the Rays suffered a steady decline in attendance.

Following their four division titles and a wild card in seven years from 2000 to 2006—thanks to Billy Beane's Moneyball philosophy—the A's did not have another winning season for five years. Along the way, Beane traded Oakland's best players, notably young starting pitchers Trevor Cahill and lefty Gio Gonzalez and closer Andrew Bailey, for prospects to build for the future. In February 2012, Beane splurged four years and $36 million on Cuban star Yoenis Cespedes, who had just defected from his country. The Cespedes signing and Beane's trades paid off for the A's with back-to-back division titles in 2012 and 2013. Cespedes slugged 49 homers those two years, and third baseman Josh Donaldson—a first-round draft pick by the Cubs in 2007 for whom Beane traded in 2008—broke through to superstar status.

Fresh off two division-winning seasons with one of the lowest player payrolls in the game, Beane apparently made the decision to compete for a championship in 2014. By the end of the season, the A's payroll totaled $89 million—still just tenth in the league, but a big boost over the $69 million in player salaries the previous year. Oakland's blockbuster moves came in July when Beane traded top infield prospect Addison Russell to the Cubs for starter Jeff Samardzija and, 26 days later, Cespedes to Boston for Red Sox ace Jon Lester. With Oakland sporting the best record in baseball and up by 2½ games in their division, and with veteran lefty Scott Kazmir and second-year righty Sonny Gray both 12–3 at the time, the Lester trade, particularly following the one for Samardzija, was made with the clear intent to go deep into the postseason. But while Oakland's pitching held up, without Cespedes the A's went from being the highest-scoring team in the majors to 25th in scoring the last two months of the season. Oakland wound up a distant second in the AL West to the Los Angeles Angels, but did qualify for the wild-card game—a wild 12-inning game that they lost.

Having missed Beane's mark, it was back to payroll austerity for Oakland's A's. That winter Lester became a free agent and Beane traded away Samardzija and Donaldson, the second-best position player in the major leagues in 2013 and 2014 according to the WAR metric. While Donaldson promptly became the American League MVP in 2015 for first-place Toronto, the A's plummeted to last in the AL West, where they stayed the next two years. Gray, third in the AL Cy Young Award voting in 2015 on the back of his 14–7 record for a 94-loss team, and closer Sean Doolittle were both traded in July 2017 to teams with World Series aspirations—Sonny to the Yankees, and Sean to the Washington Nationals.

In 2018, both the A's and the Rays were back in contention. With by far the lowest payroll in the majors at $46 million, Tampa Bay went from four straight losing seasons to 90 wins in the AL East but could not keep pace with the Red Sox and Yankees, both 100-win teams. With baseball's second lowest payroll at $70 million, Oakland had 97 wins, good for second in the AL West and a date with the 100-win Yankees in the wildcard game. The A's lost. And in 2019, both teams finished second in their division to meet each other in the wild-card game—the Rays with 96 wins, despite still having the lowest payroll in the majors, and the Athletics, whose payroll improved to 25th in the major leagues, with 97 wins. The Rays beat the A's and then pushed the 107-win best-record-in-baseball Houston Astros, whose payroll exceeded Tampa Bay's by $110 million, to the five-game limit in their division series before bowing out of the postseason.

As impressive as what the Rays and the A's accomplished in 2019 with two of the lowest payrolls in baseball, neither team seemed poised to sneak past the Yankees and Astros to win their respective American League divisions in 2020—the surest route to making it at least as far as the five-game division series round of the postseason. Whatever advantage Tampa Bay and Oakland could leverage from their baseball geek squads, it was likely to be at the margins because both New York and especially Houston were fully committed both to data analytics *and* to spending what was necessary to be the best team in baseball.

A formidable team in their own right, the A's nonetheless looked to have a chance to contend in the AL West, even against the powerhouse Astros, for as long as they could keep their cadre of star players together. Just as they did 20 years before with first baseman Jason Giambi, shortstop Miguel Tejada, and third baseman Eric Chavez, the A's had laid the foundation for success with an outstanding trio of players at those same positions: Matt Olson, Marcus Semien, and Matt Chapman, all of whom had more than 30 homers and 90 RBIs in 2019. Olson and Chapman, both in their third year in 2019, would not be eligible for arbitration until 2021, the same year Semien, who arrived in Beane's trade for Samardzija, could declare for free agency. Tampa Bay's core of young stars lacked such an impressive track record, and one of them—Nate Snell, the 2018 Cy Young Award winner—was hampered much of 2019 with elbow problems.

As it happened, both Tampa Bay and Oakland won their division in 2020—a season limited to just 60 games beginning in late July because of the COVID-19 pandemic. At 36-24 Oakland easily outpaced Houston's Astros to win the AL West by seven games, only to lose to the Astros in their division series. Tampa Bay, with the second lowest player-payroll in the major leagues, at 40-20, had the best record in the American League, beat the Yankees by seven games in the AL East, beat the Yankees again in their division series, and made it to the World Series to be beaten by the only team in baseball with a better record—and the third-highest payroll in the game—the Los Angeles Dodgers.

9

BASEBALL'S DIVERSITY SCORECARD

In November 2004, coming off back-to-back 90-loss seasons for the first time since 1982–1983, the Mets introduced their new manager for 2005: Willie Randolph, signed to a three-year contract. Randolph grew up in Brooklyn, rooting for the Mets, but his major-league career centered on the 13 seasons from 1976 to 1988 when he was the Yankees' outstanding second baseman over in the Bronx. He returned to the Yankees as their third-base coach in 1993 and sat by Joe Torre's side in 2004 as his bench coach. Highly regarded as a coach for his interaction with players and his baseball-smarts, Randolph had aspirations of managing in the major leagues.

On at least 10 prior occasions, Randolph had been interviewed by teams looking for a new manager, including in October 2002 by the Mets, looking to replace then-manager Bobby Valentine after finishing last in the NL East just two years after going to the World Series, in October 2002. Instead of the inexperienced Randolph, the Mets settled on Oakland A's manager Art Howe. And why not? Howe had 12 years of experience managing in Houston and Oakland. He had just led the A's to their second straight 100-win season and third postseason in a row. He also wanted out of Oakland, where he chafed under Billy Beane's Moneyball approach, especially the part that interfered in his bailiwick as the manager.

It appeared as though the 48-year-old Randolph's ambition to manage would be forever thwarted. The question hovering in the background was whether Randolph's being Black stood in the way of his aspirations. Ten percent of the players on major-league rosters in 2004 were African American. Another 28 percent were Black or White Hispanic players from Latin America. But of baseball's 30 major-league managers, only three were African American—Montreal's Frank Robinson, the Cubs' Dusty Baker, and Pittsburgh's Lloyd McClendon. The Giants' Felipe Alou and Kansas City's Tony Peña, both Black Hispanic from the Dominican Republic, and the White Sox' Ozzie Guillen, White Hispanic from Venezuela, were the only other minority managers. From the end of the 2002 season until Randolph was announced as the Mets' new manager after the 2004 season, only four of the 19 manager positions that opened up went to a person of color, two of whom—Alou going to San Francisco in 2003, and Baker to Chicago that same year—were well-respected managers with 10 years of experience in the majors.

Jackie Robinson's integration of the major leagues on April 15, 1947, was a milestone in the history of American race relations from which Major League Baseball has gotten lots of mileage for being on the right side of history. But the narrative isn't so simple on either point. The civil rights movement in the United States, aimed at taking down the edifice of Jim Crow in the South and offshoots almost everywhere else in the country, had years of protests and violence, and years of marches and more violence to go before the Civil Rights and Voting Rights Acts of 1964 and 1965 became the law of the land. And even in all the years since, the scars of racism in America and virulent pushback have remained.

For baseball, Robinson's extraordinary success was not quite the post-racial shining legacy that champions of the game would have us believe. He was not welcome. And the first generation of Black players had much more to prove than their white counterparts competing for major-league jobs. The best of the first Black players—Larry Doby, Minnie Minoso, Willie Mays, Hank Aaron, Ernie Banks, Frank Robinson, and Roberto Clemente—could not denied. They were superstars, disproportionate in their number to the few Black players who became regulars on big-league rosters in the 1950s. And even as Black players became more accepted in the game, they were treated as second-class citizens in Florida spring training locales and in many of the major-league cities where they played and lived well into the 1960s.

African Americans topped 10 percent of major-league players in 1962 and 15 percent in 1971. By then, an additional 11 percent of players were from Latin America, almost all from Caribbean Basin countries. There were still no Black managers in Major League Baseball. The only Latin-born managers in major-league history—Mike Gonzalez, for 17 games in 1938 and six more in 1940, and Preston Gomez, the first manager of the 1969-expansion San Diego Padres—were White Hispanics from Cuba. Gonzalez, a former catcher and highly regarded as a coach, almost certainly could have had a successful career as a major-league manager in the 1930s and 1940s if given a chance—which he wasn't, because he was from Cuba.

In 1975, a year when African Americans accounted for more than 18 percent of major-league players, the Cleveland Indians made Frank Robinson Major League Baseball's first Black manager. Robinson was fired in June 1977. The next two Black managers—Larry Doby in 1978 and Maury Wills in 1980 and 1981—were, like Robinson, former star players. Neither lasted a full season and neither got a second chance at managing. Frank Robinson did, in 1981 with the Giants. He was fired a second time in 1984, midseason. There had not been a Black manager since then when, in April 1987, the 40th anniversary of Jackie Robinson's debut, Dodgers general manager Al Campanis made his infamous remarks on *Nightline* about Black baseball professionals not having the "necessities to be a field manager." Perhaps what Campanis said was not what he really believed, but his words were a damning indictment that forced the hand of Major League Baseball.

Over the next six years—although not for any of the four midseason managerial changes in 1987—there was a flurry of hiring Black managers. Frank Robinson was brought back a third time in 1988 to manage the Baltimore Orioles. In 1989, Cito Gaston was given charge of the Toronto Blue Jays. In 1991, Hal McRae was named manager of the Kansas City Royals. In 1992, Felipe Alou was finally given a chance to manage the Montreal Expos, in whose minor-league system he had managed since 1977. The 1993 season began with new managers Don Baylor in Colorado with the expansion Rockies, Dusty Baker in San Francisco, and Cuban-born Tony Perez in Cincinnati. But still, that was just six Black former major-leaguers chosen for the 54 managerial changes made by major-league teams between 1988 and 1993. And Robinson was fired as a manager for the third time in May 1991.

One can argue that teams were playing it safe with the Black baseball professionals they hired to be managers in that five of the six had renowned playing careers and were respected for their leadership and gravitas as major leaguers. Robinson and Perez played in five World Series, McRae in four, Baker and Baylor in three, and Alou in one. Robinson was one of baseball's all-time great sluggers (retiring with 586 home runs) and had already been a major-league manager. Baylor and Baker combined for 580 career homers in playing careers encompassing most of the 1970s and 1980s. Alou was a premier player in the 1960s, even if he was overshadowed by superstars Mays and Aaron on the teams he played for. Perez was a cornerstone of Cincinnati's 1970s Big Red Machine and McRae a cornerstone of the Kansas City team that won four division titles in five years in the 1970s. Gaston, however, was not a star in his 10-year playing career, only the first half of which he played as a regular.

Perez was the only one of the new Black managers not to last long—just 44 games in 1993, with the Reds at 20–24, when team owner Marge Schott decided to replace him with Davey Johnson. That he was not given a chance to prove himself over a full season was perhaps not surprising. Perez may have been a star on the Big Red Machine, but he did not have Johnson's managerial pedigree, which included managing the powerhouse Mets to two division titles in the mid-1980s, including a World Series championship in 1986. And Schott had drawn unseemly notice for allowing her dog to poop on Cincinnati's playing field, saying that Hitler "was OK at the beginning; he just went too far," and using racial slurs. Gaston, Baker, and Alou, however, had immediate competitive success as major-league managers, shooting down the canard that Black men were somehow not up to the job. What mattered was having a good team to manage.

Cito Gaston was the first Black man to be named manager of a team with realistic competitive prospects. Even though the team got off to a terrible 12–24 start in 1989, the Blue Jays had won the AL East in 1985 and came within two games of the division title in 1987 and 1988. No team had a better record in baseball than Toronto from the day Gaston took over. His first year on the job, Gaston became the first Black manager to manage a team in the postseason. After another division title and failure in the ALCS in 1991, Gaston became the first Black manager to manage in a World Series in 1992—and the first to win a World Series. And Gaston's Blue Jays did it again in 1993. That same year, Dusty Baker, in his first year as a manager at any level, became the first Black manager to lead a team to 100 victories. His Giants, whose roster was bolstered by free agent Barry Bonds, won 103 games in a scintillating race for the NL Western Division title that they lost to the 104-win Atlanta Braves in the last year that there was no wild card to fall back on. And in 1994, Felipe Alou, in his third year managing a rising Expos team whose roster included his son Moises and nephew Mel Rojas, had his team in first place with the best record in the majors when the players went on strike.

Five of baseball's 28 teams were led by Black managers when baseball went on strike. In 1995, Major League Baseball returned with just four. Gone was Hal McRae, fired in September in 1994 during the strike, despite his Royals being on a 15–4 roll when the game was shut down; only Alou's Expos had a better record in that span. Kansas City's general manager later said that firing McRae was his worst mistake. Alou, Baker, Baylor, and Gaston remained in place. Don Baylor joined Gaston as one of the only Black managers to manage in the postseason by leading the Rockies, in only their third year, to the National League wild card. Colorado's biggest-impact player was outfielder Larry Walker, one of the many in-their-prime stars on Alou's 1994 Expos who were no longer there, or soon to be gone, because the Expos' owners refused to invest in keeping a very good team together for a run at a championship. Felipe Alou went from managing the front-runner in all of Major League Baseball in August 1994 to the bottom of the NL East heap in 1995.

Perhaps there was nothing insidious about it, teams just choosing the best man for the manager's job, without regard to race. And four major-league teams already had Black managers. But of the 27 manager openings in the first three years after the strike, 1995 to 1997, not one went to a minority. Gaston was fired with just days remaining on the 1997 schedule, not unexpectedly, since the Blue Jays were enduring their fourth losing season in a row since their back-to-back championships. The number of African American managers remained at four, however, because the White Sox hired Jerry Manuel to manage in 1998. Manuel, who had an inconsequential big-league career of just 96 games over parts of five seasons, had coached for Alou in Montreal and was Jim Leyland's bench coach on the 1997 World Series champion Florida Marlins. There were four other new managers at the start of the 1998 season—including for the expansion Tampa Bay Devil Rays and Arizona Diamondbacks—and two managerial changes during the season. None went to a minority.

Baseball had just celebrated the 50th anniversary of Jackie Robinson's breaking the major-league color barrier in 1998, so the fact that Manuel was the only minority hired to fill 39 manager vacancies since the start of the 1993 season was an embarrassment for Major League Baseball. None of the four teams beginning the 1999 season with a new manager had hired a minority, either. Commissioner Bud Selig's promise on Robinson's debut anniversary two years earlier to promote diversity in all of baseball's management positions, including in executive suites, was looking disingenuous at best. In April 1999, Selig addressed the issue, sending a memo to all team owners mandating that they consider—and interview—minority candidates for all manager and front office vacancies. The commissioner said he told the owners they were limiting themselves by "just recycling" the same people as managers.

His mandate had an impact. Not including interim managers, of the 32 manager positions that opened up from then until the end of the 2002 season, 10 went to Black or Caribbean-born Hispanic candidates. Three were in fact "recycled" managers with at least four years of previous managerial experience: Baylor, who took over the Cubs in 2000; McRae, hired by Tampa Bay early in the 2001 season; and Frank Robinson, now 66 years old and working in the commissioner's office, who was asked in 2002 to return to the dugout in Montreal, whose Expos had let Alou go in May 2001 and were now a ward of Major League Baseball. Alou taking over the Giants and Baker the Cubs in 2003 would also be "recycled." Only two of the first-time managers—Lloyd McClendon, hired by the Pirates in 2001, and former long-time White Sox shortstop Ozzie Guillen, who replaced Manuel in 2004—would manage at least five years in the major leagues.

Dusty Baker became the third Black manager to lead his team into the postseason when the Giants won the NL West in 1997, and Jerry Manuel became the fourth when his White Sox captured the AL Central Division title in 2000. Like Baylor's 1995 Rockies, none of those teams made it past the division series round. Finally, in 2002, Dusty Baker joined Cito Gaston as the only Black men to have managed a team in the World Series. First it went well. Baker's Giants held a three-games-to-two lead in the series against the Angels and a 5–0 lead going into the seventh inning of Game Six in Anaheim. But it ended badly. The Giants lost the sixth game, 6–5, and the seventh game, 4–1. Following that calamity and the season-long friction between Baker and franchise owner Peter Magowan, the Giants did not renew his contract for 2003, thus opening the revolving manager's door for Felipe Alou in San Francisco and Baker in Chicago. In 2005, Guillen led the White Sox to the best record in the American League and an 11–1 romp through the postseason to bring the franchise—and the city of Chicago—its first World Series title since the 1917. Baseball now had two minority managers whose team had won a World Series.

In 2006, his second year in charge of the Mets, Willie Randolph came close to being the third Black American and fourth minority (after Guillen) to manage in the World Series. The Mets, tied with the Yankees for the best record in baseball, won the NL East decisively but lost the NLCS to St. Louis in seven games. As if that was not hard enough to swallow, the next year his Mets blew a seemingly secure seven-game division lead over the second-place Phillies with 17 games remaining by losing 12 of them. Rather than give Randolph an immediate vote of confidence following his team's late-September collapse, the Mets waited several days before announcing he would indeed be returning as manager in 2008. It was a short-lived reprieve. A sluggish 34–35 start to the 2008 season put an end to Randolph's tenure as Mets manager. The front office indictment of Randolph was that he had underachieved as manager of a team that included stars the caliber of Carlos Beltran, David Wright, Jose Reyes, and left-handed ace Johan Santana. After giving the job to Jerry Manuel, the Mets had the National League's best record the rest of the way. But history repeated itself; the Mets squandered a 3½-game lead by losing 10 of their final 17 games. The blame for that September meltdown could not be placed on Willie Randolph. He wasn't there.

Notwithstanding Randolph's misfortune, the years between 2007 and 2010 were a high point for the number of minority managers in Major League Baseball: Every year there were at least eight. Four of the 11 minorities who managed major-league teams during those years were from Caribbean countries. Three were veterans with managerial résumés dating back to the 1990s: Baker, Manuel (Randolph's replacement), and Gaston, brought back in June 2008 for a return engagement in Toronto, 11 years after the Blue Jays had fired him for not being able to respond "to the challenges of the American League East." (Gaston's second, forgettable tenure ended in 2010.) Eight were first-time managers, including Guillen since 2004 and Randolph when he still had the job.

The most successful of the first-timers was Ron Washington, whose first season managing the Texas Rangers was 2007. Three years later he became just the third Black manager to manage in the World Series, guiding the Rangers there for the first time in franchise history. The Rangers were back in 2011, making him just the second Black manager in major-league history to take his team to the World Series two years in a row. Neither year, however, did Washington's Rangers win, leaving Cito Gaston as still the only African American and Ozzie Guillen as the only Hispanic manager to have won a World Series. Meanwhile, Felipe Alou's managerial career came to an end in 2006 after consecutive losing seasons with the Giants. In his 14 years as a manager, Alou managed in only one postseason—in 2003, his first year in San Francisco as Baker's successor, when the Giants won their division handily but lost to the wild-card World Series–bound Marlins in their division series. Deprived of managing in the World Series in 1994 because of the strike, Alou could only wonder what might have been for his Expos had the season and postseason played out.

Selig's hiring rules paid dividends in the front office, including for women, but ultimately has not really changed the complexion of baseball's executive suites. In 1999, the year he mandated that teams interview minority candidates for all field manager and executive positions, minorities and women accounted for only 3 percent of front office positions in Major League Baseball. By 2013, that number was up to 20 percent. The most high-profile minority executives in the Selig era were African American Ken Williams, the White Sox general manager from 2000 until he was promoted to executive vice president in 2012, and Dominican-born Omar Minaya, appointed by Major League Baseball to be the Expos' GM in 2002 and subsequently hired by the Mets to be general manager as the 2004 season came to an end. Both men hired minority managers—Williams giving Ozzie Guillen his opportunity in 2003 and Minaya hiring Randolph and then Jerry Manuel to replace him. And both teams had competitive success. The White Sox won the 2005 World Series; the Mets made it to the NLCS in 2006.

And then there was Kim Ng, of Chinese-Thai descent. She grew up in Queens and loved baseball, rooting for the Yankees (not the Mets). She became assistant general manager of the Yankees at the age of 29 in 1998, left New York for Los Angeles to become vice president and assistant general manager of the Dodgers in 2001, and in November 2005 was a leading candidate to be the Dodgers' next GM. Dodgers owner Frank McCourt, however, passed on the opportunity to break the gender barrier as the Dodgers had the color barrier with Jackie Robinson. The job went instead to an older white guy, certainly qualified, whose experience as an assistant GM was only one year more than Ng's—and that was with the archrival Giants, of all teams. When Ng left LA in 2011 to return to New York as a senior vice president of baseball operations for Major League Baseball, she was one of only three women to have served as an assistant GM for a major-league team. In November 2020, Ng was named GM of the Miami Marlins, becoming the first female general manager in major league history.

At baseball's winter meetings in December 2019, the White Sox' Ken Williams and Marlins' Mike Hill were the only Black men in charge of baseball operations for their teams. The Giants' president of baseball operations, Farhan Zaidi (of Pakistani descent), and Detroit GM Al Avila (White Hispanic, born in Cuba), were the only other minorities in a senior executive position responsible for baseball decisions. Only five Black men have ever been GM of a major-league team, and there have been none since Dave Stewart was fired by the Arizona Diamondbacks in 2016. Major League Baseball defensively points to its programs to develop minorities and women for senior front office positions, but Dusty Baker thought institutional discrimination abounded in baseball.

Selig's initiative to promote diversity has been a qualified success at best, not only in baseball front offices but in the dugout. By the mid-2010s, the paucity of minority managers—particularly African Americans—was once again an issue for Major League Baseball. None of the 10 open manager jobs in 2015 went to a minority, and in the five years from 2011 to 2015, only four of 41 manager vacancies were filled by a minority, one of whom was a US-born White Hispanic. Two of the four—Cuban-born Fredi Gonzalez, taking charge of the Braves in 2011, and Lloyd McClendon, returning to manage Seattle in 2014—had appreciable prior big-league managerial experience, Gonzalez with the Marlins from 2007 to 2010 and McClendon with the Pirates from 2001 to 2005. They were the major leagues' only minority managers in 2015. Commissioner Rob Manfred, in his first year succeeding his mentor Bud Selig, explained in October that front offices "hire who they feel to be the most qualified person for the job." The commissioner felt compelled to add, "That's the American way," as if that explained it. Selig's rule on interviewing minority candidates for every opening was still in effect, but Black and Hispanic coaches and former players who aspired to be managers—and who were widely thought by baseball professionals to be fully capable of running a major-league team—thought the "rule" was, in practice, meaningless.

The Los Angeles Dodgers and Washington Nationals both hired Black managers to take over their clubs in 2016. Washington went with experience, bringing Dusty Baker back for his 21st year as a manager, two years after he was let go by Cincinnati. Los Angeles went with first-time manager Dave Roberts. Along with Gonzalez, they were the only minority managers in Major League Baseball. Both led their team to a division title. In 2017 Roberts joined Gaston, Baker, and Washington as the only Black managers to have ever managed a team on baseball's biggest stage: the World Series. The Dodgers lost. That milestone aside, they were baseball's only Black managers that year. While Rick Renteria, an American of Mexican descent, was in his first year managing the White Sox, there were no Latin-born managers in the major leagues in 2017. Yet, 42 percent of players on major-league rosters were nonwhite—African Americans, US-born Hispanics, and Latin-born Hispanics—according to Major League Baseball's own data for the previous year. This time Manfred's explanation for why there were so few minority managers was that the game had evolved to be "much more focused on analytics," making it a "very different interview process"—which implicitly sounded a lot like Al Campanis saying in 1987 that Blacks lacked the "necessities" to be competitive for manager jobs.

Because Baker was fired for failing to get the Nationals beyond the division series, the 2018 season began with Roberts as baseball's only African American manager and three Hispanic managers—Renteria, born in California; Dave Martinez, of Puerto Rican descent born in New York, who replaced Baker in Washington; and Alex Cora, from Puerto Rico, as the new rookie manager in Boston. Roberts's Dodgers and Cora's Red Sox met in the World Series—the first Fall Classic where both teams were managed by a minority. The Red Sox prevailed. In 2019, Charlie Montoyo, also Puerto Rican, joined Cora as baseball's only Caribbean-born managers, and Roberts was still the only Black manager. Martinez led the wild-card Nationals to a World Series championship.

Part of the frustration for minorities aspiring to major-league managerial careers was that there were so few second chances for those getting a first opportunity and then, as is ultimately par for the course, being fired. Willie Randolph never got another chance to manage after being dumped by the Mets in 2008, at the age of 53, much to his frustration. "I've made no secrets about my desire to manage," he said years later, adding that he would be a "really good" manager. Nor did former star catcher Tony Peña, Black Hispanic from the Dominican Republic, get another chance after managing very bad Royals teams from 2002 to early in the 2005 season; Cecil Cooper, an African American manager who brought the Astros to a barely winning record of 171–170 from late in the 2007 season to late in the 2009 season; or Bo Porter, also a Black American, manager of the Astros from 2013 to 2014—years that were deliberately scripted to be losing seasons by Houston's front office.

In defense of Randolph's perspective, it would be remiss not to mention that a fellow Brooklyn-bred manager of some renown, Hall of Fame skipper Joe Torre, in leading his 1982 Braves to the NL Western Division title, presided over the fourth-worst record in the National League after the All-Star break, including one stretch of 19 losses in 21 games that turned their runaway into a dogfight not decided until the final day of the season. A similar unfolding of events happened the next year, when Torre's Braves held a half-game lead three days short of September only to falter with the NL's worst record the rest of the way. That did not stop the Cardinals from hiring him to be their manager in 1990, or the Yankees, despite Torre's lack of success in St. Louis, from making him their manager in 1996. Similarly, Grady Little's decision to leave an exhausted Pedro Martinez in to face the most dangerous part of the Yankees batting order in the eighth inning of Game Seven in the 2003 ALCS cost Boston its 5–2 lead, a chance to play in the World Series for the first time since 1918, and Little his job—but it didn't keep the Dodgers from hiring him to be their manager in 2006.

If Randolph and other minority baseball professionals struggled to gain traction as managers, and competitively successful managers like Cito Gaston and Ron Washington did not get a chance to manage in other cities despite having taken teams to back-to-back World Series, Frank Robinson and Dusty Baker were the Morgan Freeman of major-league managers: steady, disciplined, accountable, and dignified. They were beyond reproach, authoritative voices of integrity in the dugout, the club-

house, with the media. And they were specifically asked to take over
troubled teams to restore their credibility. Robinson was asked by Major
League Baseball to return to the dugout in Montreal in 2002, 11 years
after he had last managed a game. Baker, 66 years old and retired for two
years, was hired by Washington in 2016 to get an underachieving but
strong Nationals team into the World Series, and again by Houston in
2020, at the age of 70—two years since being fired by the Nationals for
failing to get them to the promised land—to restore faith in an outstanding Astros team discredited in a just-surfaced scandal for cheating during
their championship season of 2017.

Major League Baseball's problem with diversity, however, was not
just about the underrepresentation of minorities in positions of authority
in the dugout and executive suites. It was also about its waning popularity
with Black Americans. Diversity itself was not a problem on the playing
field—not when 27 percent of the players on big-league rosters in 2019
were from Latin America or Asia. But in the 100th anniversary year of
Jackie Robinson's birth, Black players accounted for only 7.7 percent of
major-league teams' Opening Day rosters in 2019, and 11 of baseball's
30 major-league teams did not have a single African American player in
their dugout.

The numbers of Black Americans on major-league rosters had steadily
declined from a high of 18.7 percent in 1981 to as low as 6.7 percent in
2016. A large part of the reason was that baseball did not have the same
cultural relevance as basketball and football for Black youth—not in
youth leagues, not in high school, not in college, and not even sitting at
home watching on TV. Major League Baseball had begun addressing the
problem of declining Black youth interest in the 1990s by promoting and
investing in outreach programs, most notably its Reviving Baseball in
Inner Cities initiative. That Dusty Baker and Dave Roberts were the only
African Americans chosen to fill the 35 managerial vacancies from 2016
to the start of the 2020 season, however, has sent decidedly mixed sig-
nals.

Layered on top of this in 2020 was the Black Lives Matter movement.
In the midst of an out-of-control coronavirus pandemic sweeping the
United States that delayed the start of the major-league season for more
than four months, the death on May 25 in Minneapolis of George Floyd,
an unarmed Black man, unable to breathe because a white police officer
had him pinned face down against the pavement with his knee on the

back of Floyd's neck, provoked massive protests across America, coast to coast, north to south. Major League Baseball issued a statement deploring racism and racial injustice, in effect taking a stand in support of Black Lives Matter. And after another Black man was shot in the back by the police in Kenosha, Wisconsin, in August, the Milwaukee Brewers refused to play their August 23 game in solidarity with Black Lives Matter, and the Cincinnati Reds—their opponent—declined to accept a forfeit and supported the Brewers' stand. Three games were not played that day, and seven more the day after, as major-league players—white, Latin, Asian, and Black—stood up by standing down in support of social justice. This was a pivot turn for Major League Baseball.

One would think it shouldn't have been, not for a sport that struck a blow against segregated America when Jackie Robinson took the field on April 15, 1947. But it was, because Major League Baseball has always been leery of social activism, especially by its players and especially concerning race. In the two decades after Jackie Robinson integrated the major leagues, as the civil rights movement gained momentum in the 1960s, Black players were mindful to keep a low profile—really, to not say anything implying support for even peaceful protests, because they were disruptive.

Major League Baseball's insensitive response to the assassination of Black civil rights leader Martin Luther King Jr. on April 4, 1968—four days before Opening Day—provoked unprecedented pushback on the game's institutional powers-that-be by Black players. It began with many Black major leaguers refusing to play in the final few exhibition games before the scheduled first games on April 8, out of respect for Dr. King. It gained momentum when Commissioner William Eckert made no decision one way or the other about whether to move back Opening Day until after King's funeral on April 9, leaving the decision instead to team owners. With pent-up Black rage over bigotry, persistent discrimination, and po-lice brutality manifesting itself in rioting and vandalism in the streets of many US cities, the Washington Senators and Cincinnati Reds decided against playing on April 8, never mind their cities' tradition of hosting the first two games of every new season. Houston's Astros planned to go ahead with their home opener that night; their opponents, however—Pittsburgh's Pirates, with 11 Black American and Black Hispanic players on their roster, including star players Roberto Clemente, Willie Stargell, and Maury Wills—refused to go along, voting unanimously as a team not to take the field until after King's funeral, even if it meant forfeiting games.

It was a unifying moment in the Pirates' well-integrated clubhouse, with white players supporting their Black teammates. Perhaps civil rights were not talked about much among Pirates teammates in the interest of avoiding a fraught subject, but on this they were clear. Noting that Pittsburgh's Black players were emphatic about honoring King by not playing, pitcher Steve Blass said, "We were white and we felt the same way." The Pirates' stand won the support of Houston's Black players. The game was cancelled. No games were played on April 8. No games were played on April 9, either, the day Martin Luther King was laid to rest. The 1968 season began the next day.

This was a rare moment for Major League Baseball, because until the urgency of Black Lives Matter forced the league's hand in the summer of 2020, social activism by players continued to be discouraged. While some NFL, NBA and WNBA players were vocal in their support of the Black Lives Matter movement against police brutality and social injustice after NFL quarterback Colin Kaepernick began kneeling in solidarity during the national anthem in 2016—a politically explosive gesture, it turned out—major-league players were mostly silent. George Floyd's death changed that. Major-league stars spoke out in support of Black Lives Matter, including prominent white ballplayers like Houston's Alex Bregman, the Mets' Pete Alonso, and the White Sox' Lucas Giolito.

In the first game of the 2020 season, which was not played until July 23 because of the pandemic, New York's Yankees and Washington's Nationals, lined up on their dugout's side of the foul lines, put a hand to a 200-yard black cloth and knelt in silence for a full minute to pay tribute to Black lives mattering. No fans were in the stands, for obvious health reasons, but it was a unifying moment for a country besieged by the pandemic. As Steve Blass had said 52 years before, "You didn't have to be black or white to be aware of doing the right thing and respecting the whole situation."

10

THE LATIN TSUNAMI AND THE
SECOND CUBAN WAVE

The World Baseball Classic, first held in March 2006, again in 2009, and every four years thereafter, was another of Bud Selig's legacy initiatives to boost Major League Baseball's profile outside the United States. It has not just showcased the excellence of national teams from baseball-obsessed countries in the Asian Pacific Rim and Latin America—Japan won the first two Classics, the Dominican Republic in 2013, and the United States in 2017—but is a vivid reminder of how many of the best major-league players come from Caribbean Basin countries. Three of the teams from Latin America in the first World Baseball Classic—the Dominican Republic, Puerto Rico, and Venezuela—had star-studded rosters filled almost entirely by major leaguers. That year, nearly one in four (24 percent) major-league players were from Latin America. On Opening Day in 2020, nearly one in three (31 percent) were.

The large numbers of players from the Caribbean on major-league rosters is a relatively recent development. Through the end of World War II, only 43 of the 5,897 players who had played Major League Baseball since 1901 were born and grew up in the island nations, including the US territory of Puerto Rico, and Latin countries enveloping the Caribbean. All but four of them were from Cuba. Even though baseball was ingrained in the culture and Caribbean winter leagues attracted many Major League and Negro League players, except for the Washington Senators beginning in the 1930s, major-league teams did not scout prospective talent south of the border. A big reason why was that so many of the best players in Cuba and Puerto Rico were Black, and therefore not acceptable, at a time when Major League Baseball was uncompromising in its stand against integrating the national pastime.

The integration of Major League Baseball that took root after World War II, with Jackie Robinson and Larry Doby leading the way, was the catalyst for an unprecedented influx of players from the Caribbean Basin in the 1950s. By 1960, there were 50 players from the Caribbean on major-league rosters, including future Hall of Famers Roberto Clemente and Orlando Cepeda from Puerto Rico, Juan Marichal from the Dominican Republic, and Luis Aparicio from Venezuela. Beginning with Minnie Minoso in 1951, Cubans were at the leading edge of the globalization of Major League Baseball. They numbered nearly half (23) of the 50 major-league players from the Caribbean Basin in 1960. But the first wave of players leaving Cuba in hopes of a big-league career came to an end in the chaotic first years after Fidel Castro's seizure of power in 1959. By the mid-1960s, Castro's imposition of severe travel restrictions, part of his crackdown on political liberties, made it difficult if not impossible for Cubans to come to the United States. The success of outstanding players like Minoso, Camilo Pascual, Tony Oliva, Tony Perez, and Luis Tiant, who had left Cuba to play big-league baseball, turned out to be at the expense of being able to return to family still in Cuba.

The number of Latin-born players who had ever played in the major leagues doubled between 1960 and 1975. A third of the Caribbean players on major-league rosters in 1975 were from Puerto Rico. Just 13 were from Cuba—almost all of whom came to the United States to play ball before Castro's crackdown. By 1991, the number of Latin-born players to have ever played major-league baseball doubled again. Having surpassed the number from Puerto Rico in 1978, Dominican-born players now accounted for the largest share of non-Americans on major-league rosters. But it wasn't until after the players' strike that the Caribbean wave to major league baseball became a tsunami, the epicenter of which was the Dominican Republic, sharing half the island of Hispaniola with Haiti (where baseball, disdained as cultural imperialism, was not a sport of any consequence).

Two of baseball's biggest and most dynamic stars straddling the turn of the twenty-first century were from the DR: Sammy Sosa and Pedro Martinez. The star-studded 2006 Dominican team in the World Baseball Classic, whose roster was entirely major leaguers, included Albert Pujols,

David Ortiz, Vladimir Guerrero, and Adrian Beltre. Pujols, whose family moved to the United States when he was 16, was already in the conversation about the greatest first basemen ever. Guerrero, like Pujols, hit for power and average. Beltre was a third of the way through a career that would establish him as one of the best all-around third basemen of all time. Ortiz, mostly used as a designated hitter, teamed with Dominican-born Manny Ramirez, whose family moved to New York City when he was 13, to give the Red Sox a feared pair of sluggers in the middle of the batting order. More than half of the Latin players making it to the majors between 1995 and 2006 were from the Dominican Republic.

The explosive increase in Dominicans reaching the major leagues was tied directly to teams' investment in building and staffing baseball academies to develop young players, of which the impoverished country had an abundance, hoping to make a living at the game—preferably in the major leagues. The Dodgers opened the first academy in the DR in 1987, modeling it on the old complex of training fields and dormitories large enough to accommodate the Brooklyn Dodgers and its minor-league affiliates that Branch Rickey established in Vero Beach, Florida, in 1948. Every major-league team soon had baseball academies in the Dominican Republic. (It helped that Juan Marichal was the DR's Minister of Sports in the 1990s.)

The Dominican academies were baseball factories that provided not only skills training in baseball but formal education, including learning English and the basics of US culture. Major-league teams gave teenage prospects as young as 16 signing bonuses to attend their academy and paid them a stipend while they were there (in addition to providing room, board, and an education). Graduating from the academy to a minor-league contract was no easy thing. As many as 500 Dominican teens were signed by major-league teams to attend a baseball academy in any given year. In a highly competitive environment, the kids had to prove they had major-league potential. According to a 2013 investigative report in *Mother Jones* magazine, of the 832 players in Dominican baseball academies in 2006, fewer than half made it to the rookie level in minor-league baseball and less than 3 percent eventually wore a major-league uniform.

The academies spurred a robust industry of local agents—*buscones*—trying to cash in on the signing bonuses being offered to young Dominicans. Because Major League Baseball does not have an annual draft for amateur players in foreign countries, as it does in the United States, those who have not played professionally in their home country are considered international free agents who can sign with whichever team offers the most bonus money. *Buscones* networked in the DR exploit teams' competitive bidding for teenage prospects by scouting and recruiting players even younger than 16, helping develop their skills, and aggressively promoting them to major-league scouts. Their price? As much as 30 percent of a kid's signing bonus.

Given the stakes and widespread poverty in the Dominican Republic, *buscones* have not been above bribes, falsifying proof of age and other legal documents, and even providing steroids to young players to boost their prospects. In 2000, for example, the Cleveland Indians signed a promising young Dominican right-hander named Fausto Carmona, presented as 17 years old. After a year pitching in Cleveland's baseball academy in the DR, Carmona was given a minor-league contract. By 2006, at the presumed age of 22, he was pitching in the majors. In 2007, his first year as a starter, Carmona's 19–8 record helped Cleveland win the AL Central. Five years later, as Carmona was seeking to renew his work visa for the United States, it was discovered his birth certificate had been fraudulently edited; his name was really Roberto Hernandez and he was actually three years older than the Indians thought. In part due to injuries, Hernandez was not nearly as good in the second half of his career as when he was Fausto Carmona.

These kinds of shenanigans, along with *buscones*' efforts to drive up signing bonuses and an investigation by Major League Baseball of young-player development programs in the Dominican academies led to a decision in 2012 to establish limits on how much any team could spend in signing bonuses for international free agents. That didn't mean local *buscones* and some major-league clubs didn't try to conduct business as before to nab the best young prospects. In 2017, Major League Baseball gave a lifetime ban to Atlanta Braves general manager John Coppolella for violating the rules governing international signings. Soon thereafter, the US Justice Department began an investigation of possible corruption involving major-league teams in signing international amateur free agents in the Caribbean.

The exponential increase of Venezuelan ballplayers in the major leagues since the mid-1990s was facilitated by major-league teams establishing baseball academies in Venezuela, just as they had in the Dominican Republic. Baseball is as ingrained in Venezuela as it is in Cuba and the DR, with youth development programs as well as a history of professional winter leagues dating back to the 1930s. In the strike year of 1994, there were 19 Venezuelan players on major-league rosters. With 23 of major-league baseball's 30 teams having opened academies in Venezuela during the 1990s, by 2002 there were 63 Venezuelans in the majors, surpassing for the first time the number from Puerto Rico—among them that year, future Hall of Famers Roberto Alomar and Ivan Rodriguez, the Yankees' Bernie Williams and Jorge Posada, and Carlos Beltran and Carlos Delgado. Accounting for 6.6 percent of players making their major-league debut over the next six years, by 2008 Venezuela had pushed ahead of Puerto Rico as the second-largest Caribbean source of players all-time in Major League Baseball, after the Dominican Republic.

The payoff for major-league teams' investment in Venezuela—until then a country best known for turning out lithe, acrobatic shortstops, from Luis Aparicio to Dave Concepcion to Ozzie Guillen and Omar Vizquel—has been elite players at every position. Johan Santana (in 2004 and 2006) and Felix Hernandez (in 2010) won Cy Young Awards. Francisco Rodriguez led the American League in saves three times in four years between 2005 and 2008, including a major-league record 62 in 2008. In 2012, Miguel Cabrera became the first player in 45 years to win the Triple Crown and won the Most Valuable Player Award that year and the next. Jose Altuve won three batting titles between 2014 and 2017, led the league in hits all four years and twice in stolen bases, and was the American League MVP in 2017. Ronald Acuna Jr. was NL Rookie of the Year in 2018.

Venezuela, however, has been plagued by a rapidly deteriorating—in fact, disintegrating—economy, skyrocketing crime, and political violence since Hugo Chavez, a Fidel Castro acolyte, won the presidency in 1998 and proceeded to rule by decree. Instability reigned. Venezuelan players returning home for the off-season, and their family members still living in the country, were vulnerable to threats and extortion precisely because of the big-league money they made. The threat was vividly brought home in November 2011 when Washington Nationals rookie catcher Wilson Ramos, who earned a modest $415,000 during the season, was kidnapped at gunpoint from his family home in Venezuela and rescued by police commandos in a firefight two days later. In earlier years, Detroit closer Ugueth Urbina's mother was kidnapped in 2005 and held five months before being rescued, and Colorado catcher Yorvit Torrealba's son was kidnapped in 2009 and eventually released. It is not known if Torrealba, who earned $3.7 million that year, paid the ransom. Urbina was paid $4 million in 2005.

Escalating civil unrest and political violence after Chavez died in 2013 and was replaced by Nicolas Maduro, his handpicked successor, forced a retrenchment by Major League Baseball in Venezuela. All but four major-league teams had closed their academies in the country by 2015. Major- and minor-league players, including those from Venezuela, were cautioned about the risks of playing in the Venezuelan winter league. Venezuelan players not affiliated with Major League Baseball began abandoning their country's baseball league to play professionally in the Dominican Republic and Mexico. Young Venezuelan ballplayers were fleeing their country, many for the DR, where they hoped to be signed by a major-league team. These developments had a severe impact on Venezuelan baseball. Attendance suffered badly, and the dramatic drop in revenue forced the Venezuelan league to limit roster size and cut back on equipment, including the supply of baseballs.

Mostly missing from Major League Baseball's vastly increased Caribbean demographic were players from Cuba. The generation of Cuban players in Major League Baseball born after Castro seized power, including Jose Canseco and Rafael Palmeiro, were mostly raised in the United States after arriving as children on so-called freedom flights from the mid-1960s to early-1970s that were organized by the United States and tolerated by Castro as a way to defuse dissent in Cuba. Love of the game was perhaps in their Cuban genetic makeup, but they learned the game on American diamonds. Whereas there were 73 Cuban-born players who debuted in the major leagues between 1950 to 1970, during the'70s, '80s, and '90s up till the 1994 strike, there were just 14.

In the face of US sanctions against the Castro regime, however, the dominance of Cuban teams in international tournaments—including the Pan American Games, the Baseball World Cup, and the Summer Olympic Games—was a major part of Cuba's revolutionary identity. The Cuban league's regular season was the proving ground for players to be selected to play for their country in international competition, including Cuba's highly regarded national team. From 1987 through 1997, the Cuban national team ran off a string of 152 consecutive wins. Many players on Cuba's national team, their lack of opportunity because of the cold war between the United States and Castro notwithstanding, were thought to be good enough to play and to star in the major leagues. Major-league scouts also had the opportunity to assess Cuban players on national and "junior" teams participating in "friendly" exhibition series against US collegians that began in 1987, alternating between Cuba and Millington, Tennessee, which were permitted by the US government as a cultural exchange.

The collapse of the Soviet Union and the end of the Cold War in 1991 changed the dynamic. Russia was in no position to bail out Castro's perpetually failing economy, instigating a new wave of Cubans fleeing their country as economic refugees. The situation became a headache for the United States in 1994. Congress tightened US sanctions on Cuba, to be alleviated only once Castro was gone and Cuba moved in a democratic, free-market direction. President Clinton's administration reached an agreement with the Castro regime to control the refugee crisis, which included the safety valve (for both countries) of allowing 20,000 Cubans to legally come to the United States each year and eased restrictions on travel and money transfers to Cuba by Cuban Americans.

Baltimore Orioles owner Peter Angelos, seeing an opening in the more relaxed US policy under Clinton, began lobbying the administration to allow him to take his team to Cuba to play the Cuban national team. Institutionally, Major League Baseball had his back, if for no other reason than that it hoped to open a gate to scout Cuba's baseball talent. It was not the first time Major League Baseball had sought to establish a rudimentary relationship with Cuba's baseball federation, but because of fierce political opposition to any engagement with Castro, previous efforts at "baseball diplomacy" in the 1970s were squashed by the US government's unwillingness to even consider a replication of the Nixon administration's "ping-pong diplomacy" to open up China.

After initial pushback, the key obstacle being that US law prohibited any revenue from going to the regime, Clinton agreed. During spring training in March 1999, the Orioles visited Havana. Orioles star and Cuban exile Rafael Palmeiro refused to go. Fidel Castro, sitting alongside Commissioner Bud Selig, watched Cuba's national team lose a tight 11-inning game to the Orioles. In a reciprocal visit, the Cuban national team traveled to Baltimore in May and beat the Orioles in their home park. But no US dollars went to Castro's regime, and the brief détente between Major League Baseball and the Cuban Baseball Federation went nowhere.

The Castro regime's decision to legalize US currency for use in Cuba to prevent a complete economic collapse after Soviet aid was cut off had a profound effect on Cuban ballplayers. Their privileged status in revolutionary Cuba—the regime had always insisted as a propaganda selling point that they played for their love of the game and their country, not for big paydays like in corrupt, materialistic America—could no longer compensate for the fact that their meager salaries were now below a livable income, even in Cuba. Motivated by money and a desire to choose their own destiny—*and* with right-hander Rene Arocha having set an example in July 1991 by asking US authorities for asylum at Miami's international airport instead of returning to Cuba with his team following their exhibition in Tennessee—a second Cuban wave to the major leagues took off in the mid-1990s. In 1996, right-hander Rolando Arrojo's defection from the Cuban team about to play in the 1996 Olympic Games in Atlanta, coming just after the latest series against American collegians in Tennessee, caused the regime to put an end to the "friendly" series.

The second Cuban wave of players were defectors, although they rejected the insinuation of that word because they did not "defect" from their country, only from a repressive regime that hardly lived up to the socioeconomic aspirations of Castro's revolution. Most Cuban players defecting did so when their team traveled to international tournaments in other countries, where they would simply walk off the team, as Arocha did in Miami, and ask for asylum. A few were elite stars playing on their country's indomitable national team; Arocha and Arrojo were both star pitchers on the national team. Others were rising stars in the Cuban league or even at the very beginning of their careers, on Cuba's junior national teams. Two of the most coveted junior team players seen by major-league scouts were shortstop Rey Ordoñez, 22 years old when he defected during the World University Games in Buffalo in 1993, and right-hander Livan Hernandez, age 20 when he walked off his team during a tournament in Mexico in 1995.

Major League Baseball was caught flat-footed by players leaving Cuba because they could not directly enter the United States legally. There were no protocols for how to deal with them. Instead, the contractual rights to Arocha and Ordoñez after their defections in the United States were awarded based on a no-bid lottery of interested teams, with neither player having a say in the matter. The Cardinals won the lottery for Arocha in 1991 and the Mets for Ordoñez in 1993. Arocha, 11–8 as a starter in his 1993 rookie season, suffered an elbow injury two years later that ended his big-league career. Ordoñez, presented as the Mets' answer to the Yankees' Derek Jeter in their mutual rookie seasons in 1996, proved a disappointment in the seven years he played in New York.

It wasn't long before a handful of anti-Castro Cuban exiles in Miami began opportunistically exploiting baseball's lack of an established policy for dealing with Cuban player-defectors to cash in themselves by serving as facilitators for Cuban ballplayers to flee their country for the chance to play in the major leagues. Joe Cubas, the most prominent among them, forged a career of shadowing Cuban players at international tournaments, gaining their trust to persuade them to leave Castro's Cuba behind, and helping to arrange their departure from the island nation—not to the United States, but to a welcoming third country in the Caribbean Basin where they could establish residency and become international free agents, free to sign with whichever major-league team offered the most money. This paradigm absolved Major League Baseball from having to come up with a coherent policy for dealing with Cuban players.

Cubas's first big score was Livan Hernandez, whom he flew from Mexico, where he defected, to the Dominican Republic, where he signed a $4.5 million contract in January 1996 with the Florida Marlins, whose home city was Miami, a hotbed of Cuban-exile anti-Castro sentiment. Even though Cuban national team star pitcher Rolando Arrojo defected in the United States on the eve of the 1996 Olympic Games, Cubas persuaded him to establish residency in Costa Rica so that he too could be signed as an international free agent; in April 1997, he signed with the expansion-Devil Rays in Florida's Gulf Coast Tampa-St. Petersburg metropolitan area, also with a large Cuban population, in a deal that included a $7 million signing bonus. Arrojo was the Rays' ace, their only starter with a winning record, in their inaugural 1998 season. Already in his 30s, Arrojo's 1998 season would be the best of his five in the major leagues.

Livan Hernandez quickly became a star. Of the Cuban players making it the majors in the 1990s, Hernandez was the most successful—9–3 in his rookie year with a 4–0 record in the postseason for the wild-card 1997 World Series champion Marlins, and a 178–177 record in his 17-year major-league career. But Livan's defection and contract with the Marlins caused trouble for his much older half brother, Orlando "El Duque" Hernandez, an accomplished pitcher with a 126–47 record from 1986 to 1995 in Cuban regular-season play. Star pitcher though he was, El Duque was dropped from Cuba's national team as it was preparing to compete in the 1996 Olympics in Atlanta. Later that year, the Cuban Baseball Federation banished him and two other players for life following the arrest, trial, conviction, and sentencing to 15 years in prison of a Miami-based agent for traveling to Havana to orchestrate their defection from Cuba to Venezuela. The evidence against the agent—Cubas's cousin—included large amounts of US currency and phony Venezuelan work visas for the players.

Unable to play baseball and ostracized as a would-be traitor, Orlando Hernandez had every incentive to flee Cuba—which he did in December 1997, just months after Livan's star turn in the World Series. He fled by boat from a remote beach in Cuba, a 35-nautical-mile open-sea journey to an island off the Bahamas. From there, Cubas arranged to fly him to Costa Rica to establish residency, making him an international free agent. By the end of March 1998, with Cubas as his broker, Hernandez had in hand a four-year, $6.6 million deal and a $1 million signing bonus from the Yankees. El Duque made his major-league debut in June, went 12–4 as a rookie for the 114-win 1998 Yankees, and was 17–9 the next year and 12–13 in 2000. The Yankees won the World Series all three years, with Hernandez winning his first nine postseason starts, including two in World Series games, before losing to the Mets in Game Three of the 2000 World Series.

Although defecting in foreign countries carried the risk of being caught by the security minders accompanying Cuban teams, the risk of trying to leave from the island nation itself was far greater. El Duque's escape from the Cuban beach to the Bahamas was dramatically sensationalized by Cubas, with Hernandez playing along, for anti-Castro propaganda purposes as being on a rickety raft through rough seas in shark-infested waters. Their narrative played up the heroic extent to which Cuban ballplayers—not to mention ordinary Cubans—would risk their lives to flee a repressive regime for the promise of liberty and finding their true destiny in a free society. Except: "It wasn't a raft," according to the boat's owner. "It was a good boat." And, "We never saw any sharks." A marlin, maybe. The part about being stranded for days on the beach where they landed before being rescued by the US Coast Guard? That was true, if embellished to give it a Robinson Crusoe vibe, but only because a bigger launch that was supposed to meet them there and take them to Florida failed to arrive. Afterward, Cubas got involved to make certain Orlando

Hernandez and his talented right arm went to Costa Rica rather than America, where he would have been subject to baseball's annual amateur draft and would not have commanded the kind of international amateur free agent contract the Yankees gave him.

The major-league exploits of defector players like Ordonez, the Hernandez half brothers, and Arrojo were closely followed back in Cuba, giving momentum to the second Cuban wave, which continues to this day. Their success, and their country's economic travails, made leaving Cuba for an opportunity to play baseball for big money in the United States an attractive option, notwithstanding having to leave behind family and friends. The failure of the "baseball diplomacy" played by the Orioles and the Cuban national team in 1999—which was inevitable once George W. Bush was elected president in 2000, given the widespread anti-Castro sentiment in his party's base—left no alternative but defection for Cuban players wanting to play in the major leagues.

Ever on the lookout for international talent, especially since baseball no longer had the kind of hold on American youth—particularly Black Americans—that football and basketball did, Major League Baseball remained intrigued by Cuban players. Although big-league scouts were handicapped by only being able to see Cuban players in international tournaments, the performance of star-powered Cuban national teams in international competition—including the first World Baseball Classic in 2006, where Cuba advanced to the final before losing to Japan—left them with little doubt that Cuba's top stars were capable of being successful in the major leagues if given the chance. The talent level of young Cuban players still at the beginning of their careers had become an open question by the mid-2000s; major-league scouts assessed that Cuba's impoverished economy was having a deleterious impact on the Cuban league, reducing its competitiveness to no better than Double-A. Some Cuban prospects still in their mid-teens defected straight to baseball academies in the Dominican Republic, hoping for their big break without even playing for Cuban developmental teams.

All of the top Cuban stars who have defected since 1999 had immediate success in the major leagues: Jose Contreras, who pitched eight shutout innings against the Orioles in the March 1999 exhibition game in Havana, signed in 2002 by the Yankees; infielder Alexei Ramirez, signed by the White Sox in 2008; outfielder Yoenis Cespedes, signed by Oakland in 2012; first baseman Jose Abreu, signed by the White Sox in 2013;

and corner infielder Yuli Gurriel, signed by Houston in 2016. Unlike other Cuban ballplayer defectors, whose new major-league teams started them out with a minor-league affiliate for at least part of their first year in the United States before calling them up, Ramirez, Cespedes, and Abreu went directly to the majors. A few highly touted rising stars in Cuban baseball when they defected—Kendrys Morales (21 when he left Cuba in 2004), Aroldis Chapman (21 in 2009), and Yasiel Puig (20 in 2011)—also had immediate success in the majors after a relatively brief stay in the minor leagues: Morales with the Angels, Chapman with the Reds, and Puig with the Dodgers.

Contreras in Mexico, Ramirez and Gurriel (along with his younger baseball-playing brother Lourdes) in the Dominican Republic, and Chapman in the Netherlands jumped their Cuban teams during or while returning from international tournaments. Morales, Puig, Cespedes, and Abreu endured more perilous journeys from Cuba by sea. Morales, whose Cuban career was derailed when security officials shipped him back to Cuba and banned him from baseball after concluding he was a risk to defect during a 2003 qualifying tournament in Mexico for the 2004 Olympics, failed in numerous attempts before finally making it off the island to the Dominican Republic. Puig, also considered by Cuban authorities to be a flight risk and banned from the national team, fled by sea to Mexico; Cespedes, to the DR; and Abreu, to Haiti. Like all Cuban defectors, these stars established residency outside the United States so that they could be international free agents, free to accept the best offer from teams competing to sign them.

The escape of players directly from Cuba was typically orchestrated by agents expecting a sizable cut of their future major-league contracts and signing bonuses. They relied on criminal networks skilled in human smuggling, often linked to drug-trafficking organizations, to get them out. The perils to players fleeing Cuba directly were not only the risks of being caught or being lost in rough seas, but also being extorted after the fact for a sizable portion of their new big-league contract—or even held hostage, as Puig briefly was by smugglers associated with the notoriously violent security arm of a Mexican drug cartel. As if succeeding in the major leagues wasn't hard enough, after they their big-league careers began with immediate success, Puig and Abreu were both harassed for more money, they and their families threatened. Abreu paid out $5.8 million after the fact, according to court records submitted by US prosecutors in 2016 in a case against the agent and some of his confederates involved in smuggling Abreu and other players out of Cuba.

President Obama's decision in 2014 to establish diplomatic relations with Havana, now ruled by Fidel's younger 83-year-old brother Raul Castro, and to eliminate or reduce many restrictions on trade and travel to Cuba gave new impetus to Major League Baseball's interest in forging a productive relationship of its own with the Cuban Baseball Federation. In December 2015, major leaguers—including Jose Abreu and Alexei Ramirez, who were assured there would be no problems entering or leaving the country—conducted a goodwill tour in Cuba. Three months later, during spring training, the Tampa Bay Rays beat the Cuban national team in a game in Havana. The US and Cuban presidents were together in attendance. By late 2018, the two sides had reached an agreement to systematize and legalize the process whereby players at least 25 years old, or with at least six years playing in the Cuban league, would be free to play in the United States (and bring along their families) and negotiate their own contracts in exchange for a portion of their signing bonus going to the Cuban federation. Cuba already had agreements along those lines that effectively "leased" star players to professional leagues in Japan, Korea, and a few other countries. For its part, Major League Baseball agreed not to sign for two years any players younger than 25 who chose to defect for the chance to be an international free agent.

For Cuban baseball, the agreement offered a lifeline to reverse years of competitive erosion resulting from the defection of star players and even young prospects in their teens being lured to play in other countries, where they would be in a better position to sign with major-league teams. And by imposing a mid-20s age limit for Cuban players wanting to play in the major leagues, the Cuban league would benefit from continuing to develop homegrown talent and keeping its best players through at least the early portion of their prime playing years. For Cuban players, it meant no longer having to defect from their team in games played outside the country, risk their lives by undertaking a hazardous journey by sea to reach another shore, or—as had become more common—rely on people-smuggling networks demanding an exorbitant share of the players' future major-league earnings, with its own attendant risks of being caught. Perhaps even more important, it also meant not being barred from their country of birth, including years-long separation from their families. The

Cuban federation said that 34 players were eligible to sign with major-league teams.

The agreement, and the potential for major-league teams to establish a foothold in Cuba to scout young players and perhaps even establish training academies, never happened. It ran afoul of the US embargo still in effect on Cuba that prohibited US money going to the Cuban government. Major League Baseball officials negotiated the 2018 agreement with the understanding that the Trump administration's rollback of Obama's opening the door to more normal relations with Cuba would not affect existing contracts, licenses, and deals in the works. Their understanding was misplaced. "A payment to the Cuban Baseball Federation," the Trump administration explained to Major League Baseball when it terminated the agreement in April 2019, "is a payment to the Cuban government." The administration was not sympathetic to Major League Baseball's argument that "the goal of the agreement . . . is to end the human trafficking of baseball players from Cuba."

11

THE DARK (STEROIDS) SIDE OF RECOVERY

Defensive about accusations that he turned a blind eye to superstar Barry Bonds's use of performance-enhancing drugs, former Giants owner Peter Magowan told the *San Francisco Chronicle* in 2016, "People say, 'Why didn't you know Barry was taking steroids? What am I supposed to do? Go to his locker and see if there's a steroid bottle?"

The bottle of androstenedione, then a legal supplement designed to mimic an anabolic steroid, spotted by a sharp-eyed reporter in Mark McGwire's locker during his 1998 chase of Roger Maris and the single-season home run record is exactly what called attention to the use of steroids in Major League Baseball. Not that anyone paid it much attention at the time, given the compelling feel-good story line of indisputably nice guys McGwire—then with 51 homers and 36 games remaining to hit at least another 11—and Sammy Sosa going after 61. But it was now out there.

It did not go unnoticed that McGwire was a big guy. Not just tall, at 6-foot-5, but a monster of a man—much bigger of build and stronger than when he broke in as a rookie with 49 home runs as a 23-year-old with the Oakland Athletics. Now looking much the part of an outdoorsman with his red hair, goatee, broad chest, and muscular biceps, Mark McGwire— "Big Mac"—was baseball's Paul Bunyan. He made Roger Maris, six feet tall and lean when he hit 61 homers in '61, look small and unprepossessing in comparison. *All* the other home run hitters in Maris's day looked small compared to Big Mac. Mantle, Mays, and Aaron: While strong with sinewy muscles, none of them are over 6 feet or tilted the scale much above 190 pounds in their prime. Even Harmon Killebrew, baseball's most brawny slugger in the 1960s, was not as nearly as Herculean in physical stature as Big Mac. And Sosa, too, had undergone a metamorphosis since his rookie year in 1989. The Cubs' 6-foot-tall Dominican-born outfielder had gone from a lithe 165 pounds at 20 years old to about 220 now that he was 29. He was solid, pumped, and ripped like a bodybuilder. Sammy Sosa was baseball's Arnold Schwarzenegger, except not as tall.

That bottle of andro in McGwire's locker presented Major League Baseball with an immediate public relations problem just as Big Mac and Sosa were bearing down on Maris's 61 homers. Everyone, especially the baseball media and fans, loved the thrill of the chase. The friendly duel between McGwire and Sosa to be the first to 62 and to see which of them by season's end would be baseball's new home run champion, and with how many, was appropriately understood by Commissioner Selig as the capstone to Major League Baseball's recovery from the devastation of the 1994–1995 players' strike that had many frustrated and angry fans vowing never to return to the national pastime. It captivated the nation even beyond people who paid the game just casual attention. Suddenly, that bottle of andro raised questions about whether a new single-season home run record set by McGwire would be legitimate, or the product of, as a *New York Times* headline put it on August 23, 1998, "Popeye Spiking His Spinach." It didn't help that a few days later, commenting on the McGwire story, Sosa said he used creatine, a natural supplement popular among bodybuilders to gain muscle and improve strength.

What the heck *was* that stuff? Andro was a supplement that raised the body's level of the male hormone testosterone, which both builds lean muscle and facilitates recovery from injury. McGwire said he had been using it for more than a year, that it was "natural" in terms of its effect on male hormones, and that "everybody that I know in the game uses the same stuff that I do." Even though the Olympics, US college sports, and the NFL banned the use of the substance among their athletes, the fact that androstenedione was legally sold and readily available in gyms and health stores throughout the country—notwithstanding its health risks to the heart—allowed Major League Baseball to deflect the issue that was souring the feel-good aura around McGwire as he closed in on the record.

The fact that it was a legal supplement also gave cover to McGwire, the players' union, and Major League Baseball to insist he had done nothing wrong, assert that players' rights to privacy should be respected, and scold sportswriters (and others) trying to sully his quest by implying he was cheating. Actually, many of baseball's most influential sportswriters went out of their way to affirm that because the supplement was legal, there was nothing untoward about Big Mac's pursuit of Maris and that it was wrong to create a controversy where there really wasn't one.

The andro revelation had no bearing on baseball's celebration of McGwire's 62nd home run. Baseball fans, not to mention television and radio broadcasts, were certainly not inclined to have misgivings about the legitimacy of his accomplishment. America was witnessing a feel-good historical moment. Big Mac was an American hero. Even better, the race had been one between two personally appealing power hitters to break the record, and both soared past 61—Sosa to 65 and McGwire all the way to 70. It was in many respects, 68 years later, Babe Ruth blasting an unheard-of 54 homers in 1920, shattering the record 29 he had set the year before, all over again. It was a big deal. And big was definitely in—including for the players.

It was obvious in the 1990s, in a trend that began *before* the strike, that ballplayers were bigger and bulkier than they had ever been. After every off-season, there were more players showing up in Florida and Arizona for spring training bigger than their teammates, not to mention the fans, had last seen them. And they were not just bigger; they were more buff, ripped, stronger. Some were showoffs, flaunting their muscles and ripped abs, shoulders, and backs. And a few were self-aware about it. They preened in less than their baseball jerseys and pants as if posing for pinups, as if they were supermodels for a male swimsuit issue of *Sports Illustrated*. They were chiseled beefcakes, glamorous male specimens with home run clout. Even top-of-the-order batters were becoming sluggers. Everyone could see the changes taking place, but nobody was seriously questioning why.

For people in the baseball profession, including sportswriters, this was perhaps because they did not want to know the answer—not really. Not with ever more home runs soaring over the fences. Dramatic physical changes in players taking place during the winter months were attributed to tailored diets often prepared by personal chefs, to protein shakes, to nutritional supplements, to lifting weights, to intense exercise regimens devised by personal trainers. And the fans? Well, fans dig the long ball. And they appreciated the off-season work ethic of players wanting to excel at their craft. As for steroids—performance-enhancing drugs that had scandalized the Olympics and had reached the level of notoriety in the NFL—nobody wanted to consider they might be a problem in the major leagues.

It got to the point of caricature—including by Major League Baseball itself in a commercial promo for the 2002 All-Star Game depicting cartoon renditions of mightily pumped-up ballplayers and ending with the word "POW." Thus were sluggers Barry Bonds and Mike Piazza, Alex Rodriguez and Sammy Sosa lionized. Even slender players not known for their power hitting—like pitcher Randy Johnson, shortstop Derek Jeter, and outfielder Ichiro Suzuki—were depicted with exaggerated musculature. The Yankees' Jason Giambi, a huge guy in the manner of McGwire, took home the top prize in the Home Run Derby that was an annual part of All-Star break festivities with 24 moon shots at Milwaukee's Miller Park, home to the franchise formerly owned by Bud Selig, who, as commissioner, was quite at home watching the proceedings.

A month before that 2002 All-Star Game, relying on "dozens of interviews" with players and others in professional baseball, Tom Verducci of *Sports Illustrated* put it all into perspective with a damning article entitled "Totally Juiced." A decade earlier, he wrote, steroids were considered "taboo," even if a handful of "renegade sluggers" used anabolic steroids hoping to power up their performance—most notably Oakland slugger Jose Canseco, who was serenaded by "Steroids! Steroids!" at Fenway Park during the 1990 American League Championship Series (during which, by the way, he had only two hits in the four games, none of them home runs). But now the game had become a "pharmacological trade show" in which it was not just steroids but an array of other drugs, such as human growth hormone (HGH), that were used, and not just bulky sluggers but "even pitchers and wispy outfielders" who were "juicing up." Some players believed that as many as half of major-league players were on steroids.

The centerpiece of the *SI* article was former all-star Ken Caminiti discussing the impact steroids had on his career. Until 1996, in seven prior seasons as an everyday third baseman—six in Houston and one in San Diego—Caminiti had never gotten a single vote for Most Valuable

Player, had never been elected by the fans to start in the All-Star Game, and had been named to an All-Star team just once. Not one of baseball's prominent players, he nonetheless was a solid major-league veteran. In 1995, his first year with the Padres, Caminiti had the best year yet of his career with 26 home runs, 94 runs batted in, and a .302 batting average. But that was nothing compared to what he did in 1996—40 homers, 130 RBIs, and a .326 batting average—which earned him all 28 first-place votes for the National League MVP. Bill James called it "one of the top fluke seasons of all time." Caminiti attributed his great season to steroids he began using after injuring his shoulder in April, just days after turning 33, confessing that they not only helped his recovery but made him a much better player, particularly when it came to hitting for power. "I'd crush the ball 450 feet with almost no effort," he told Verducci. It also gave him a mental edge in believing the odds were always in his favor when he faced opposing pitchers.

And it was not just the sluggers using the stuff to hit the ball harder and drive the ball farther more consistently than they ever had before. Position players whose calling cards were defense or their ability to hit for average and advance runners on base believed that adding a power dimension to their game would substantially increase their value to the team, even if it didn't get them into the no-longer-exclusive 30-homer club. And pitchers were learning that taking steroids allowed them to throw harder than before—and for longer in their careers. It did not go unnoticed that some starting pitchers in their late 30s began throwing at velocities they had not shown in years, or that bullpens were increasingly populated by relievers, young and old, consistently throwing in the mid-90s (miles per hour) or higher. Baseball was rapidly becoming a power game.

The steroids issue had been out there as an awkward problem for Major League Baseball since at least McGwire's bottle of andro, but the *SI* exposé thrust it into the realm of an out-of-control crisis. Major League Baseball had put forward a steroids-testing program with tough penalties during the 1994 negotiations with the players' union, but it went nowhere because the only issues that mattered in those talks were about free agency. Once the strike was over, the issue was largely shelved. Revenue sharing and luxury taxes on player payrolls exceeding a certain amount were the commissioner's and owners' priorities in negotiations with the union, and the players' union was adamant that testing would be a violation of players' privacy—a violation it could not endorse. Unlike in Judge Landis's day, when he embodied the commissioner of baseball as an all-powerful czar who ruled by fiat—his decisions final—Selig could not simply impose mandatory drug testing with prohibitive penalties on major leaguers. He required the approval of the players' union. In any case, until 1998's McGwire and Sosa race to 62 homers and beyond, steroids use was dismissed as a problem limited to a handful of players like Canseco. Even as it subsequently became clear that steroid use was more prevalent than had been acknowledged, the issue was mostly buried by the barrage of home runs that threatened sacred records and delighted fans.

Players certainly understood that boosting performance through anabolic steroids was cheating the game. To the extent they commented on the issue, it was to say they personally did not and never would use performance-enhancing drugs. They pleaded ignorance or refused to say anything about whether their suddenly muscle-bound teammates used steroids. Some invoked the sanctity of the clubhouse vow of silence to deflect the issue. Owners claimed ignorance. Selig insisted it was not a problem, at least not a serious one, and pointed to baseball's having tested for the drugs in the minor leagues since the 1980s and having implemented year-round mandatory minor-league testing for anabolic steroids in 2001, with penalties for subsequent violations that escalated, after a fifth offense, to a lifetime ban. Any minor leaguer on a major-league 40-man roster was exempt, since there was no provision for drug testing in their collective bargaining agreement.

Notwithstanding the stigma on player reputations, including star players, in the event of public disclosure, and notwithstanding testing in the minor leagues, there was a culture of steroid use at every level of professional baseball. The perceived benefits of making it to the majors and relatively light penalties for failing drug tests caused many minor leaguers to gamble on their future with steroids. Selig was surprised to learn that the results for 11 percent of nearly 2,000 minor leaguers, knowing they were subject to mandatory testing, returned positive for steroids. And any player who made it to the majors or earned a spot on the 40-man roster knew, as things then stood, there would be no testing. In major-league clubhouses, players injecting steroids was an open secret respected by all who had access, including reporters. Players traded on their experiences and shared where and how they got the stuff with each other.

Anabolic steroids, illegal in the United States and some of which were powerful drugs given to animals, were readily available over the counter south of the border. There was a thriving legal steroid market in the Dominican Republic, where they were easily accessible to Dominican players. Caminiti, playing in San Diego, got his across the border in Mexico.

The *SI* article made it impossible for drug testing *not* to be a part of the new collective bargaining agreement being negotiated in the summer of 2002. The union's long-standing resistance to testing for performance-enhancing drugs on privacy grounds allowed Selig and Major League Baseball to seize the ethical high ground from the players, never mind that the commissioner and the owners had previously turned a self-serving blind eye to the problem. The new collective bargaining agreement, ratified in October, included mandatory testing of every major-league player at least once during the 2003 season, with 240 players selected randomly to be tested a second time. The union's demand that all results be anonymous to protect players' privacy was acceptable to the commissioner and the owners. Nobody wanted the game to be further sullied by identifying drug cheats, who might also be prominent stars adored by fans. If 5 percent of players tested positive in 2003, testing would be extended for at least another season, this time with penalties that obviously would make it impossible to hide the names of sanctioned players. In the best of all worlds, if there were to be further survey testing in 2004 but the anonymous results showed less than 2½ percent of major leaguers were doping in any two consecutive years afterward, then the commissioner, the owners, the players, and the union could all say baseball really didn't have a steroid problem.

Caminiti and others interviewed for the *SI* article cast baseball's steroid problem as not just about cashing in on more lucrative contracts in salary arbitration or free agency than they might otherwise have earned, although that was a major motivation for many established veterans who were not quite superstars. For many players, especially those beginning to see age-related declines in performance, it was about keeping their starting positions or even just hanging on in the competitive world of Major League Baseball. For younger players, it was about winning jobs and rising to stardom. It was an open secret in clubhouses that lots of players were using steroids, and there was a widespread perspective that the prevalence of steroids-inflated ballplayers made it necessary for other players to take them just to keep up.

Paralleling the motivations of players using steroids to just stay in the game, or of good players wanting to become great players, was peer envy. So it was for Barry Bonds, envious of all the attention McGwire and Sosa were getting during their race to catch and eclipse the Maris single-season record. Since the early 1990s, Bonds also had to put up with the much more fawning publicity given to Ken Griffey Jr., his rival for best player of their generation. Part of it was a matter of personality. In addition to being a great player, Griffey was infectiously joyous—impossible not to like. McGwire and Sosa, neither of whom came close to measuring up to Bonds as a complete ballplayer, were also appealing personalities—genuinely likable guys. Barry Bonds, as great as he was, did not have an endearing way about him; he was often dismissive and surly.

Bonds, however, expected and wanted his due as not only the best player of his generation but one of the greatest of all time. His game was a combination of speed and power—like that of his godfather, Willie Mays, even if it could still be said that Barry Bonds was not quite—not yet, anyway—the second coming of the Say Hey Kid. From his rookie year with Pittsburgh in 1986, his coming to San Francisco as a free agent in 1993, and through the end of the 1998 season—13 years in all—Bonds had hit 411 home runs and stolen 445 bases with a career batting average of .290. Still going strong at 33, there was little doubt he'd exceed 500 homers and 500 stolen bases. He already had his ticket to Cooperstown printed and validated in his pocket, just awaiting the guardians at the gate of baseball's Mount Olympus to take it.

With due respect to McGwire and Sosa, Bonds was the most feared hitter in the game. In 1998, while they were soaring past Maris, Bonds drew the most intentional walks in the major leagues for the third year in a row, and it was the seventh straight year he led the National League. But he was sorely vexed by the accolades that went to sluggers just for hitting long-distance home runs—especially McGwire and Sosa in 1998. And he surely also noticed that Griffey had back-to-back seasons of 56 homers in 1997 and 1998. Bonds had never hit more than 46 (his first year with the Giants) and had hit as many as 40 only three times in his career so far.

Back in the 1920s, Ty Cobb, with 12 batting titles to his credit and whose .366 batting average over 24 major-league seasons remains the highest in history, took umbrage at the accolades for Babe Ruth and his gargantuan clouts. Insisting that he could hit with that kind of power *if he wanted to*, Cobb in May 1925 set out to prove the point by belting three homers in one game against the St. Louis Browns, and the next day hitting two more, making him at the time only the second player in history to hit five home runs in consecutive games. (The other player was *not* the Babe; in fact, although he already had 284 career home runs, Ruth had yet to hit three in a game. In the years ahead, Ruth would hit three homers in a game twice in the regular season and twice in the World Series, but he never totaled five home runs in back-to-back games.) But that was not the kind of hitter Cobb was, or wanted to be. Having shown he could do it, Cobb was not enticed to swing for the fences just because fans loved the Babe's long balls and home runs made Ruth baseball's first big-time celebrity personality. Cobb never again hit three homers in a game.

Looking askance at the celebrities McGwire and Sosa became as they chased Maris, Bonds became obsessed with the long ball—even though that was already a part of his game. Bonds returned in 1999 a changed man. Bonds, Barry Bonds, was powering up. It's not like he needed to take steroids to be better than he was; his legacy as one of baseball's all-time greats was already secure. But that was the direction he chose, hooking up with a personal trainer in the Bay Area who introduced him to steroids supplemented by an intensive weight-training program. Gone was the lean 6-foot-1, 190-pound, mean, intimidating hitting machine Barry Bonds had been. Steroid use ballooned his muscle mass—Bonds was now in the neighborhood of 220 pounds—as well as his head (literally), to the point that he was almost unrecognizable. Bonds was more than ready to compete with the likes of McGwire and Sosa for the home run title, as well as drawing gasps for how hard he hit them and how far they went.

The new Bonds had a rough start when, just 13 games into the season, after clobbering four home runs in his first 41 at-bats and being walked 11 times, he was forced out of action for two months with elbow problems—including a damaged triceps tendon that was attributed by Giants' manager Dusty Baker to "20 years of throwing," although it might also have been caused or aggravated by the strain of supporting so much new muscle mass. For all the benefits players derived from using the stuff, extensive use of steroids also made them more prone to injuries from strained muscles, tendons, and ligaments. Caminiti was frequently side-lined by likely steroid-related injuries in the years after his 1996 MVP season, ironically shortening his career to what it might have been any-way. Bonds finished the 1999 season with 34 homers in 355 at-bats, bringing him within 55 of the coveted 500 mark. He might have made that the next year if not for missing 18 games; nonetheless, his 49 home runs in 2000 were a new career high and just one short of Sosa's major-league-leading 50.

Bonds reached 500 career home runs early in the 2001 season. At the end of August, his total for the year stood at 57. With 27 games remain-ing, a slump could mean McGwire's record 70 was out of reach. Three home runs blasted at altitude in Colorado on September 9 vaulted Bonds past Maris and gave him 63. And then baseball came to an end—not for the reasons it had in 1994, but because of al-Qaeda's terrorist attack that collapsed both World Trade Center towers in New York and destroyed part of the Pentagon in Washington, DC, on 9/11. It looked like the season might have just ended, but in a testament to the resilience of America and President Bush's admonition that al-Qaeda's attack would not destroy the American way of life, Major League Baseball resumed its schedule a week later and Bonds resumed his quest to set the new single-season home run record. He tied McGwire's 70 in Houston with three games remaining.

The next day, at home against the Dodgers, Barry Bonds wasted no time making the single-season home run record his own by hitting his 71st in the very first inning off Chan Ho Park, and his 72nd, for good measure, two innings later. On October 7, in game 162, Bonds clobbered home run number 73—a season-ending total that even at the time, in this era of behemoth sluggers, seemed unassailable. And he did not play in nine games, leading one to wonder whether he might have hit 75 or more. Bonds now had 551 home runs. He had turned 37 in late July. He was old in baseball years, but he felt great and was going strong. Having taken down McGwire's single-season record, Bonds's next target was Aaron's career total of 755.

His record-setting 71st on October 5, 2001, was a soaring, majestic, moon shot deep into the right-field stands at San Francisco's Pacific Bell Park. It was greeted with a barrage of fireworks. Bonds was greeted at home plate by his 11-year-old son, a batboy for the Giants. Pandemonium swept the stadium. But unlike the handshakes and pats on the rump McGwire got from opposing Chicago Cubs infielders when he broke the Maris record, the Dodgers infielders stood their ground. Part of it was likely because the Dodgers were bitter historical rivals of the Giants dating back to when both teams were in New York. Part of it was that Bonds's surliness did not invite celebration of a grouch. But there was also an ambivalence about his setting a new record. Even though Verducci's *Sports Illustrated* article exposing steroids in baseball was still nine months from being published, there was more than a little wonder about how exactly Bonds was able to do it. Bonds insisted his bulky new muscular physique was from a designer diet and the intensity of his weight training and had nothing to do with steroids.

The steroids scandal caught up with Barry Bonds, and with Bud Selig, and with the players' union, and with all of baseball and its fans a year and a half after the *Sports Illustrated* article alerted the world that the major leagues had a steroid problem far more serious than anyone was willing to admit. In December 2004 the *San Francisco Chronicle* published an investigative report by Mark Fainaru-Wada and Lance Williams on grand jury testimony by Bonds in a federal investigation concerning the role of BALCO—the Bay Area Laboratory Co-operative, which described itself as a health supplements company—in providing illegal steroids and other performance-enhancing drugs to world-famous athletes, including Olympians, and devising detailed protocols for their use to maximize their impact. Bonds, whose personal trainer was associated with the group, was among BALCO's world-famous athlete clients called to testify before the federal grand jury. Another was New York Yankees slugger Jason Giambi.

Giambi was a good-hitting prospect in 1995 when he broke in with the Oakland A's, for whom McGwire still played, after two full minor-league seasons in which he hit a total of 28 home runs in 913 at-bats—not exactly a slugger arising. During his first four years in Oakland from 1995 to 1998, he averaged 18 homers a year while driving in 295 runs and batting .289. Over the next three years Giambi ramped up his game, crashing 114 home runs—averaging 38 a year—with 380 RBIs and a .330 batting average. Voted the American League MVP in 2000 and finishing second in 2001, Giambi told the BALCO grand jury he started injecting steroids in 2001, the year he became a free agent once the season was done. His .342 batting average was second in the American League that year, his on-base plus slugging percentage second in the majors only to the incomparable Barry Bonds, and he was the best position player in the American League based on wins above replacement. That made him the most attractive free agent on the market. He went to the Yankees for seven years and $120 million.

The Yankees couldn't have been happier with their investment. The first year of his new deal in 2002, Giambi smashed 41 homers. That off-season, Bonds introduced him to BALCO, where Bonds's trainer switched him to a different steroid that was much more difficult to detect in the drug tests that were to be given to major leaguers for the first time in 2003. Giambi was also introduced to human growth hormone to strengthen his joints, helping his body bear the muscle added from using steroids. Giambi again hit 41 home runs for the Yankees. The next year, however, was a nightmare for the Yankees' slugger. Giambi showed up to spring training in 2004 a much thinner version of himself. He felt weak and played in only 70 of the Yankees' first 95 games, hitting just 11 homers, before missing most of the rest of the season after a tumor in his pituitary gland was discovered to be the cause of his ailments. Then in December, he and the Yankees were hit by the details of his presumed-secret BALCO grand jury testimony.

The Yankees scrambled about what to do with the revelation that one of their cornerstone players was a cheat. Reports immediately circulated that they were looking to void the rest of his contract. Aside from that being a chancy proposition to begin with, the Yankees should have known Jason Giambi was taking performance-enhancing drugs based on his agent's request that the word "steroids" be replaced by more nebulous language when he signed his free agent deal.

Giambi's pituitary tumor was also a cautionary tale about the potential negative health impacts of pumping up on steroids. Although steroids were not necessarily the cause of his illness, pituitary growths can result from excessive steroid use. Steroids can also ravage the heart and arteries. Two years after Ken Caminiti told *SI*'s Tom Verducci about how steroids bolstered his career, he was dead from cardiac arrest at the age of 41. Giambi rebounded in 2005 to hit more than 30 homers in three of the next four years, but his reputation never recovered. It didn't help that he didn't explicitly say he used steroids when he apologized to Yankees fans in the immediate wake of the *Chronicle*'s report on his BALCO testimony.

The *Chronicle*'s exposé prompted a quick call to action by Congress. While spring training was in progress in March 2005, the House Committee on Oversight and Reform convened hearings on steroid use in baseball and what should be done about it. Featured witnesses included a handful of prominent current and former major-league stars as well as Commissioner Selig and Donald Fehr, his counterpart as head of the players' union. It did not go well for Major League Baseball. Nobody accepted accountability, and Congress wasn't buying that. Hall of Fame pitcher Jim Bunning, now a United States senator, told them that using steroids was cheating and, moreover, that records set by any player pumped up on steroids shouldn't count.

Mark McGwire, retired since 2001, looked ashamed as he repeatedly said he would not "discuss the past" when asked whether he had used steroids and, "That's not for me to determine" when asked whether players using steroids were cheating. His was a sad performance. Sammy Sosa, traded by the Cubs to the Orioles in February with 574 home runs on his résumé (on his way to 609), said, "To be clear, I have never taken illegal performance-enhancing drugs. I have never injected myself or had anyone inject me with anything." Orioles power-hitting first baseman and DH Rafael Palmeiro, about to begin his 20th major-league season with 551 home runs and 78 hits shy of 3,000, agreed that anyone using steroids was cheating and emphatically stated, "I have never used steroids. Period. . . Never." Five months later, having recently become just the fourth player with both 3,000 hits and 500 homers, Palmeiro was suspended for 10 days after testing positive for steroids. He had 3,018 hits and 569 homers at the time, returned in mid-August, and played just seven more games, going 2-for-26 without any home runs, before retiring in disgrace 31 homers short of joining Aaron and Mays as the only players in history with 600 homers and 3,000 hits.

The commissioner insisted his office was pretty much ignorant of the problem until the story about McGwire's andro broke, that he had instituted a new testing program that would work, and that his "stated goal" on performance-enhancing drugs was "zero tolerance." But "do we have a problem?" Selig rhetorically asked. "No"—even though the anonymous testing in 2003 showed that 104 players—7 percent of all players in the major leagues—tested positive for steroids, and about 2 percent in 2004.

With Congress warning that it was prepared to consider legislation mandating comprehensive drug testing and penalties in US professional sports leagues if Major League Baseball did not crack down much more effectively on doping, Selig and the owners acted quickly to impose tougher penalties.

Fehr and the union resisted going along until the Palmeiro affair made that position untenable. The fact that Hank Aaron, whose record 755 home runs was being threatened by Barry Bonds (who had 708 by the end of the 2005 season, almost all of which he missed because of knee surgery), and fellow Hall of Famer Lou Brock both advocated tougher penalties for performance-enhancing drug use in follow-up congressional testimony in September ripped the rug out from under Fehr's last-ditch argument that Selig's penalties would have more a punitive than deterrent effect.

Major League Baseball was now imposing 50-day suspensions for the first time a player tested positive for performance-enhancing drugs, 100 days for the second time, and a lifetime banishment for the third time. Selig in 2006 also commissioned former senator George J. Mitchell to do an independent historical review and assessment of steroid use in baseball. Mitchell worked around resistance from the owners and players' union alike—most players refused to talk to Mitchell's investigators—to gather the information he needed through hundreds of interviews with people having access, medical records, and documents corroborating transactions involving performance-enhancing drugs. The federal prosecutor for the BALCO case shared information with Mitchell, but not the 2003 survey test results on individual players (which, inexplicably, were not destroyed once the testing was done) that the government seized as part its investigation because the legality of that action was being contested by the players' union in court. While Mitchell did not have access to those records, his investigation benefited from information provided by personal trainers Kirk Radomski and Brian McNamee, both of whom supplied various performance-enhancing drugs to major-league players whose names they gave after being pressed by federal prosecutors to cooperate in Mitchell's investigation.

Mitchell's report to the commissioner, *The Illegal Use of Steroids and Other Performance Enhancing Substances by Players in Major League Baseball*, released in December 2007, was devastating in its findings and conclusions. Steroid use was widespread. The 7 percent positive rate for the drug in Major League Baseball's 2003 survey "almost certainly" understated the level of player use because players were warned they would be tested during the season and because HGH could not be detected in the urine tests that were conducted. A negative test did not necessarily mean a player had not been using performance-enhancing drugs if he had cycled off the drugs before being tested. And in 2004, when tests were supposed to be unannounced, Mitchell heard credible allegations that some players were given advanced notice of when it would be their turn, which could have allowed them to "evade effective testing."

Perhaps Mitchell's most damning judgment was that players using steroids "did not act in a vacuum": "Everyone involved in baseball over the past two decades—Commissioners, club officials, the Players Association, and players—shares to some extent in the responsibility for the steroids era." And there you had it. Mitchell's report gave a name for the period arguably bookended by McGwire and Sosa running down Maris's record in 1998 and Barry Bonds passing Hank Aaron in career home runs with number 756 off Washington's Mike Bacsik in San Francisco on August 7, 2007, just four months before Mitchell completed his report. Mitchell called it "the steroids era." There seemed to be as many people in the country rooting against Bonds as for him as he closed in on Aaron's record.

The sensationalism surrounding the Mitchell Report, however, was not his bottom-line conclusions and recommendations—which basically amounted to Major League Baseball adopting more reliable and rigorous testing procedures, including for HGH, and imposing harsher penalties for failed tests. It was the star prominence of some of the 89 current and former players Mitchell identified as having injected steroids and HGH, principally from information derived from the BALCO investigation and provided by the trainers Radomski, who worked for the Mets in the 1990s, and McNamee, who worked for the Blue Jays and Yankees. McGwire's name was *not* among those 89, notwithstanding that bottle of andro and Jose Canseco's 2005 tell-all book, *Juiced*, in which he talked about the two of them injecting steroids in bathroom stalls and called McGwire "a thriving example of what steroids can do to make you a better player."

It was telling that most of the 89 names were players destined to be lost in history as marginal major leaguers, getting directly to the point Caminiti emphasized in the *Sports Illustrated* article in 2002 about players trying for whatever advantage they could to make it to—and stay in—the major leagues, knowing that many of their fellow wannabe big-leaguers were doing the same. Others of the 89 were aging former star players like Chuck Knoblauch, David Justice, and Mo Vaughn trying to extend their careers—that, too, was one of Caminiti's points—although it could not be said definitively that they had *not* taken steroids to make a name for themselves in the 1990s. It was the biggest of the big names, aside from Bonds and Giambi, whose alleged steroid-use had already been surfaced by a federal investigation and leaked grand jury testimony, that caused the biggest stir: outfielder Gary Sheffield; shortstop Miguel Tejada; pitchers Kevin Brown, Andy Pettitte, and Roger Clemens—especially Clemens, whose 354 career victories had him considering whether to come back for a 25th season in 2008 to surpass Warren Spahn's 363 wins for the fourth most since 1901.

Clemens, like Barry Bonds, had a Hall of Fame–bound career before he ever used steroids—although, in the context of the times, one cannot be certain that he didn't, especially given his bizarre and extraordinarily ill-timed meltdown in the 1990 ALCS, when his angry tirade of expletives directed at the plate umpire got him thrown out in the second inning of his Game Four start to prevent his team from being swept (which is what happened) by Canseco, McGwire, and the Oakland A's. From 1986 to 1992, pitching for the Boston Red Sox, Clemens put together one of the most dominating seven-year runs by any pitcher ever. Three times a 20-game winner, winning 68 percent of his decisions, four times leading the league in earned run average, striking out nearly 8.4 batters every 9 innings while averaging 257 innings a year, and completing over a third of his starts (at a time when complete games were trending towards extinction)—Rocket Roger's legacy was assured immortality. But he turned 30 in 1992, and the next four years saw him slide toward what looked like the twilight of his career. He was barely a .500 pitcher, at 40–39, and although he averaged 8.7 K's per 9 innings from 1993 to 1996 and led the league with 257 strikeouts in 242⅔ innings in 1996, Clemens was no longer the dominant force he had been.

Saying that Rocket Roger was in fact "in the twilight of his career," the Red Sox were unwilling to give their ace and arguably best pitcher in franchise history (which Cy Young himself could also claim) the contract he wanted to keep him in Boston when he became a free agent in 1996. Instead, Clemens took his 192–111 career record in Boston to Toronto for a four-year, $40 million contract and became perhaps even more dominant than he was in his prime. In 1997 and 1998, at the ages of 34 and 35, Clemens won 21 and 20; led the league in wins, strikeouts, and ERA both years; won 76 percent of his decisions for a Blue Jays team whose winning percentage those years was .506; blew away by the K over 10 batters per 9 innings both years—the first time he had done that in his career; and won back-to-back Cy Young Awards to put on his mantle alongside his three as a Red Sox, making him the first to win more than four.

According to Brian McNamee, hired by the Blue Jays as a strength and conditioning coach in 1998, it was that summer that Clemens first asked him to inject him with Winstrol—an anabolic steroid—that Rocket Roger himself supplied. Through the end of May, Clemens had a mediocre 5–6 record and 3.50 ERA in his first 11 starts. The rest of the way, Clemens was 15–0, had a 2.29 earned-run average, and averaged 11 K's per 9 innings. McNamee told investigators he did not inquire how or from where Clemens had obtained the steroids. Although the earliest McNamee could know the Jays' ace was injecting steroids was 1998, the fact that Clemens gave him the drugs leaves open the possibility he used them in 1997 to boost his record from 10–13 and a 3.63 ERA with Boston in 1996, to 21–7 and 2.05 his first year in Toronto.

Clemens's pair of dominating seasons meant George Steinbrenner had to have him for the Yankees, never mind that they had just put together one of the most dominant seasons by any team ever—114 regular-season wins and an 11–2 postseason run to win the World Series. And get him Steinbrenner did, giving up 18-game winner David Wells, the same age, whose 1998 contributions included winning all four of his postseason starts. After a less-than-stellar first year in the Bronx in 1999—a 14–10 record, a very high 4.60 ERA, and his worst strikeouts-per-inning ratio since 1993—Rocket Roger urged the Yankees to hire McNamee as strength and conditioning coach. The Yankees obliged. Clemens improved to 13–8 with a 3.70 earned run average in 2000, and the next year led the majors with a 20–3 record, picking up his sixth Cy Young Award, as the Yankees went to their fourth straight World Series. Clemens by now was much more physically imposing than he had been with the Red Sox.

One of the signature moments of Clemens's career came in his Game Two start at Yankee Stadium in the 2000 World Series against New York's *other* team—the Mets. It came against the backdrop of his having hit Mets star slugger Mike Piazza on his batting helmet in their teams' interleague series in July. The Mets thought Rocket Roger's headshot was deliberate, perhaps as payback for Piazza's having entered the July game 7-for-12 lifetime against Clemens with three home runs and only once having been a Clemens strikeout victim. Clearly, Piazza was not intimidated by Rocket Roger. Facing Piazza in the World Series for the first time since then, Clemens came hard-inside with a fastball. Piazza fisted it off. His bat shattering, Piazza started running to first base, not knowing the ball had gone foul. Clemens picked up the barrel of Piazza's busted bat, which had flown toward the mound, and fired the "jagged, pointed, sharp piece of wood," as broadcaster Joe Buck described it on national television, side-armed right in front of the Mets' best player as he was heading up the line. Buck's partner Tim McCarver called it a "blatant act" for which Piazza had "every right to be upset."

The dugouts emptied. There was no fight on the field. Clemens, whose "blatant act" could have resulted in serious injury had he hit Piazza, did not get tossed from the game, as he had been for his importunate words ten years earlier in the ALCS. He went on to pitch eight dominant shutout innings, allowing just two hits, before the Mets' five-run ninth-inning rally off Yankees relievers, keyed by Piazza's two-run homer, came up a run short of tying the game. At the time, it certainly seemed Clemens's competitive aggressiveness was out of bounds and out of control. In retrospective context, there were those wondering whether his lack of impulse control was a manifestation of "'roid rage."

Although the Yankees let McNamee go after the 2001 season for reasons unrelated to anything having to do with performing-enhancing drugs, he remained a personal trainer for both Clemens and Yankees southpaw Andy Pettitte, sometimes traveling with the team at Clemens's expense. Bonding as fellow Texans, where both grew up even though neither was born in the Lone Star State, Pettitte and Clemens were as close as any two teammates could be. They were workout buddies. By McNamee's account, Pettitte began inquiring about performance-enhancing drugs after the 2001 season, and in the spring of 2002 asked him for HGH to help speed his recovery from elbow tendinitis. Clemens was called to testify before the congressional committee looking at steroids use in baseball on the Mitchell Report's revelations about him. Pettitte provided an affidavit under oath in which he admitted taking HGH and claimed Clemens, his good friend and teammate, told him as early as 1999 and 2000 that he used HGH. Clemens denied before the committee ever taking steroids or HGH, saying that McNamee was a liar and his good buddy Pettitte "misremembered."

Part of the fallout from Mitchell's Report was that neither Barry Bonds nor Roger Clemens returned for the 2008 season. They retired instead, both forgoing career goals on the near horizon. Bonds, with his record 762 home runs and stunning 1.051 on-base plus slugging percentage— fourth all-time behind Ruth, Ted Williams, and Gehrig—was just 65 hits short of 3,000. Clemens remained 10 wins short of passing by Spahn. Pettitte continued on, genuinely humbled and apologetic for cheating when he reported to spring training in 2008. With 164 of his career 201 wins so far earned as a Yankee, Pettitte needed just 36 more, perhaps requiring three more seasons, to become only the third pitcher in franchise history to win 200.

Unlike the repentant Pettitte, Bonds and Clemens both persisted in denying the evidence. This had already resulted in Bonds being indicted for lying to a federal grand jury, and Clemens was soon to be indicted for lying to Congress. It also made Clemens and Bonds much less sympathetic figures. That Greg Maddux, four years younger, eclipsed Clemens in career wins with 355 to Roger's 354 seemed poetic justice; the two were rivals—the studious Mad Dog versus the intimidating Rocket Roger, both supercompetitive—for the best of their generation of pitchers. As for Bonds, probably most baseball fans today consider Aaron's 755 to be the "real" record, even while acknowledging that the "official" record belongs to Bonds (however it was that he got there).

Many baseball fans were putting their hopes in Alex Rodriguez, the enigmatic Yankees superstar third baseman, to eventually blow past Bonds's 762 to return integrity to the career home-run crown. He seemed a good bet. A-Rod had just been voted the American League's 2007 MVP with 54 home runs to give him 518 home runs in the 13 years since his rookie season in 1995. He was the youngest player to ever reach 500, and he was only 32 years old. The Yankees thought so too, even after he stunned team executives and embarrassed Major League Baseball by opting out of the remaining three years of the 10-year, $252 million contract he signed in 2001 just as the Red Sox were on the verge of sweeping the 2007 World Series. With Rodriguez suitably repentant for his impetuous opt-out and the Yankees wanting to cash in on the possibility he would set the new home run record in their uniform, the two sides agreed to a new record-setting 10-year, $275 million deal that also included $6 million bonuses for eclipsing Mays, Ruth, and Aaron—and another $12 million for breaking Bonds's tainted record.

Savoring his new contract, Rodriguez agreed to an interview with *60 Minutes*, which coincidentally took place just after the Mitchell Report was released. Asked the journalistically necessary and inevitable question about whether he ever used steroids, A-Rod said, "No," and implicitly said he'd have no need to even consider steroids because "I've never been overmatched on the baseball field." That turned out to be his Rafael Palmeiro moment, because, even as the legality of the government's seizure of the 2003 survey test results was still in legal limbo and the evidence was under seal, by the winter of 2008–2009, the names of the players testing positive for steroids began slowly leaking out.

For the purpose of the 2003 "anonymous" survey of steroid use, player samples sent to the lab were labeled with corresponding code numbers to hide their identities. That list was kept by the company hired by Major League Baseball to oversee the tests. The lab got only the coded identities, with no names attached. Players' anonymity was preserved by the company. Major League Baseball and the players' union received only the aggregation of results from the lab, not the coded individual results. Federal prosecutors in the BALCO case now had their hands on both the coded results *and* the master list, allowing investigators to put names to those testing positive for performance-enhancing drugs. That was not information to be used in any prosecution—or released at all—until the courts ruled it was legal. In August 2009, the federal circuit court of appeals in San Francisco ruled in favor of the players' union, which argued that the government had no right to all the test results. But as several players pointed out, that decision was too little, too late because the names of prominent players testing positive for steroids had already been leaked.

One of the first names to leak, in February 2009, was that of Alex Rodriguez. A-Rod wasted no time trying to get ahead of the story by telling ESPN's Peter Gammons, one of nation's most esteemed baseball reporters, that "I did take a banned substance," but only from 2001 to

2003 when he was on the Texas Rangers, after he signed his original record-setting contract. A week later, on the first day of spring training, he publicly confessed before his Yankees teammates. In June, Sammy Sosa was revealed to have tested positive for anabolic steroids in 2003, putting the lie to his congressional testimony and a figurative asterisk on his three 61-plus homer seasons in four years. In July, Red Sox sluggers Manny Ramirez, now with the Dodgers and having just finished serving a 50-day suspension for a recent failed drug test, and David Ortiz were reported to have been among the 104 failed performance-enhancing drug tests in the 2003 survey.

The fallout from the BALCO investigation and the Mitchell Report forced Major League Baseball to adopt, and the union to accept, more frequent mandatory testing of players without any anonymity, including blood testing for human growth hormone, and much tougher penalties for those caught cheating, including a lifetime ban for the third positive result. But baseball had suffered an eternal black eye in that the power-hitting exploits of the steroids era would always be viewed as mostly fraudulent. Twelve batters have crossed the exclusive 500-homer milestone since McGwire and Sosa's epic 1998 season. Only four—Ken Griffey Jr., Frank Thomas, Jim Thome, and Albert Pujols—have not had their names sullied by failed drug tests or credible evidence of steroids use.

Baseball may have moved beyond the steroids era, but embarrassments from star players failing tests continued, even after suspension penalties were increased in 2014 to 80 games for the first violation and 162 games—a full season—for the second. Manny Ramirez, now with Tampa Bay, was suspended for 100 games for failing a second test in April 2011; he retired with 555 career home runs. In 2012, Giants outfielder Melky Cabrera, leading the National League in batting average, was suspended for the rest of the season. In August 2013, outstanding Brewers outfielder Ryan Braun—the National League MVP two years before and runner-up in 2012—was suspended for the rest of the season and none other than Alex Rodriguez for the rest of the year and the entire next season—211 games in all—not for having failed a drug test, but for documented evidence they were on a supervised regimen of performance-enhancing drugs that was designed specifically to evade testing. Braun accepted his suspension, the better to move on with his baseball career. A-Rod, just coming off the disabled list with a hip injury and sitting on 647 career home runs, insisted on a hearing and played the rest of the season. He was just 14 long balls away from passing Willie Mays's 660 and cashing in on the first of his $6 million home run milestone bonuses.

All four were clients of Biogenesis, an anti-aging clinic in Coral Gables, Florida, whose founder, Anthony Bosch, provided them with steroids, HGH, and other performance-enhancing drugs in concoctions, amounts, and staggered doses intended to make them undetectable in baseball's more stringent drug-testing environment. The Biogenesis scandal broke in January 2013 when the weekly alternative newspaper *Miami New Times* published a detailed investigative report that was kicked off when a disaffected internal whistleblower provided files Bosch kept on his ballplayer clients. The fact that Ramirez, Cabrera, and Braun—in October 2011—failed baseball's drug tests suggested, according to the *Miami New Times*, that "either Bosch isn't particularly gifted at crafting drugs that can beat performance tests or his clients aren't careful." Bosch would later say it was the latter.

Ryan Braun was able to skate by his failed test during the 2011 division series in the year he won the MVP because his high-priced attorney convinced the arbitrator hearing his appeal that there had been an unacceptable break in the chain of custody before the sample got to the testing lab, leaving open the possibility it had been tampered with, even though Braun's sample was properly stored and the seal unbroken. It wasn't enough that Braun got off on a technicality—the chain-of-custody violation did nothing to compromise his blood sample—he also attacked the personal integrity and motives of the courier, accusing him of an anti-Braun conspiracy.

Proclaiming innocence and blaming someone else was what most players did when confronted with a failed drug test. Bonds and Giambi insisted they didn't know what, exactly, was in the topicals BALCO gave them. In his 2009 mea culpa, even while admitting he failed his 2003 steroid test, A-Rod qualified that by saying, "I'm guilty for being negligent, not asking the right questions," and, "I don't know exactly what substance I was guilty of using." Sosa, while denying *ever* taking steroids, also said in his testimony that he did not break any laws, which one congressman interpreted as leaving open the possibility he took steroids only in his home country, the Dominican Republic, where over-the-counter sales were legal. Rafael "I have never used steroids, period" Palmeiro blamed his subsequent failed test on a "contaminated" B-12 vitamin shot he was given from teammate Miguel Tejada's stash. Tejada, when asked about the B-12, said he had gotten shipments from the Dominican Republic, where B-12 doses, sometimes deliberately laced with steroids, often euphemistically referred to performance-enhancing drugs.

Braun's blame game, however, backfired on him and trapped A-Rod by infuriating Bud Selig, notwithstanding that Braun was the best player on the commissioner's favorite team—the one he used to own. Selig ordered an investigation into the *Miami New Times* story. Major League Baseball filed a lawsuit against Bosch, forcing him to cooperate in exchange for dropping the lawsuit. Bosch's information gave Selig what he needed to suspend Braun even in the absence (because of a technicality) of his failed drug test. Even though Bosch provided all the details, Alex Rodriguez, denying it all, went on a quixotic quest to slime Selig's investigation, and—no matter the irreversible damage he was doing to his already irreparably tarred reputation by acting like a jerk—refused to back down. Finally, in January 2014, he relented, admitted it was all true, and accepted being suspended for the entire 2014 baseball season in the interest of continuing on with his career with the ever-diminishing hope he might hit the 109 homers he still needed to pass Barry Bonds. A-Rod also received immunity from any federal investigation.

In 2015, Alex Rodriguez returned to a team that really didn't want him. A-Rod passed the Say Hey Kid in May without much fanfare. Home run number 661 was anticlimactic and almost embarrassing. His 33 home runs in 2015 brought him to 687—just 27 behind the Babe. Major League Baseball was spared the awkwardness of Rodriguez eclipsing Ruth and Aaron because he had become a wreck of a ballplayer at 40 years old. Discredited, hobbled by his surgically repaired right hip, relegated to a DH role, and no longer an impact player, Rodriguez was told in early August 2016 that the Yankees, having a forgettable season in fourth place, were looking to the future that he would not be a part of—not even for the rest of the year. The Yankees agreed to pay the rest of his contract and A-Rod would become a special advisor to the club. Alex Rodriguez retired with 696 home runs.

None of the Hall of Fame–worthy players explicitly implicated in baseball's steroids era have passed muster with the baseball writers whose votes guard the doors in Cooperstown. McGwire's highest vote total in his 10 years on the ballot—players must be among the 10 names on 75 percent of ballots to be elected—was 24 percent; Sheffield reached 30 percent and Ramirez 28 percent in 2020, their sixth and fourth years on the ballot; Sosa's was 12.5 percent; and Palmeiro was eliminated from consideration after just four years on the writers' ballot. Bonds and Clemens both got significantly more votes their first year on the ballot and were named on an increasing number of ballots in subsequent years, but consistently fell short of the total necessary. That Clemens and Bonds have gotten much more consideration that their fellow steroid users is attributable to their having established solid Hall of Fame credentials in the first half of their careers—before they became obsessed with enhancing their careers to achieve historic milestones.

In contrast to Bonds and Clemens, given that Alex Rodriguez admitted to using steroids as early as 2001—only his seventh big-league season, when he was in the prime of his career—and that he did so again at least as late as 2012 with Biogenesis, nobody knows how much of his stellar career was a fraud. Perhaps all of it.

Part III

New Thinking in the Old Ball Game

12

THE OWNERS' TAKE

Show Me the Money

When George Steinbrenner passed away a week after his 80th birthday in July 2010, he left a complicated legacy. Steinbrenner was "The Boss." An abusive bully, he also had a sentimental side. He was suspended twice by baseball commissioners: once for a federal felony for which he served no jail time, and once for hiring a scurrilous con man to dig up dirt on Yankees star outfielder Dave Winfield, whom Steinbrenner had soured on. The Boss presided over two revivals of the Yankees' "forever" dynasty—first when they ended a 12-year pennant drought by winning four pennants and two World Series between 1976 and 1981, and then when they ended a 14-year postseason drought by going to the postseason 13 straight years and winning four of the six World Series they played. After failing to make the playoffs in 2008, the Yankees rebounded to win a fifth (and final) World Series for the Boss in 2009. Notorious for firing managers in his first 19 years as Yankees owner, after his second suspension, Steinbrenner settled on a strategy of stability in the dugout; in the 18 years from 1992 till his dying day, the Yankees had just three managers—Buck Showalter, followed by Joe Torre in 1996, followed by Joe Girardi in 2008.

And George Steinbrenner presided over the Yankees' becoming a billion-dollar baseball franchise. A Cleveland-based shipping magnate, the Boss and his partners bought the club in 1973 for a mere $8.8 million, of which he personally ponied up less than 2 percent. (Nine years earlier, the franchise had been purchased for $14 million.) By 2006, the Yankees were worth more than $1 billion. At the time of Steinbrenner's death, the franchise was valued at $1.6 billion, according to *Forbes*. Part of that, of course, was attributable to the storied history of the Yankees, including their extraordinary record of success—total domination of the AL East, if not always the American League—since 1996. Part of it was the value of their outstanding core of player assets. But also important in that $1.6 billion valuation was the revenue the Yankees earned from advertising and merchandising agreements, including from a concessions company called Legends Hospitality, which Steinbrenner formed in partnership with NFL Dallas Cowboys owner Jerry Jones. Far more important than all that, however, were the proceeds from cable television broadcasts of Yankees games, an area magnified when the Yankees formed their own network—YES, for Yankees Entertainment and Sports—in 2001.

It wasn't just the Yankees. Every major-league club earned income from advertising, merchandising, and cable television broadcasts. But it was the hallowed franchises in big media markets that made the most—in particular New York's Yankees, Chicago's Cubs, Boston's Red Sox, and LA's Dodgers. They capitalized on local and regional cable networks paying large sums for almost-exclusive broadcast rights to their baseball games. For six years, 1998 to 2003, the Dodgers were even owned by Rupert Murdoch's Fox Entertainment Group, which bought one of baseball's highest-profile franchises for the purpose of using their games as the foundation for a new regional sports cable television network it was planning for Southern California. Teams in small media markets, by contrast, earned significantly less from cable broadcasts of their games. Not surprisingly, most big-market clubs initially put up fierce resistance to Bud Selig's insistence that revenue sharing was critical for smaller-market franchises to survive, especially in the face of escalating player payrolls resulting from arbitration and free agency.

Steinbrenner was the most vocal in opposition, contending that his Yankees earned and deserved their huge revenue advantage and should not have to subsidize teams with lesser revenues. Selig, however, had the collective weight of the small-market teams behind him and the winning argument that revenue sharing was necessary to get the players' union to agree to a permeable salary cap in the form of a "luxury tax" on teams whose player payrolls exceeded a certain threshold. Steinbrenner's Yankees, by virtue of their unmatched revenue streams and willingness to spend liberally on players to maintain their competitive advantage, were hit hard on both counts—putting far more into revenue sharing than any other team and paying more in "taxes" than any other team for exceeding player payroll thresholds every year.

By the second decade of the new century, big-market teams were signing billion-dollar deals for broadcasting rights to their games extending many years into the future. Most were negotiated agreements that gave them an ownership stake—often a big one—in local regional sports networks. Having an equity stake in the networks allowed franchise owners to exclude a significant portion of their regional cable television earnings from baseball's revenue-sharing mandate by claiming that portion as profits earned by their broadcasting business, not their ballclub. In 2016, at least half of baseball's 30 major-league teams had an ownership stake in a regional sports network or local cable network. The Dodgers, being in the huge Los Angeles media market, earned by far the most in broadcast revenue—more than $200 million; the Yankees were in the neighborhood of $100 million; 13 teams in 2016 earned at least $50 million in television revenue; and the bottom six earned about half that. By this time, the post–George Steinbrenner Yankees, now ruled by his sons, had sold most of its ownership shares in YES, which claimed the largest audience of any regional sports network, to Murdoch's entertainment behemoth 21st Century Fox for nearly $4 billion.

That major-league teams profited handsomely from lucrative deals with regional sports networks was not necessarily beneficial to their loyal fan base watching games at home. Millions of fans in the greater Houston, Los Angeles, and New York metropolitan areas could not watch most games of the Astros, Dodgers, and Yankees after they entered into joint ventures with major media conglomerates because major cable and satellite TV providers refused to pay the exorbitant carriage fees that the teams' media partners were demanding for the regional sports networks broadcasting their games. The Astros' joint venture went bankrupt after two years in 2014. In New York, Comcast insisted in a stinging rebuke to the notion of Yankees games as must-see TV that fewer than 10 percent of its customers watched even a quarter of their games, which made carrying the network cost-prohibitive at the price Fox was demanding for YES network. The Yankees bought back control of YES from Fox in 2019.

Aside from leveraging the intrinsic value of their broadcasts for lucrative long-term deals with media outlets that often included an equity stake, franchise owners did not hesitate to exploit a city's identification with its team for public funding and tax breaks to build new fields of dreams to replace aging stadiums. This was not a particularly new development. As far back as 1928, voters in the city of Cleveland approved funding for a huge multipurpose stadium, good for both baseball and football, that the Indians used mostly for Sunday and holiday home dates after it opened in 1931 before moving full-time into the cavernous ballpark in 1947. (In the meantime, Cleveland's Indians played most of their games in twice-renovated League Park, which, like all other big-league ballparks at the time, was not publicly funded.) In the 1950s, Milwaukee, Baltimore, Kansas City, and Minneapolis all used public money to renovate and expand the seating capacity of existing minor-league stadiums in hopes of attracting major-league teams. They all did.

All but four of baseball's 30 major-league teams currently play in ballparks built or renovated with substantial public funding. Of those that were not, Boston's Fenway Park and Chicago's Wrigley Field both opened before World War I; the building of Dodger Stadium in 1962 would not have been possible without the city of Los Angeles selling 352 acres of land in Chavez Ravine to Walter O'Malley's transplanted Brooklyn Dodgers for well below market value and evicting the families that lived there; and the Giants' new home in San Francisco, which opened for baseball in 2000, is the only ballpark built since Dodger Stadium whose construction did not rely on any public money.

O'Malley was the first franchise owner to demand public dollars or tax breaks for new stadiums with the implicit threat—sometimes made explicit—of moving elsewhere if funding was not forthcoming. He warned two years in advance that Brooklyn's beloved Dodgers would leave town unless New York City's urban development czar Robert Moses made available the real estate he wanted for a new ballpark at a cost-effective price *and* built the supporting infrastructure for a new home for the Dodgers. Moses didn't. O'Malley wasn't bluffing: The Dodgers moved to LA with the promise they could build a modern new stadium in Chavez Ravine. The tactic of holding fan loyalties hostage, even if it meant the fan base had to pay higher sales taxes or diverted government spending from other public works to get their way, has been repeated again and again.

Steinbrenner used that tack when he began lobbying for a new Yankee Stadium in the 1980s to replace the original, which opened in 1923 and had been repaired and renovated in the 1970s with the assistance of public funding. Originally wanting the new stadium to be in Manhattan before settling for staying at the same location in the Bronx, the Yankees' Boss suggested he would move his team out of the city and across the Hudson River if the city or New York State did not subsidize the cost of construction. They would still be the *New York* Yankees, only in New Jersey. While requiring the Yankees (and the Mets, who were simultaneously building a new stadium in Queens) to pay the cost of construction for the new stadium, the city approved tax breaks that allowed the Yankees to save tens of millions in financing costs, as well as exemptions from paying rent or property taxes on the new stadium built on city-owned land. Moreover, public funds from both city and state taxes would cover nearly $300 million of the cost in surrounding infrastructure, including new parking garages and a new metro rail stop. The city's economic development corporation warned the mayor that failure to provide tax-free financing would result in "the loss of the New York Yankees." The Yankees' team president later told a congressional hearing that had the city not provided the financing, the franchise would have left town.

On April 13, 2009, after 45 years calling Shea Stadium their home, the New York Mets opened a new stadium at the same location in Flushing, Queens. Three days later, just two days short of the 86th anniversary of baseball's greatest coliseum being informally christened "The House That Ruth Built" when the Babe hit the first-ever home run at Yankee Stadium, the New York Yankees opened a new stadium on the same hallowed ground in the Bronx. In deference to tradition (the Yankees are probably the major-league franchise most bound by tradition) and history—they are the "forever" dynasty, after all—they called their new stadium Yankee Stadium. Brand new stadium, same old name—because nothing says Yankees like "Yankee Stadium." The Mets' new home also honored tradition—just not theirs—by specifically replicating the iconic rotunda entrance behind home plate that made Brooklyn's Ebbets Field, built in 1913, an architectural classic and a lost treasure after the Dodgers left town for Los Angeles in 1958 and their Brooklyn ballpark was demolished two years later. The Mets' new home further honored tradition by devoting the rotunda to the groundbreaking career and memory of Jackie Robinson.

Notwithstanding that the Mets' owners financed nearly two-thirds of the $632 million it cost to build the new stadium, it was named not for the team, nor for the city whose tax dollars and tax breaks contributed mightily to its construction, nor even for Jackie Robinson—an American hero whose integration of Major League Baseball in the face of considerable nasty opposition was a pivotal point in the battle for equal rights for all American citizens. Instead, in deference to the Almighty Dollar, the Mets would henceforth be playing in Citi Field. Citigroup, one of the world's largest investment banks and headquartered in New York, agreed to pay the Mets $20 million a year for 20 years to have their name emblazoned on the new stadium. Though the deal was signed in 2006 when ground was broken for construction across from Shea Stadium, the stadium's name was not without considerable controversy when the ballpark opened on the heels of Citigroup's being bailed out at the expense of billions in taxpayer dollars from the consequences of the 2008 financial collapse it had a role in precipitating.

Historically, major-league ballparks were named for geographic characteristics in the urban areas they were built, or for the owner of the franchise that built the thing, or occasionally for the team that would play there. Many of the wooden-grandstand ballparks in the first decade of the twentieth century were known by their location in the city—in Chicago, West Side Grounds for the Cubs and South Side Park for the White Sox; in Boston, South End Grounds for the National League team and Huntington Avenue Grounds for the American League team; and in New York, Hilltop Park for the AL team called the Highlanders (because they were on the highest hilltop in Manhattan) before they were the Yankees in either name or excellence.

In the first round of new concrete-and-steel stadiums that were constructed in the early twentieth century, Boston's Fenway Park was named after the Fens area where it was built and Pittsburgh's Forbes Field was named in honor of a British general whose forces liberated the area in a decisive battle of the French and Indian War in the mid-18th century. Shibe Park in Philadelphia, Comiskey Park in Chicago, Navin Field in Detroit, and Ebbets Field in Brooklyn bore the names of franchise owners. At the end of this round of stadium construction in 1923 came Yankee Stadium, named for the team that played there rather than for the name or any distinguishing characteristic of the place it was built (in the Bronx) or for team owner and brewery magnate Jacob Ruppert, who financed its construction. Stadium names often changed when a new owner took over the franchise, such as Washington's National Park being renamed Griffith Stadium in 1920 after Clark Griffith assumed ownership of the Senators; Weeghman Park in Chicago becoming Wrigley Field in the mid-1920s when chewing-gum magnate William Wrigley became owner of the northside team in the Windy City; and Redland Field in Cincinnati becoming Crosley Field and Navin Field in Detroit being re-named Briggs Stadium in the 1930s after new owners Powel Crosley and Walter Briggs.

During the stadium-building boom in the 1960s and 1970s, 'twas the team name Dodger Stadium or Royals Stadium—or geography that most often found its way onto the nameplate. Candlestick Park in San Francis-co was named for the windswept and often brutally cold (in the summer-time) promontory on which the stadium was built; on the banks of the Ohio River, the Reds' new ballpark in Cincinnati was called Riverfront Stadium; and the new Three Rivers Stadium in Pittsburgh was so called because it stood at the nexus of the Allegheny, Monongahela, and Ohio Rivers. Stadiums that were publicly funded had names like Metropolitan Stadium in the suburbs of Minnesota's Twin Cities, Fulton County Sta-dium in Atlanta, and Anaheim Stadium for the California Angels in Orange County. Seattle's Kingdome acknowledged both that it was pub-licly financed by King County in Washington State and that it was an indoor domed stadium, following in the wake of Houston's Astrodome, which was so named because Houston was the new mission control cen-ter for NASA's space missions.

The opening in June 1989 of Toronto's SkyDome, named for its roof that retracted so that Blue Jays fans could look up at the sky on nice days, began a new wave of stadium construction. Twenty-two of Major League Baseball's 30 fields of dreams have been built since 1990. For the most part, following the example of Baltimore's Oriole Park at Camden Yards, which opened in 1992, they were designed to appeal to baseball fans' nostalgia for the classic, more intimate ballparks in urban settings that reflected their city's character—except not as cramped, with all the mod-ern conveniences twenty-first-century Americans expect, and with very high-priced field-level seats and luxury suites lucrative for franchise bot-tom lines. They all benefited, to one degree or another, from some combination of public financing or tax benefits for the stadium or surrounding infrastructure such as parking garages and off-freeway access. These ballparks were often the centerpiece of gentrification projects in old and even impoverished neighborhoods, such as in southeast Washington, DC, where Nationals Park was built in 2008, bringing in well-heeled residents and businesses to boost city revenues and appeal as a desirable place to live and work.

But there was a new naming trend afoot. Now it was all about the money. Stadium names were for sale to big corporations willing to pay for the privilege. It was a trend that began in the 1990s, not just for new ballparks but for older ones as well. Candlestick Park, for example, became 3Com Park in 1996 before being abandoned for a new stadium in San Francisco, which has gone through four corporate-name changes since opening in 2000. Traditional naming conventions—such as for the team, the unique geography or location, or the franchise owner or some other prominent person—had become quaint. Purchased naming rights consigned the founding father of the White Sox to the history books when the new Comiskey Park, which opened in 1991, became US Cellular Field in 2003 and then Guaranteed Rate Field in 2017.

Chasing corporate dollars for naming rights to their new publicly funded ballparks sometimes proved embarrassing, as happened when Enron Corporation, a major energy conglomerate, was hauled into federal court in 2001 for accounting fraud to hide financial losses. Notwithstanding Enron's 30-year, $100 million deal with the Astros to have its company name proudly displayed on Houston's new ballpark, nearly 70 percent of whose construction was funded by the city, by 2002 Enron Field was Minute Maid Park. And the new home of the Texas Rangers, which opened as the Ballpark in Arlington in 1994 and was renamed Ameriquest Field in 2004, reverted to Rangers Ballpark in Arlington three years later when Ameriquest was being investigated for predatory lending. The insurance company Globe Life then bought naming rights that extended to an even newer stadium for the Rangers that opened in 2020.

Of the 30 current ballparks in Major League Baseball, 20 bear the name of financial or corporate enterprises. Most of the new stadiums are admired and loved for their design and setting, enough so that they might be destinations themselves, especially where they nod to old-time ballparks of the past. But corporate names are impersonal, and corporate branding of ballparks is perhaps even sacrilegious to a game that evokes the more pastoral America of a century ago. Part of the charm of the old-time fields of dreams was in their names—Ebbets Field, Crosley Field, Comiskey Park, Briggs Stadium; the still-existing Fenway Park and Wrigley Field; and even Candlestick, as cold as it was for the fans that endured games there. To many, back in the day (or today in Boston and Chicago), their names were synonymous with the teams that played there. The same cannot be said for ballparks named for corporations that pay for the privilege. Baltimore's Oriole Park at Camden Yards (named both for the team that plays there and the historical site where the Baltimore & Ohio Railroad, America's first railroad chartered specifically to carry public passengers, had its terminus for routes traveling both northeast and west), Nationals Park in Washington, the new Yankee Stadium, and Marlins Park in Miami are the only ballparks built since 1990 whose franchises resisted any temptation for lucrative naming-rights deals from some corporate or financial institution. Their names *are* synonymous with the teams that play there.

13

WHERE LOSING WAS A WINNING PROPOSITION

Major-league teams historically have always worked to be as competitive as possible within the reality of fiscal constraints and the rules governing player-team contractual relationships fundamentally defined, even since free agency, by the reserve clause. The most successful franchises are those with the most money to spend on players or that have invested in productive farm systems. Those with few pennants to show on baseball's historical scorecard, and with many more losing seasons than winning ones, are those bunched at the other end of the financial spectrum because they are in small-market cities or have had parsimonious owners. They did the best they could under the circumstances, every now and again being able to assemble and keep together a team that was competitive for some number of years—rarely more than half a decade—before falling back to years of mediocrity (or worse).

Whether franchises were competitive or not, roster turnovers were rarely abrupt. They were evolutionary, typically recycling every five to seven years, depending on how competitive the team was, with young minor-league talent phased in, aging veterans phased out, and player acquisitions through trades, cash transactions, and free agency providing ballast to carry teams from one year to the next. The worst teams would recycle their rosters more quickly than the best teams, although in the era before free agency, that was not necessarily true of bad teams that nonetheless had a core of very good players—like the Cubs in the first half of the 1960s with Ernie Banks, Ron Santo, Billy Williams, and Dick Ellsworth.

Historically, richer franchises had a significant advantage in both scouting and signing the best amateur players, all of whom were, in effect, free agents to sign with the highest-bonus bidder. That changed in 1965 when Major League Baseball instituted a draft for high school and college players that helped rectify competitive imbalance by establishing a draft order for teams that was the inverse of the previous year's final standings. This prevented the best-capitalized teams from cornering the market on the best amateur players and from being able to outbid other teams for a highly coveted player because the team that drafted him had exclusive negotiating rights (unless the player opted out of beginning his professional career that year).

The earliest beneficiary of the amateur draft was Kansas City's hapless Athletics, a perennial bottom dweller since moving from Philadelphia in 1955. With the first pick in 1965's first amateur draft (following their AL-worst record in 1964), the A's chose college outfielder Rick Monday. With the second overall pick the next year, after finishing last again, Kansas City selected college outfielder Reggie Jackson, and with their second-round pick in 1968, the 27th pick overall, Vida Blue was welcomed into the A's minor-league system. Those selections were instrumental to the Athletics, now in Oakland, becoming a baseball dynasty in the first half of the 1970s with five straight division titles and three consecutive World Series championships. (Monday was traded after their first division title in 1971 for Ken Holtzman, a cornerstone starting pitcher for the A's the next four years.) Even as the Athletics were winning, however, their best players were demanding to be paid more than their owner could afford. The Oakland dynasty came to an abrupt end in 1976, when free agency was granted for players with six years in the major leagues. The reserve clause could no longer serve as a firewall for the Athletics, or any other club, to keep their best players eligible for free agency from signing with any team offering them the best deal.

The significant role the amateur draft played in Oakland's becoming a baseball dynamo did not cause any franchise to decide on a strategy of building the foundation for a contending ballclub by deliberately fielding a noncompetitive team sure to be one of the worst in the game for several seasons in order to ensure a top pick in successive annual players drafts. To the extent it was thought about at all (which might have been more along the lines of "on the bright side of all this losing"), a "tanking" strategy would probably have been considered both untenable, from the perspective of competitive integrity—fans and the media were not shy in lambasting ownership for not doing more to make their team better *right now*—and impractical, in the context of the inherent uncertainty of any player's development, even that of a top draft pick. Having to be really bad to get really good would not have seemed a winning strategy.

That changed in the 2010s when the Chicago Cubs and Houston Astros both did precisely that. Both franchises took advantage of new rules in the player-approved 2012–2016 collective bargaining agreement that imposed a cap on amateur draft spending but also gave the teams with the worst records and the best positioning in the draft order the largest pool of bonus money to sign the players they selected. It was not as though either franchise had not been successful. As rivals in the National League's Central Division, the Cubs had won three division titles and a wild card since the major leagues went to a three-division alignment in both leagues, and the Astros had finished first four times and been the wild card twice. While the 2003 Cubs were cursed by one of their own—the fan reaching for a possibly catchable fly ball down the left-field line heading into the grandstand—and failed to make it to the World Series, the Astros did play in the 2005 World Series, where they were swept by the other, much less celebrated team from Chicago, the White Sox.

The decision to lure Theo Epstein away from the Boston Red Sox to become president of baseball operations in November 2011 is a milestone in Chicago Cubs history that five years later brought them their first pennant since the last year of World War II and first World Series championship since the days of "Tinker to Evers to Chance" and Three Finger Brown way back in 1908. Epstein inherited a team that had finished fifth in the six-team NL Central each of the two previous years. They had lost 91 games in the 2011 season just ended. They had the third-highest player payroll in the National League. Five of their eight players with the most plate appearances in 2011 were 33 or older; two of their three starting pitchers with the most innings pitched in 2011 were over 30 with earned run averages close to 5.00. One of the few bright spots was 21-year-old second-year shortstop Starlin Castro, signed by the Cubs as a 16-year-old in the Dominican Republic, who had a .304 batting average in 283 big-league games. He was a keeper—the only one, really, as far as Epstein was concerned.

Rather than building toward ending the Cubs' epic championship drought by incrementally improving the club over the next few years to be as competitive as possible, Epstein was willing to make Chicago's Cubs the worst team in baseball for the immediate future so they could hopefully become one of the best teams in baseball by the middle of the decade. The city of Chicago, at least the North Side, was going to have to endure a few years of very bad baseball for the purpose of positioning in baseball's annual draft. Their 87 losses in 2010 had already resulted in the Cubs selecting infielder Javier Baez as the 11th overall pick in the 2011 draft. Epstein's first consequential move was to trade pitching prospect Andrew Cashner to San Diego for first baseman Anthony Rizzo, who was promoted to Chicago in June 2012.

Epstein's first year in charge saw the Cubs finishing fifth again with the second-worst record in the major leagues. Only the Astros, a team adopting the same strategy, kept the Cubs from the NL Central basement and baseball's worst record in 2012. But that got them the second overall pick in the 2013 amateur draft, which Epstein used to select and sign third baseman Kris Bryant. The Cubs improved to lose only 96 games in 2013, earning them the fourth overall pick in the 2014 draft. They took catcher Kyle Schwarber. In 2014, the Cubs finished last in their division again, with 89 losses. In July, Epstein took advantage of the Oakland A's needing starting pitching in their bid to win the AL West by trading two of his starters—Jason Hammel, 8–5 with a 2.98 earned run average at the time, and Jeff Samardzija, whose excellent 2.83 ERA belied his 2–7 record—for outstanding shortstop prospect Addison Russell. Oakland wound up with a wild-card berth; the Cubs got a coveted prospect and, by virtue of their record, the ninth overall pick in the 2015 draft.

After five consecutive losing seasons, the last three in his first three years in Chicago, Epstein decided the Cubs were finally ready to compete. He traded for veteran center fielder Dexter Fowler to help guide his core of dynamic young players. He signed former Red Sox ace Jon Lester to bolster the starting rotation. But Epstein's first, most important move after the 2014 season was to hire Joe Maddon as manager—the same Joe Maddon whose homespun savvy and unorthodox ways of connecting with players and building clubhouse cohesion and astute use of data analytics as a situational decision-making tool in managing ball games had turned around the fortunes of the dismal Tampa Bay Rays.

Maddon's deal was for five years. What he and the Cubs accomplished the first year was more than probably even Epstein expected. Although never in serious contention for the 2015 division title, the Cubs nonetheless won 97 games—a 24-win improvement from the previous year—for the third-best record in the division, the entire National League, and all of Major League Baseball. Russell at second and Bryant at third both made their major-league debuts in April. Bryant hit 26 homers, drove in 99 runs, and was unanimously voted Rookie of the Year. Rizzo hit 31 home runs. Schwarber was called up in June; by August he was starting in left field. And right-hander Jake Arrieta, a struggling pitcher Epstein acquired in 2013, was a revelation. He finished with a 22–6 record and 1.77 ERA to win the Cy Young Award. Arrieta was 18–2 in his last 23 starts; ended the season with 11 straight wins, including a no-hitter against the Dodgers in August; and pitched a masterful five-hit shutout to defeat the 98-win Pittsburgh Pirates in the wild-card game. The Cubs then took down the 100-win St. Louis Cardinals, to whom they and the Pirates lost the NL Central Division race, in four games in their division series before being swept by New York's Mets in the NLCS.

It was now going on 71 years since the Cubs last played in a World Series, and 108 since they last won one. Epstein decided that, as phenomenal a year as the Cubs just had, *now* was the time to go for that championship. On the same day in December, Epstein traded Starlin Castro to the Yankees and signed free agent Ben Zobrist to a four-year, $56 million contract. Castro had been something of an enigma, alternately brilliant in his play and frustrating in his work ethic, in his six years at Wrigley. Epstein preferred Addison Russell—Castro's superior defensively—at shortstop and knew he had hot-prospect infielder Javier Baez waiting in the wings. Zobrist had played for Maddon in Tampa Bay, where his versatility and heady play made him a favorite of his once and future manager. Epstein also raided the National League's best team in 2015— the Cardinals—for their best position player and pitcher, according to the wins above replacement metric, to sign free agents Jason Heyward to solidify the outfield and veteran right-hander John Lackey to give the Cubs five solid frontline starting pitchers.

The 2016 Cubs got off to a fast start by winning eight of their first nine games. On July 25, with the Cubs nursing a comfortable seven-game advantage in their division but just a game and a half better than the NL East and NL West division leaders, Epstein traded with the Yankees for elite closer Aroldis Chapman and his frequently thrown 100-mile-per-hour blow-them-away fastball. The Yankees had acquired him from Cincinnati to be their closer before the start of the season but by mid-July were all but out of contention and planning for the future. In the 287 innings he brought to Chicago since becoming a closer in 2012, Chapman had given up just 156 hits while striking out exactly 500 batters—an average of 15.7 K's per 9 innings. To get him, however, Epstein had to part with one of baseball's top ten minor-league prospects—shortstop Gleyber Torres, still in the lower minors.

Aiming for a World Series championship in 2016, assessing that Torres was probably two years away from the Big Time (which proved true) and knowing that a major Cubs strength was their core of talented young infielders, Epstein was willing to part with his exciting young prospect to acquire the power closer he felt was necessary for the Cubs to finally end their century-plus championship drought, even though Chapman would be a free agent at the end of the year. The Cubs won 44 of their 63 games after acquiring Chapman, who had 16 saves, a 1.01 ERA, and 46 strikeouts in 26⅔ innings the rest of the way. Their 103 wins were the most in baseball and the most in franchise history since 1910. Bryant led the team with 39 homers, which was third in the league and was the National League MVP; Rizzo had 32 homers, and his 109 runs batted in were second in the league; and Lester was 19–5, Arrieta 18–8, Kyle Hendricks 16–8, Jason Hammel 15–10, and Lackey 11–8 while starting all but 10 of the Cubs' regular-season games.

After spending every day but one atop the NL Central, Chicago beat San Francisco in their division series; Los Angeles in the NLCS, winning three in a row to overcome a two-games-to-one deficit; and Cleveland in the World Series, winning three games in a row to overcome a three-games-to-one deficit. Chapman could not hold a 6–3 Cubs lead in the eighth, giving up a game-tying home run. But it ended well with a two-run 10th and a celebration on the infield in Cleveland. Chicago's Cubs were World Series champions for the first time since 1908.

Epstein's mission accomplished, the Cubs seemed destined to be a dynasty—the National League team to beat every year—till at least the end of the decade. Even though Chapman re-signed with the Yankees as a free agent less than two months after the World Series, Chicago had a solid core of outstanding young players—Rizzo, Bryant, Baez, and Russell under team control until the early 2020s—and highly regarded prospects in their minor-league pipeline. Baez and Bryant, who played 69 games in the outfield in 2016, were both versatile players in the Zobrist mold who could play multiple positions wherever Maddon might want them in any given game. Joe Maddon's managerial creativity was by now legendary; Theo Epstein was the model of front office creative genius, sure to ensure that the Cubs would have the players needed to remain a top-tier ballclub for years to come; and Chicago's Cubs had the financial resources to make that happen.

Although the Cubs won their division by a comfortable six games, the 2017 season was more of a struggle. Their 92–70 record was only fourth best in the National League. Bryant had another outstanding season, as did Rizzo. The Cubs' pitching was more problematic. Their starters' ERA was over 4.00—more than a run higher than their 2.96 earned run average in 2016—which meant Cubs relievers had to work nearly 20 percent more innings in 2017. Epstein's biggest move was to trade outfielder Eloy Jimenez, the team's top minor-league prospect, to acquire lefty Jose Quintana from the White Sox in mid-July. Quintana was excellent the rest of the way, with a 7–3 record in 14 starts. Although not favored against the better 97-win Washington Nationals in their division series, the Cubs beat them in five games, but they proved to be no match for the 104-win Dodgers in the NLCS, losing in five games.

Epstein moved to improve the pitching in 2018 by signing free agent Yu Darvish to a six-year, $126 million contract. Averaging 11 strikeouts per 9 innings in his five major-league seasons and 131 big-league starts, Darvish had been one of baseball's most compelling pitchers since leaving Japan in 2012. Darvish, however, made only eight starts for the Cubs in 2018 before being sidelined by an elbow injury. Even without him, the Cubs improved to 95–68, but had to settle for second place and a wild-card slot after losing a one-game playoff to Milwaukee to decide the division winner. They then lost the wild-card game, 2–1, to Colorado in 13 innings.

Cubs fans may have been disaffected that Epstein did not make any off-season splash by signing or trading for high-impact players to facilitate a bid to get back to the World Series in 2019. Team owner Tom Ricketts claimed the Cubs did not have the financial resources to add appreciably to their player payroll, despite trailing only the Yankees,

Dodgers, Red Sox, and Giants in revenue earnings. Ricketts's line was consistent with nearly all other team owners in Major League Baseball in emphasizing the importance of fiscal restraint and being conservative in the free agent marketplace as a way to control expenses. In June 2019, however, he did invest $33 million for three years to sign elite closer Craig Kimbrel and his 333 career saves and 14.7 strikeouts per 9 innings in nine major-league seasons. The Cubs were tied for first with the Brewers at the time; Kimbrel was sitting at home because teams were unwilling to give him the higher-value longer-term contract he was seeking. Beset by knee and elbow problems, Kimbrel's first year in Chicago went badly—he blew three leads in 16 save opportunities and had a horrendous 6.53 earned run average. The Cubs ended up third in their division, with only the eighth-best record in the National League.

Their failure to make the postseason in 2019 raised questions as to whether the remarkable team the Cubs had built through tanking and astute trades and free-agent signings of established veterans had run its course. Maddon's magic, it seemed, was gone. He was not asked to return for 2020.

Like the Cubs, the Astros, now in the American League's Western Division, emerged from five years of deliberate tanking to be unexpectedly competitive and win a wild-card berth in 2015. Following their wild-card trip to the World Series in 2005, the Astros tried maintaining the pretense of competitiveness by signing some of their own best players to expensive contract extensions—most notably outfielder–first baseman Lance Berkman and top starting pitcher Roy Oswalt, both through the 2010 season—and playing in the free agent market. After the 2006 season they invested $100 million in a six-year deal for power hitter Carlos Lee as a long-term replacement for the now-retired Hall of Fame first baseman Jeff Bagwell, and $12.5 million in a two-year deal for right-hander Woody Williams, who had just turned 40, to help reinforce a starting rotation handicapped by the free-agency departures of pitching aces Andy Pettitte and Roger Clemens, both returning to the Yankees. And in 2008 Houston committed to three years and $16.5 million for Kazuo Matsui to replace another future Hall of Famer, Craig Biggio, at second base, even though Matsui's transition from Japanese baseball to the major leagues had not gone smoothly. Houston also traded with Baltimore for shortstop

Miguel Tejada, assuming the remaining two years and $29.6 million on the six-year deal he signed in December 2003.

None of the Astros' big free agent signings met expectations. The result of Houston's strategy was the fifth-highest payroll in the National League from 2006 to 2010 that resulted in three losing seasons and the Astros winning just 48 percent of their games. The best they finished was second in the NL Central in 2006, barely above water with an 82–80 record. The contract extensions they offered their best players and the free agents they signed meant their roster was consistently one of the oldest in the National League. Meanwhile, their big-spending focus on major-league salaries that ended up having no competitive payoff in terms of reaching the postseason resulted in a significant atrophying in the depth and quality of their minor-league system. According to *Baseball America*'s farm-system ratings, by 2008 theirs was the second worst of the 30 major-league franchises, and in 2009 and 2010 it *was* the worst.

With attendance dropping dramatically, their chances for a competitive turnaround seeming bleak, and their owner preparing to put the franchise up for sale, the Astros slashed their payroll from $93 million to $71 million in 2011, $30 million of which went to three players signed as free-agents in previous years. During the season, they also traded two of their best young players—outfielders Hunter Pence and Michael Bourne, both having capitalized on their eligibility for salary arbitration in salary negotiations—neither for high-value prospects, just to shed their combined $11.3 million in salary. Houston lost 106 games—the only team in either league to lose over 100. It was the first time in franchise history the Astros had lost 100 games—something they had not even done as a 1962-expansion club. That did not prevent the Astros from being sold for the second-highest price paid for a major-league franchise up to that time, after the sale of the Cubs to Ricketts in 2010.

Under new ownership, the Astros in 2012 reduced their payroll to the lowest in the majors at $37 million. In July they traded their two remaining players with salaries over $10 million. Houston lost a major-league-high 107 games, six more than the tanking Cubs. And in 2013, the Astros celebrated their first year in the American League, courtesy of Major League Baseball's realignment into two 15-team leagues, with 111 losses. They did this with a microscopic major-league payroll of just $14.7 million—$10 million less than Miami's Marlins, with the next lowest payroll. Only three Astros players earned more than $1 million; all were signed to one-year deals as free agents before the season to provide ballast for Houston's big-league roster of young, inexperienced players. Two of the three didn't make it through the season. Houston, meanwhile, was building a player-development juggernaut by reinvesting in their farm system and giving focus to scouting young Latin players in Caribbean Basin countries.

The payoff for four years of tanking came with an unexpected 86-win season in 2015 to qualify as the American League's second wild-card team. Twenty-five-year-old Venezuelan second baseman Jose Altuve, whose 225 hits and .341 batting average in 2014 led the majors, topped the AL again in hits with 200. Twenty-year-old Carlos Correa, from Puerto Rico, chosen with the very first pick in the 2012 amateur draft that the Astros "earned" by having baseball's worst record the previous year, won Rookie of the Year honors after being called up to Houston in June. Left-hander Dallas Keuchel, 20–8 in his fourth big-league season, won the Cy Young Award and stymied the Yankees in the wild-card game. The Astros also had the benefit of the second pick in the June 2015 amateur draft, which they used to select third baseman Alex Bregman, whose big-league debut would come in July the next year.

The 2015 Astros were not quite ready for prime time, however, losing their division series in five games to the eventual World Series champion Kansas City Royals. And in 2016, Houston fell back to third with 84 wins. But with outfielder George Springer (selected by Houston with the 11th overall pick in the 2011 draft) having his breakout season with 29 homers in 2016, Altuve winning his second batting title, Correa emerging as a top-tier player, and Bregman waiting in the wings, there was little doubt Houston was primed to be a dominant club—perhaps even the American League team to beat—for the foreseeable future.

In 2017, a Houston Astros dynasty was born. It was the first of three consecutive 100-win seasons. The Astros survived a tense seven-game ALCS with the Yankees, then took down the Dodgers in an epic seven-game World Series in which the two teams combined for 25 home runs—15 by Houston, five of which were by Springer to tie the World Series record set by Reggie Jackson in 1977 and matched in 2009 by Chase Utley. In 2018 the Astros improved from 101 to 103 wins and seemed on the road to repeating as World Series champions when they won the first game of the 2018 ALCS against Boston's 108-win Red Sox. 'Twas not to be, however; Boston steamrolled Houston, winning the next four games.

But it was back to the World Series for the 107-win 2019 Astros, whose potent lineup, hammering out 288 home runs, was compared to the historic 1927 Yankees' Murderers' Row. It took them six games to beat the 103-win Yankees in the ALCS, but the Astros lost the 2019 World Series to Washington's NL wild-card Nationals in seven games, ironically winning three in DC but losing all four games at home.

As important as tanking was to give the Astros top player selections in the annual amateur draft, so too was the decision of the Astros' new owner soon after his deal for the franchise was concluded in November 2011 to lure Jeff Luhnow from the Cardinals—a division rival at the time—to be in charge of baseball operations. Luhnow, whose focus in St. Louis was scouting and player development, prioritized data-driven analysis for player acquisition, improving player skills, and helping players make necessary adaptations in their pitching or batting mechanics to correct flaws or accommodate changed circumstances such as diminishing abilities associated with aging.

In addition to building a contending team through top amateur draft picks, Luhnow—like Epstein in Chicago—was active on the trade and free agent fronts to complement the Altuve-Correa-Springer-Bregman core of homegrown talent as soon as he felt the Astros were on the threshold of competing—and once there, to keep them an elite team. Soon after taking over, he traded for versatile minor leaguer Marwin Gonzalez, capable of playing both infield and outfield positions. In 2014, Luhnow traded for right-handed batting outfielder Jake Marisnick to provide a platoon option against southpaws. In July 2016, Luhnow wasted little time trading with the Dodgers for Cuban defector Yordan Alvarez, whom LA had just signed for $2 million. Before the Astros' 2017 championship season, he signed free-agent Josh Reddick to improve Houston's outfield deficiencies and traded for catcher Brian McCann and signed free agent Carlos Beltran, both nearing the end of their careers, less for what they might contribute on the playing field than for the veteran leadership they could provide to the Astros' core of up-and-coming stars. And prior to the 2019 season, having fallen to Boston in the 2018 ALCS, Luhnow signed veteran catcher Robinson Chiniros and veteran outfielder Michael Brantley as free agents both to shore up positions of weakness and for their veteran savvy. They all played key roles helping Houston dominate the AL West.

Pouncing on the availability of veteran starting-pitcher aces, however, was the most decisive factor in Houston's rise to dynasty aspirations. Luhnow began by acquiring longtime Tigers ace Justin Verlander (and most of what remained of his costly multiyear contract) at the end of August 2017, when Houston held a comfortable division lead. With Keuchel as their ace since 2014, the Astros already had one of the league's best starting staffs to begin the 2017 season. But pitchers are inherently vulnerable to injuries and pendulum-like swings in performance. Keuchel started 9–0 in his first 11 starts, then missed two months with a pinched nerve in his neck. Collin McHugh, without whose 19–7 record in 2015 the Astros would not have made the wild-card game, missed the first half of the season with arm problems. Free agent pickup Charlie Morton missed seven weeks. By trading for Verlander, Luhnow was fortifying his starting rotation for the competitive rigors of the postseason. Verlander won all five of his starts, giving up just four runs and 17 hits in 34 innings; beat Boston twice in their division series, including getting the win in 2⅔ innings of relief in Houston's series-clinching win in Game Four; and won both his starts against the Yankees in the ALCS.

Less than three months after winning the 2017 World Series, Luhnow traded for Pittsburgh ace Gerrit Cole to send the unmistakable message the Houston Astros intended to be *the* favorite to repeat. Cole did the most with his two Astros years before becoming eligible for free agency after the 2019 season—35–10, a 2.68 ERA, 602 strikeouts in 412⅔ innings—helping the Astros to two more division titles, two more appearances in the ALCS, and another trip to the World Series. And in July 2019, Luhnow made it three aces in Houston's starting rotation by trading for Diamondbacks veteran right-hander Zack Greinke, who was 8–1 in 10 starts the rest of the way. The Astros' farm system had sufficient depth in talent that Luhnow could surrender one of their previous first-round picks in each of his trades for Verlander, Cole, and Greinke without surrendering the prospects he considered most important to sustaining a dynasty—most notably Alvarez and outfielder Kyle Tucker, chosen by Houston fifth overall in the 2015 amateur draft. Alvarez was promoted to Houston in June and Tucker in July. Blasting 27 homers with 78 runs batted in and a .311 batting average in just 87 games, mostly as a DH, Alvarez was voted 2019 Rookie of the Year.

As accomplished as they were, both Verlander and Cole benefited from the Astros' emphasis on analytics to improve their recent performance after they got to Houston. Based on their data, the Astros encouraged the 34-year-old Verlander to throw more sliders than he had in Detroit and Cole to throw more curveballs than he had in Pittsburgh. The strikeout ratios of both pitchers increased dramatically, and opponents' batting average against both pitchers plummeted after they were given the data-driven insight that "helped show guys what they do well," as Verlander put it. In his 73 starts for the Astros from September 2017 through 2019, Verlander boosted his strikeout ratio to 12.1 from 9.5 K's per 9 innings and held opponents to a .183 batting average compared to .215 in his last 73 starts for the Tigers dating back to August 2015. Cole had averaged just 8.4 strikeouts per 9 innings in his five seasons with the Pirates, and opposing batters hit .254 against him. In his two years as an Astro, Cole boosted his strikeout ratio to 13.1 and held opponents to a .192 batting average.

That both the Cubs and the Astros rose so quickly from the depths of their division to become two of baseball's powerhouse teams in the second half of the 2010s popularized tanking as a rebuilding strategy. The basic model was to dramatically cut player payroll; endure a handful of very bad seasons of 90, 100, or even more losses for the payoff of being one of the first teams to choose among the most coveted players in the annual amateur draft; develop talent depth in the minor leagues; promote top-tier prospects to the majors as soon as they are ready; and as a new core of young players begins to take root on the major-league club, complement them with experienced, often high-priced veterans through targeted trades and free agent signings.

By 2020, several other teams were on the path of self-destruction blazed by Chicago and Houston. In 2017, the year after the Cubs put an end to their "lovable losers" history, Detroit's Tigers, winners of 86 games the year before with a largely veteran roster but a fallow farm system and carrying the burden of several expensive long-term contracts, decided it was time to start over. After enduring a summer of mounting losses, the team traded Verlander and outfielder Justin Upton, their best position player, at the end of August in a salary dump. Detroit ended the season with 98 losses, lost 98 again the next year, then lost 114 games in 2019 for not only the worst record in the majors, but the worst record in baseball since an earlier Tigers team had lost 119 in 2003.

As soon as former Yankees icon Derek Jeter, the face of the Miami franchise's new ownership group, assumed responsibility as CEO of the Marlins in October 2017, he began tearing the club apart to build anew. The Marlins had not had a winning record since 2009. They did, however, have an outstanding core of increasingly expensive young players—outfielders Giancarlo Stanton, Christian Yelich, and Marcell Ozuna, all three outstanding hitters and the presumed foundation for a contending Miami team in the years ahead. The previous franchise owners had given Stanton a record-setting 13-year, $325 million contract in 2014 and Yelich a seven-year deal worth nearly $50 million in 2015, and Ozuna was likely to earn a hefty salary increase in arbitration. Jeter quickly determined that the Marlins were not close to competing for a division title and thought Miami's star players, just entering their prime years, would be too costly to build around—particularly Stanton and Yelich, whose deals were backloaded for huge salaries in the years ahead. Before spring training in 2018, Jeter had traded all three. The Marlins went on to have the worst record in the National League in Jeter's first two years as their boss.

In 2018, in the midst of a horrendous season just two years after finishing second in the tough AL East with 89 wins to capture a wild card seeding in the postseason, Baltimore's Orioles traded virtually all of their best players—including shortstop–third baseman Manny Machado, considered one of baseball's premier players—to reduce payroll and acquire prospects to help rebuild a farm system that ranked among baseball's worst. The Orioles finished the season with a 15–40 record after the July 31 trade deadline, ending up with a franchise-worst 115 losses. Baltimore followed up by losing 108 games in 2019

None of those teams, however, could be sure their approach would lead to the same level of success—several years as an imposing contender, World Series championship included—as it had for the Cubs and Astros. Tanking is a viable and potentially successful strategy for those franchises in the middle of the linear spectrum of willingness to be very bad for several years in order to emerge, phoenix-like, as a championship-caliber team. On one end, franchises like the Yankees, the Dodgers, and likely the Red Sox can't ever sell being deliberately very bad now to be very good later to their fan bases, which expect, almost as a birthright, their teams to be consistently competitive. When the 2016 Yankees gave up on the season by trading top relievers Aroldis Chapman to the Cubs and Andrew Miller to the Indians for prospects, it was *not* to give up on the *next* season. Their expectation was to compete in 2017, which indeed they did, ending up a wild-card team, just two games behind in their division.

On the other end of the spectrum, small-revenue teams in "tank" mode—like Detroit, Baltimore, and Miami—risk finding themselves constantly having to start over. Their limited revenues make it difficult to acquire high-priced expensive veterans—like the Cubs did with Heyward, Zobrist, and Chapman and the Astros did with Verlander, Cole, and Greinke—to complement players developed in their farm systems. And assuming their top draft picks and prospects traded for pan out, keeping them together for long before they became too expensive to keep becomes a challenge. The Astros and Cubs, by contrast, were both in the sweet spot of being able to justify to fans not accustomed to consistently competitive teams the merits of losing big now to win big later, while also having the financial resources to invest in expensive players around young talent and to keep them together long enough to make a year-after-year run at championship seasons—perhaps even ultimately building their fans' expectations for continued excellence that would make future tanking a problematic proposition.

14

BASEBALL'S POWER DYNAMIC

Muscling Up and Mowing Them Down

There were 6,105 home runs hit by major-league batters in 2017, shattering the old record of 5,693 set in the year 2000, at the height of the steroids era, by more than 400. That was a 9 percent increase from the 5,610 soaring out of the park in 2016 and a more than 24 percent increase from the 4,909 homers hit in 2015. Miami's Giancarlo Stanton led the majors with 59 homers. (Some might argue Stanton came the closest to catching Maris for the *legitimate* single-season home run record, given the steroids dalliance of McGwire, Sosa, and Bonds.) Yankees rookie Aaron Judge led the American League with 52. Strikeouts increased by 3 percent, from 38,982 in 2016 to 40,104. It was the tenth straight year that a new record was set for strikeouts. Twelve starting pitchers averaged more than 10 strikeouts per 9 innings. Boston's Chris Sale, Arizona's Robbie Ray, and Washington's Max Scherzer averaged more than 12.

The next year—2018, a season that saw major-league hitters collect 41,020 hits (of which 5,585 were homers)—there were 41,207 strikeouts. The pitching staffs of six major-league teams alone struck out more batters than innings pitched. Astros and Yankees pitchers struck out more than 10 a game. Houston's starting pitchers, accounting for almost two-thirds of their staff's innings, averaged 10.4 K's per 9 innings. Gerrit Cole, with 276 strikeouts in 200⅓ innings, and Justin Verlander, with 290 in 214 innings, averaged more than 12. Yankees relievers—the most imposing (and feared) in baseball—led major-league bullpens with a strikeout ratio of 11.4 per 9 innings. Throwing 41 percent of their team's innings, Yankees relievers got 42 percent of their outs by blowing away batters. Closer Aroldis Chapman had a K/9 ratio of 16.3 in 51⅓ innings, and setup man Dellin Betances had 15.5 in 66⅔ innings.

It was not only the 11th straight year that a new record was set for strikeouts, it was also the first ever in which there were more strikeouts than hits in the major leagues. The gap between hits and strikeouts had been narrowing to the extent that such an outcome was ultimately inevitable. Still, it was quite a shocking fact to have to embrace once it happened. Never for the life of them would earlier generations involved and interested in baseball have thought such a development *could*, let alone *would*, happen—not managers, not players, not sportswriters or the broadcast media, and not fans. All told, baseball's 30 major-league teams averaged 8.5 strikeouts per game, meaning that nearly one-third of all outs did not involve a fielding play.

Then came 2019. New records were set for strikeouts and home runs. And once again, for just the second time in history, there were more strikeouts (42,823) than hits (42,040). At 8.9 per 9 innings, strikeouts accounted for almost exactly one-third of all outs. Twenty-six percent of all at-bats and 23 percent of all plate appearances ended with a K. Fourteen teams averaged at least a strikeout an inning, led by the Astros with 10.3 strikeouts per 9 innings and the Red Sox with 10. Houston and Tampa Bay were the only teams whose starting pitchers averaged more than 10 strikeouts per 9 innings. Relievers in the Boston, Milwaukee, and Yankees bullpens had a K/9 ratio over 10.

But for all those strikeouts, home runs increased by 21 percent from 2018, to 6,776. In fact, pitchers in 2019 gave up 11 percent more home runs than ever before, shattering the record set just two years before by a phenomenal 671 bombs. The year proved quite the slugfest. In May, major-league hitters set a new record for home runs in a month. They broke that record in June and again in August. On August 30, Minnesota's Twins broke baseball's single-season team record of 267 home runs, set by the Yankees just the previous year. There was still one month, 28 games, to go. Five days later, on September 4, the Dodgers passed the 249 homers hit by the Astros in 2000 to set a new National League record with twenty games remaining on their schedule. Just six days after that, on September 11, with 18 days of the regular season left to play, the 2017 single-season record for home runs was breached at Camden Yards in

Baltimore when the Orioles' Jonathan Villar blasted the 6,106th homer of 2019 off Dodgers reliever Caleb Ferguson. The irony was that three weeks earlier the Orioles had broken the record for home runs *given up* by a team in a single season.

New York Mets rookie first baseman Pete Alonso led the majors with 53 homers, eclipsing Judge's rookie record from two years before. By the end of the year, the new major-league team record for home runs was Minnesota's 307. The Yankees blasted 306, and the Astros (now in the AL) with 288 had also surpassed the previous record. Home runs accounted for more than half the runs scored by the Yankees and Twins— 51 percent for both teams. The Dodgers ended up with 279 home runs for the new National League record. The Cubs and Brewers also finished with more homers than the Astros hit in 2000, and the Braves matched them. Baltimore pitchers watched baseballs they threw soar beyond outfield fences 305 times.

Major League Baseball has been defined by the power game—home runs and strikeouts—since the steroids era bracketing the last decade of the twentieth century and the first of the twenty-first. In baseball's eternal battle between pitcher and batter, the power game has always mattered. With runners on base, the strikeout is the pitcher's (and his team's) most formidable weapon because it negates the risk of a ball carrying over the fence, a base hit, or a fielding mishap or misjudgment if the ball is put into play. With or without runners on base, the home run is baseball's most formidable offensive weapon because it reduces the need for a string of hits or a combination of hits, walks, and errors to score runs before three outs are made.

The 5,000-homer barrier was crossed for the first time in 1998—the year McGwire blasted 70, Sosa 65, Griffey 56, and Greg Vaughn 50. That was the first of nine consecutive years of more than 5,000 homers hit in the major leagues, including the record-setting 5,693 in 2000. Whereas for most of the last half of the twentieth century between 30 and 34 percent of all runs scored on a home run, from 1998 to 2008 the figure was always at least 35 percent and sometimes as high as 37 percent. Even when scoring dropped to its lowest levels since the early 1990s between 2010 and 2015, after the 2007 Mitchell Report broke the steroids scandal wide open, it was significant that the long ball continued to account for between 34 and 37 percent of total runs scored. Coincident with the resurgence in home runs in 2016, when 5,610 were blasted—the most since 2000—the percentage of runs that scored on the back of the long ball reached 40 percent for the first time ever. By 2017, when a new record for home runs was set, that number was 42 percent, and in 2019, when the home run record was broken yet again, 45 percent of runs trotted home thanks to the long ball.

Since the artificial redline of the steroids era, baseball had gotten homer-happy. Major League Baseball was going through what was arguably the long-delayed sequel to—if not a reimagining of—the power revolution in offense Babe Ruth had kicked off nearly a full century earlier. When major-league batters breached 6,000 homers for the first time in 2017, five players hit more than 40 and a total of 117 had at least 20 home runs. Two years later, 129 batters contributed to another record-setting year with 20 or more homers, 10 of whom had more than 40. When the previous record (once removed) was set in 2000, there were 102 players with 20 or more homers and 16 with 40.

Clearly, it was not just bona fide sluggers reaching for the fences with unprecedented frequency. It was almost everybody in the lineup, from the top of the order (traditionally the get-on-base table-setters), through the middle of the order (traditionally where power hitters were slotted for the express purpose of driving in runners on base), to the bottom of the order (traditionally the place to park the team's weakest hitters, who typically played the most important defensive positions). In 2019, the leadoff and second-place hitters in their teams' batting order combined for 25 percent of baseball's record-setting 6,776 home runs. Twenty-one years earlier, when McGwire and Sosa made their epic run at the Maris record, those spots contributed only 17 percent of the majors' home run total.

From the earliest days of the 2019 season, baseball's homerfest raised questions about why it was. Pitchers were frustrated, angry, and even outspoken about the unprecedented number of home runs they were giving up. Justin Verlander had perhaps the best year of his Hall of Fame–worthy career with a 21–6 record and 300 strikeouts in 223 innings. He was virtually unhittable, giving up just 66 runs. But 45 of those runs, more than two-thirds, trotted home courtesy of the 36 homers hit off him. The 36 long balls were not only far more than he had surrendered in any previous year, they accounted for 26 percent of the 137 hits he allowed to opposing batters. In Verlander's 14 previous big-league seasons, by contrast, only 11 percent of the hits against him were home runs, scoring 34 percent of the runs he gave up. Half of the 66 runs (59 earned) given up by fellow Astros ace Gerrit Cole, 20–5 for the year with a league-best 2.50 earned run average and 326 K's in 212⅓ innings, came on the 29 home runs he surrendered among 142 total hits.

Use of performance-enhancing drugs could never be discounted, despite baseball's strict testing policies and tough penalties for violations, because of drug cocktails and dosing protocols designed to make them much more difficult to detect. But that didn't stop players from trying—and from being caught cheating. Six players in 2019 and five the previous year—including the 35-year-old eight-time All-Star Robinson Cano—received 80-game suspensions for failed drug tests. But most pitchers, including Verlander, blamed the baseball. Many said it felt different in their hand, affecting the movement they relied on to fool batters and get outs.

Commissioner Rob Manfred insisted that Major League Baseball had done nothing to change the baseball, that indeed—as much as fans might dig the long ball—franchise owners did not want to increase the number of homers in ballgames and were likewise perplexed by what was happening. Historically, that was the fallback position that baseball's powers-that-be had always taken whenever there was speculation about whether balls were "livened up" to promote the power game, such as in the 1920s when Babe Ruth's prodigious, awe-inspiring home runs were captivating fans. Two weeks before the 2019 All-Star Game, however, the commissioner suggested in an interview on Fox Sports Radio that while specifications, production processes, and materials had not changed, Rawlings—the manufacturing company now owned by Major League Baseball—had more precisely centered the core of the baseballs it was producing for the major leagues, the effect of which "could be" to reduce drag in flight.

Much commented upon was the approach batters were taking—call it a fly ball, deep into the night, revolution—to hitting the baseball. Even hitters with modest power were tailoring their swings for higher launch angles to deliberately drive the ball into the air. And they were tailoring their swings to produce *less* backspin so that balls hit into the air would travel not just higher but deeper, to outfield fences and beyond. Increasing exit velocity—how hard the ball is hit when the batter makes contact—became a key objective for improvement.

These were not only lessons learned from the accelerating advance of baseball analytics made possible by technological innovation, including high-definition motion-capture video that could break down every nano-second of baseball action with extraordinary precision, they were teach-able. Teams invested in the necessary technology to provide informative data to players and coaches. They hired coaches and trainers knowledge-able in biomechanics and skilled at helping players make even tiny ad-justments that could mean a big difference in how well they made contact with the ball. This was combined with intense study of pitchers' tenden-cies. Many players turned to private hitting coaches using biometric equipment to improve their approach at the plate.

Power pitching was the corollary to power hitting. For pitchers, the stakes were high in virtually every at-bat because so many more batters were power threats than their predecessors in earlier pitching generations had to worry about. The stakes put a premium on fighting fire with fire by overpowering batters trying to drive the baseball out of the park—for as much of the game as possible, starting with the starting pitcher and end-ing with the closer, not to mention eighth-inning setup guys and situation-al relievers called upon to get an out at a crucial time of the ballgame, all throwing blazing hard—in the upper 90s, some touching 100 miles per hour on their fastball.

In the year Mark McGwire hit 70 homers, Cubs rookie Kerry Wood fanned 233 batters in 166⅔ innings—an average of 12.6 per 9 innings—breaking Randy Johnson's K/9 record of 12.3 set the previous year. Wood and Johnson were the only pitchers until then to have averaged more than 12 strikeouts per 9 innings. Johnson had done so twice before, and did so again in 1998, pitching for Seattle and Houston, while leading the majors with 329 strikeouts. In a power pitcher tour de force, 1998 was the first of five consecutive years he led the majors in strikeouts, averag-ing 349 and 12.3 K's per 9 innings from 1998 to 2002. In 1999, Boston's Pedro Martinez became the first to average more than 13 strikeouts per 9 innings when he K'd 313 in 213⅓ innings, only to see his 13.2 K/9 ratio overtaken by Johnson's 13.4 in 2001.

To put this into historical perspective, none of baseball's premier pre–World War II strikeout pitchers with dominating fastballs that batters feared to face had a single season in which they averaged that many K's per 9 innings—not Cy Young, not Rube Waddell (who came close with

8.4 in 1903), not Walter Johnson, Dazzy Vance, Lefty Grove, or Dizzy Dean, not even Bob Feller. The first qualifying pitcher to strike out more than a batter an inning was rookie left-hander Herb Score, averaging 9.7 K's per 9 innings in 1955 and 9.5 the next year. Sandy Koufax, another lefty, became the second pitcher to strike out more than a batter an inning, and the first to fan more than 10 per 9 innings, in 1960. Not until four years later did two qualifying pitchers—Sam McDowell, also left-handed, and Koufax—have a K/9 ratio of at least 9. (Jim Maloney, in 1963, became the first right-hander to exceed a strikeout an inning.) It was not until 1997 that as many as six qualifying major-league pitchers averaged more than a strikeout an inning. Of the 110 times a qualifying starting pitcher's strikeout ratio was more than 10 per 9 innings since Koufax in 1960, all but 17 have been since the end of the players' strike in 1995.

In 2019—the Year of the Home Run—power pitching shared the limelight with power hitting; 37 of the 90 pitchers making at least 25 starts averaged at least a strikeout an inning. Twenty-three of them averaged more than 10 K's per 9 innings. Gerrit Cole led the majors with 326 strikeouts in 212⅓ innings, averaging 13.8 K's per 9 innings for the highest qualifying K/9 ratio in history—only to be broken by Cleveland right-hander Shane Bieber's 14.2 K/9 ratio in 2020. But Bieber's major-league-leading 122 strikeouts came in just 77⅓ innings over 12 starts because of the pandemic that limited the 2020 season to just 60 games. Max Scherzer's 12.7 strikeouts per 9 innings was the fifth-highest ever. And of the 119 relievers coming out of the bullpen in at least 54 games—one-third of the 162-game schedule—77 struck out a batter an inning, 54 with a K/9 ratio of at least 10. Milwaukee closer Josh Hader, averaging 16.4 Ks per 9 innings in the 61 games and 75⅔ innings he pitched, blew away 48 percent of the batters he faced. Twelve others averaged at least 13 strikeouts per 9 innings.

Year after year of record-setting strikeouts was a sharp break from the past—even the relatively recent past—attributable to the explosive increase in home runs. From the time the Babe first showcased the majesty and game-changing, bases-clearing power of his home runs after becoming a Yankee in 1920, strikeouts have always been presumed as the downside risk of swinging for the fences. Ironically, the power game Ruth inaugurated did not lead to a proliferation of strikeouts. Baseball's roaring '20s, when the number of home runs in both leagues soared, was also the decade when teams averaged fewer strikeouts per game than in any other—just 2.8, compared to 7.8 nine decades later between 2010 and 2019. Not a single player, slugger or otherwise, went back to his bench a strikeout victim as many as 100 times from 1915 until 1932. Notwithstanding his swinging for the fences all the time, Ruth never struck out more than 93 times in a season. Lou Gehrig never fanned more than 84 times.

When baseball's home run onslaught picked up steam in the 1950s with power-laden teams like New York's Yankees and Giants, Brooklyn's Dodgers, Milwaukee's Braves, and Cincinnati's Reds, strikeouts remained relatively contained. In 1956—the record-setting year for home runs (2,294) before expansion—only four batters struck out as many as 100 times. Mickey Mantle, whose 56 home runs anchored his Triple Crown season, skulked back to the bench punched out by the pitcher 99 times. It wasn't until the expansion year of 1961 that 10 batters whiffed 100 times. In 1970, Bobby Bonds reached new heights of futility by striking out an astonishing (for the time) 189 times, breaking by two the record he had set the previous year. Although Bonds, father of a six-year-old named Barry, smacked 26 home runs in 1970, what was particularly unsettling to many baseball thinkers at the time was that he was batting leadoff for San Francisco. Bonds's single-season strikeout record held up for a third of a century before Adam Dunn whiffed 195 times while slugging 46 homers in 2004.

As power hitters became less sensitive to striking out beginning in the 1960s, they nonetheless were, for the most part, practiced at protecting the plate when they faced a two-strike count, particularly with runners on base so as not to shortchange a rally by striking out. Sluggers like Frank Robinson, Willie Mays, and Hank Aaron were embarrassed by too-frequent strikeouts. For all his 755 career home runs, Aaron did not have a single 100-K season, and Mays with 660 homers and Robinson with 586 had just one with that many strikeouts—Mays, not until he was 40 years old. Most batters, meanwhile, were not cast as sluggers and did not pretend they were. They understood their job to be getting on base or advancing runners. 'Twas better to put the ball in play and force the defense to make outs than to give them outs by taking big swings that might miss or by not swinging at all on close pitches that might be called strikes.

That changed as a result of both the influential growth of advanced analytic measures and the power surge of the steroids era that began after the players' strike. Sabermetric analysts built a statistical case validating Earl Weaver's contention that "the easiest way around the bases is with one swing of the bat," as he wrote in his 1984 book *Weaver on Strategy*; that a walk was as good as a single and also had the advantage of driving up a pitcher's pitch count; and that on-base plus slugging percentages had an intrinsic value higher than batting average alone, which was a guiding principle of Oakland GM Billy Beane's Moneyball approach. Even with runners on base, for most managers an out was an out, whether by putting the ball in play or striking out trying to drive the ball a long distance. And striking out was preferable to hitting into a double play. For batters, the risk of a K next to their name was worth it for the possibility of an announcer yelling, "Going, going, gone!" over the airwaves.

The steroids era may have discredited many outsized individual ac-complishments—including those of McGwire, Sosa, and Bonds—but it did not discredit the invigorating appeal of home runs or their indisput-able value as the most efficient way to score runs. The sluggers didn't care about the strikeouts that went with them. Dunn's record 195 K's as a batter was eclipsed by Ryan Howard just three years later in 2007, when the Phillies slugger whiffed 199 times while belting 47 homers. Howard had to live with that black mark for only one year, because in 2008 the Diamondbacks' Mark Reynolds went down on strikes 204 times, for which he hit 28 home runs. It was the first of three straight years Re-ynolds fanned more than 200 times, including 223 K's (still the record) in 2009.

The 200-K threshold has been crossed 13 times by nine different players since Reynolds's first time. In 2018, an unprecedented three bat-ters struck out in excess of 200 times. Collectively, the three batters—Yoan Moncada, Giancarlo Stanton, and Joey Gallo—were strikeout vic-tims in one-third of their plate appearances. Swinging for the fences, Gallo hit 40 homers, Stanton 38, and Moncada just 17, for which he struck out a major-league-leading 217 times. Moncada, like Bobby Bonds nearly half a century before, mostly batted leadoff. Of the 129 players who clubbed at least 20 homers in 2019 to contribute to a record-setting year in home runs, 98 were also strikeout victims 100 or more times. In all, a record-setting 161 batters had at least 100 K's entered into the scorebook by their name.

And for pitchers, the challenge was to overpower hitters, particularly with runners on base, and go for the strikeout. Just as batters did, pitchers refined and even redesigned their craft to accommodate the fact that baseball was now a power game. Putting maximum effort into virtually every pitch became routine for relievers and starters alike. Velocity and movement mattered as much as location. Because pitches thrown in the upper-90s meant hitters had to decide almost immediately once the pitcher released the ball whether to take or swing, most pitchers began trying to avoid throwing in the strike zone to elite hitters, especially power hitters. They focused on establishing command—proving they *could* pitch in the strike zone without necessarily having to—and using movement to get batters to chase pitches off the plate. Nearly a third of swing-and-miss strikes in the first half of the 2019 season, and more than half (58 percent) of all pitches thrown, were outside the strike zone, according to data on pitch location, compared to less than 20 percent in 2002, the first year such data was available.

The downside, however, of the emphasis for pitchers—especially starting pitchers—on throwing as hard as they could for as long as they could was the significant risk of injury. The tremendous torque and strain on the muscles and tendons in their shoulders, upper back, arms, and elbows meant that few pitchers averaging a strikeout an inning escaped the likelihood, at least once and frequently more often, of time on the injured list or entire seasons (and more) lost to physical rehab and surgeries—predominantly Tommy John surgery to replace frayed ligaments. It happened to journeyman pitchers; it happened to elite pitchers. And past injuries, especially if accompanied by surgery, or the potential for such injuries because of how hard pitchers throw remains a factor in teams' hesitancy to give even elite pitchers in the free agent market five-to-seven-year long-term contracts. But just as fans did dig the long ball, so too were they fired up by a string of K's. In baseball's eternal battle between pitchers and batters, both sides aiming for dominance, the power game prevails.

15

STRATEGIZING PITCHING

The clash between two titans with powerful offenses in the 2019 American League Championship Series—Houston's 107-win Astros versus New York's 103-win Yankees, runaway winners in the AL West and AL East—was also a clash between pitching philosophies. The Astros, with their trio of aces—Justin Verlander, Gerrit Cole, and Zack Greinke—aligned with the long-standing tried-and-true tradition that superior starting pitching is the foundation for championships. Prioritizing starting pitching depth as the means to navigate through the month-long postseason, the Astros acquired Tigers ace Verlander on the last day of August 2017 despite having an insurmountable 11½-game lead; in January 2018, as defending World Series champions, they traded for Pirates ace Cole; and on the last day of July 2019, with a comfortable 7½-game lead but still smarting from losing the 2018 ALCS to Boston in five games, they dealt for Diamonbacks ace Greinke.

If the Astros were a throwback, the Yankees were masters of the now well-established paradigm that championships cannot be won without a reliable and stout corps of relievers fronting a shutdown closer, all of whom threw hard—very hard—to navigate through the last three innings of a ballgame where their team had the lead. They came into the ALCS with an intimidating, indomitable tag-team of four relievers earning a combined $41 million in 2019—Chad Green, often manager Aaron Boone's first call to the bullpen when Yankees starters faltered, including early in games; Tommy Kahnle and Adam Ottavino, who pitched most often in the sixth and seventh innings to protect leads; and lefty Zack

Britton, usually the eighth-inning setup man—leading up to closer Aroldis Chapman and his fearsome-velocity pitches. And that didn't include
Dellin Betances, earning $7 million in his final year before free agency,
out all season with shoulder and latissimus injuries after averaging 14.6
strikeouts per 9 innings as their setup man the five previous years. Chapman's strikeout ratio per 9 innings in 2019 was 13.4, Kahnle's 12.9,
Green's 12.8, and Ottavino's 11.9. Britton's strikeout ratio was only 7.8,
but his superb sinker limited the 245 batters he faced during the season to
a .182 batting average.

It wasn't like the Astros didn't have a solid bullpen and the Yankees
didn't have competent starting pitching. In both 2018 and 2019, Houston's bullpen was stingier in giving up runs than Yankees relievers. But
the Astros did not have the depth or overpowering pitch intimidation of
the Yankees' cadre of relievers. The Yankees' starting rotation was unex-
ceptional, not mediocre. While Houston had the best starters' ERA in the
American League in both 2018 and 2019, the Yankees were fifth and
sixth in the league, and their starters threw significantly fewer innings.
Their ace, Luis Severino, missed the entire 2019 season with injuries until
he returned for a late September tune-up in preparation for the postseason. Lefty James Paxton, acquired in a preseason trade and 15–6 with a
3.82 earned-run average, was the Yankees' only pitcher to make at least
20 starts with an ERA under 4.00. Masahiro Tanaka (11–9, 4.45) was the
only Yankees starter to throw at least 162 qualifying innings. Those were
acceptable trade-offs for the Yankees, given the depth and quality of their
bullpen.

Unlike Houston, which was willing to add substantial salary and sent a
player chosen in the first round of prior amateur drafts to secure each of
their trio of aces, the Yankees were unwilling take on high-salary multiyear contracts and reluctant to trade coveted prospects for an established
ace to bolster their starting staff for the postseason. The Astros were able
to get Verlander in 2017 in large part because the Yankees, exercising
fiscal restraint, passed on the opportunity because his salary for the two
years remaining on his contract was more than they wanted to spend. In
any case, New York had already acquired Oakland A's putative ace Sonny Gray, whose annual salary was more than $24 million less than Ver-
lander's, surrendering a first-round draft pick sidelined by Tommy John
surgery. While Verlander was nearly untouchable in winning all five of
his starts with Houston in September, Gray was a pedestrian 4–7 in 11

starts after coming to New York. That decision came back to haunt them when they lost the 2017 ALCS to the Astros in seven games, in which Verlander beat the Yankees in both his starts, giving up just one run in 16 innings.

The Pirates would have traded Cole to New York instead of Houston in January 2018 for either Gleyber Torres or Miguel Andujar, their top minor-league prospects. The Yankees said no. Then the Yankees passed on veteran lefty Cole Hamels in July, even though they were still in contention for the AL East against a Red Sox team with superior starting pitching, because the floundering Texas Rangers wanted a top prospect in exchange. Instead, the Yankees traded two lesser-regarded minor leaguers to Toronto for much less costly veteran lefty J. A. Happ, while the Cubs made a deal for Hamels to bolster their starting pitching in their fight with the Brewers for the NL Central Division title.

While the Yankees did earn a wild card and won the wild-card game in both 2017 and 2018, their relatively pedestrian starting rotation compared to the teams they were up against cost them in the postseason. In their loss to Houston in the 2017 ALCS, just one Yankees starter lasted seven innings in the seven-game series, while the Astros had three of their starters throw at least seven innings. In 2018, the Yankees were derailed in their division series by the Red Sox, whose starters pitched into the seventh inning in three of the four games. Tanaka was the only Yankees starter to go as many as five; none of New York's three other starters lasted more than three innings, giving up a combined 14 runs in their collective eight innings of work.

Despite that recent history, the Yankees, as they did on Jake Arrieta the previous off-season, passed on the top two starting pitchers on the 2018 free agent market—Houston's Dallas Keuchel and Arizona's Patrick Corbin—to fortify their starting rotation for 2019. Instead, they traded for Paxton. But injuries that decimated the Yankees' staff, including Severino's season-long tenure on the injured list and Paxton's struggles in June and July before he was sidelined for a month, quickly reinforced that lack of starting-pitching depth was a fundamental weakness in need of correction to win in the postseason. Even though the Yankees were in command of their division by mid-July, there was criticism over their decision *not* to strengthen their corps of starting pitchers for the postseason—particularly when Houston, a powerhouse team vying with the Yankees for the best record in the American League, traded for

Greinke to join their already imposing starting corps featuring Verlander and Cole. The Yankees were placing their bets on their bullpen depth in overpowering relievers to carry them to, and through, the World Series.

The formula the Yankees embraced—choosing to spend on bullpen depth in power relievers rather than higher-priced pitchers to reinforce the depth of their starting rotation—was an arguably extreme bow to the new paradigm for pitching. Complete games by now were a relic of the past. Of the 4,858 games started by major-league pitchers in 2019, only 45 were complete games—less than 1 percent. Just three years before, there were 83, and in 2000, the 234 complete games thrown accounted for nearly 5 percent of all starts. In 2019, major-league starting pitchers averaged slightly more than 5 innings, the minimum necessary for them to get credit for a win; in 2000 it was 6 innings, and 20 years earlier they averaged 6⅓ innings. Led by Verlander's 223 innings pitched, only 15 pitchers in 2019 threw as many as 200. In the not-too-distant past, 200 innings were routine for starting pitchers taking their turn every fifth day in the rotation. As recently as the year 2000—the turn of the century—36 pitchers threw at least 200 innings; 20 years before that, it was 56 pitchers with 200 innings, 16 of whom threw over 250.

In the new paradigm, in the making since the 1980s, six innings was the expectation for most starting pitchers before their velocity and command began to diminish. Top-tier starters with high strikeout totals, like Verlander, Greinke, and Cole, were counted on for seven innings or maybe even eight, depending on pitch count, the threshold for which typically was between 90 and 120 to prevent fatigue-related injuries. Most other starting pitchers were given a shorter leash. For fourth and fifth starters the expectation was often just five innings, on the premise that a pitcher with less-than-dominant stuff, having gone twice through the batting order, would be clobbered by hitters seeing him for the third time in a game. In either case, the starting pitcher's role was to hand a lead to a succession of relievers waiting in the wings, most with dominating power pitches of their own, ultimately culminating in a final-inning coup de grâce by the team's closer.

The Hall of Fame inductions of Roy Halladay, Mike Mussina, and Mariano Rivera in mid-July 2019 serves as a kind of bookend barometer to how much the game has changed in expectations for starting pitchers and end-of-game relievers. Mussina and Halladay were among the last of the old-school starting pitchers for whom pitching in excess of 200 innings every year and pitching into the late innings, completing games if their managers would allow it, was a point of pride. Rivera is the Babe Ruth of the bullpen. He stands above—far above—all the rest who have ever trotted in to save games. His accomplishments may be even more unassailable than the Babe's.

The year Mussina made his big-league debut with Baltimore—1991—was the first that complete games dropped below 10 percent. The next year he completed 8 of his 32 starts, not including the nine innings in a game that went into extra innings, and threw four shutouts. Mussina worked no fewer than 203⅓ innings in 10 of his first 12 years, and one of the years he didn't—1994—he almost certainly would have if not for the players strike that cancelled the last six weeks. By the time Halladay emerged as a top-tier starting pitcher with the Blue Jays in 2002, complete games were down to 5 percent in the American League and 4 percent in the major leagues. He completed only 2 of his 34 starts that year but led the league with 239⅓ innings. The next year his 266 innings were 24 more than anyone else in baseball, and his 9 complete games in 36 starts tied for the major-league lead with Mark Mulder and Bartolo Colón. The three of them accounted for nearly a quarter of the 110 complete games thrown by American League pitchers in 2003. From 2003 to 2011, Halladay completed 61 of his 269 starts—a phenomenal 23 percent in a time when less than 4 percent of starts were complete games—leading his league seven times in nine years, all while winning 69 percent of his decisions.

Halladay finished his career with 67 complete games in 390 starts. Mike Mussina had 57 in 536. On the day they celebrated their Hall of Fame enshrinement in July 2019, the active pitcher with the most career complete games was the Yankees' CC Sabathia, in his nineteenth year, with 38. And Sabathia had not thrown one in 112 starts dating back to April 2015, when what would be the last complete game of his career ended as an eight-inning loss; had the Yankees tied that game in the ninth, he would not have had one then either, since he almost certainly would have been replaced on the mound. None of baseball's top pitchers since Halladay's last injury-free season in 2011 have matched the 8 complete games he threw that year in 32 starts—not Clayton Kershaw or Max Scherzer; not Cory Kluber or Chris Sale: all great pitchers, along with Sabathia, with a justifiable expectation of one day joining Halladay and

Mussina in Cooperstown. The most complete games by any pitcher since then is 6.

It's worth noting that only 12 of Mussina's 57 complete games came in the 248 starts he made in his eight years in New York beginning in 2001, and 8 of those were shutouts. In 2008, his final year, on his way to the only 20-win season of his career, Mussina pitched as many as eight innings in only 3 of his 34 starts. The reason is that in all his years in pinstripes, the Yankees not only had dominating bullpens, they had the incomparable Mariano Rivera to close out victories.

Although he averaged only 8.3 strikeouts per 9 innings as a reliever and had only six seasons in which he struck more than a batter an inning, Rivera defined the model of the nearly unhittable power reliever. He did so by perfecting a vicious cut fastball that overwhelmed both right-handed and left-handed batters, no matter the excellence of their pedigree. As if his 652 career saves—to which the closest is Trevor Hoffman's 601 compiled in an 18-year career from 1993 to 2010 that earned Hoffman a place in the Hall of Fame the year before Mariano's unanimous selection—weren't enough, as if his 2.02 earned run average and holding opposing hitters to a .208 batting average against him since becoming the Yankees' closer in 1997 weren't enough, Rivera in 96 post-season games allowed just 11 earned runs in 141 innings for a 0.70 ERA, with an 8–1 record and 42 saves. In 24 World Series games, Rivera had 11 saves with a 0.99 earned run average. If Mariano does not rest comfortably on the rocking chair made of shattered bats from their turns against him that the Minnesota Twins gave him to honor his career in his final year in 2013, it is only because they were sawed off by his cutter, after all.

The balance between starting and relief pitching has been an evolutionary work in progress since the beginning of baseball time. At first, relievers replaced starting pitchers unable to pitch further because of injury or fatigue. As managers began removing starting pitchers more frequently when they were ineffective or in games that were losing causes, their relievers were drawn from a combination of young pitchers trying to make a case for themselves as starters, pitchers whose case for staying in the big leagues required a duality of roles, and veteran pitchers with vast experience but declining skills riding out the end of their careers.

For decades, top-tier starting pitchers often doubled as their team's relief ace to save close games. That 30 percent of the games thrown by Lefty Grove and Dizzy Dean—two of baseball's most prominent aces in the 1920s and 1930s, both hard-throwing strikeout pitchers—in their prime years were in relief testifies to the value managers placed on the merits of power pitching to get outs to secure victories long before the Age of the Closer. The concept of a dedicated relief ace had yet to take hold; teams did not see the need to give a quality pitcher the exclusive role as their ace out of the bullpen to save the day, and no pitcher thought "I'm a reliever" was a lucrative career path.

It wasn't until after World War II that teams began emphasizing the importance of a dedicated corps of relief pitchers. By the 1960s, as teams began to exceed an average of two pitching changes in games starting pitchers failed to finish, the number of full-time relievers on pitching staffs necessarily came to equal the number of core starters, with some specializing in long relief roles that also conditioned them for spot-starting assignments when necessary. Relief pitching was now its own honorable baseball profession, although pitching prospects still preferred the glamor of a starting role and nearly all the best young pitchers were groomed to be starters. But it was the relief ace—the "fireman"—to whom the glory went in the bullpen. Their role was to come into games to stop late-inning rallies, then pitch to the end for the win or the save. It was not unusual for them to throw two or even three innings.

The fireman era, extending into the 1980s, was in some respects the golden age of relief pitching. The first two relievers elected to the Hall of Fame pitched in this era—Hoyt Wilhelm in the 1950s and '60s and Rollie Fingers in the 1970s and '80s—as did the progenitors of the hard-throwing intimidating closer, perhaps best exemplified by Dick Radatz and Goose Gossage. The imposing Radatz, nicknamed "The Monster" for his towering 6-foot-6, 230-pound build, averaged 10.6 strikeouts per 9 innings in 207 relief appearances between 1962 and 1964. And in the era's fading years, the Yankees' Goose Gossage, also in the Hall of Fame, averaging 9.5 K's per 9 innings in 209 relief appearances from 1980 to 1983, was every bit as fiercely frightening to opposing teams.

The Age of the Fireman blended seamlessly into the Age of the Closer. The principal difference for the closer was his entry into the game in the last inning for the specific purpose of getting three outs. Unlike firemen relievers, closers rarely were called upon to put out a rally and were rarely expected to have to get more than three outs, except in the vortex of must-win games for a division title or in the postseason. Their job was not fire suppression but fire prevention. Although by the late 1980s the trend toward teams' top relievers being one-inning closers had already begun, or at least was well on the way to inevitability, Dennis Eckersley is often considered the prototype closer—and an excellent one he was. Mariano Rivera, of course, has since become the role model for closing perfection.

There has since been an ongoing debate on the relative merits of the closer paradigm versus the fireman concept in which the argument is made, including by Gossage in the role of cranky old fireman, that closers have the easier job because they typically start the last inning with no-body on base and with a lead that could be as many as three runs. Ace relievers in the fireman era of Wilhelm, Radatz, Fingers, and Gossage, frequently entering games with runners on base in the eighth and even seventh innings, typically pitched in more high-stress situations where the outcome of the game was more perilously at stake. Since the beginning of the 1980s, that role has been dispersed among specialists in the bullpen with designated roles leading up to the closer.

Relief corps are now designed to preclude even the possibility of late-inning rallies by designating eighth-inning and even seventh-inning setup men whose responsibility is to be the pre-closer to the closer. Should a lead be jeopardized in the pre-closer innings, managers can call on a situational reliever for the purpose of facing one batter to get one out, or perhaps two if a double play can be had. What they all had in common—closers, setup men, and situational relievers—was "nasty stuff" thrown hard—very hard. By the middle- to late 2010s, nearly every team had as many as four or five pitchers in the bullpen who consistently threw in the high-90s and could approach 100 miles an hour "on the radar gun." The closer on virtually every team in the majors, including every team that made the postseason in 2018 and 2019, averaged better than a strikeout an inning.

In the history of relief pitching, what began as a strategy of managing to win by bringing in a top-flight fireman or closer to save the game had evolved into a strategy of managing not to lose by not allowing a starting pitcher to blow a lead in the later innings of a ballgame. By the late 2010s, bottom-of-the-rotation starters were pulled so often in the middle innings if they allowed a runner on base, sometimes even with a lead of two or three runs, that many did not get much experience trying to pitch their way out of a jam that they might call upon in the future. A longer leash was given to elite starters, but most were on pitch counts that rarely allowed them to last eight innings, let alone pitch complete games. And even if they were in command and efficient, managers rarely let them finish close games—that's what the closer was for, after all—and even more rarely games where they had a large lead, because there is no upside to a starting pitcher throwing any more pitches than necessary in a game whose outcome is all but assured.

The new orthodoxy had other drawbacks as well. It made structuring and handling the pitching staff the most critical and complex task for front office executives and managers in the dugout. Teams were constantly value-engineering their pitching staffs. As with starting pitchers, few relievers were "elite," defined as consistently outstanding over multiple seasons. To accommodate the parade of relievers, which increased in number every year from three pitching changes per game in 2010 to 3.4 in 2019, team rosters became bullpen-pitcher heavy at the expense of position player depth on the bench. Aside from the interminable three hours it was routinely taking to play nine innings because of so many situational pitching changes, managers sometimes went to the bullpen so often in the course of a game that they depleted their cadre of available pitchers, leaving them shorthanded should the game go into extra innings. Finally, there were more unhappy returns than teams would care to admit on the strategy of not letting a starting pitcher lose his lead. Overworked hard-throwing relievers were prone to big swings in effectiveness from year to year, and even within seasons, often because of injury. And the more high-90s fastballs batters saw, the better they became at hitting them, particularly against pitchers with speed but little movement on their pitches.

The two National League teams with arguably the best starting pitching in 2019—Washington's Nationals, with Max Scherzer, Stephen Strasburg, and Patrick Corbin as their top three, and New York's division rival Mets, with Jacob deGrom, Noah Syndergaard, and Zack Wheeler as theirs—were both cursed with nightmarish bullpens. Mets relievers failed to hold the lead in 21 percent of their save situations, and their collective 4.99 ERA was the fifth worst in the majors. It wasn't supposed to be that way. During the off-season, the Mets hit the free agent market to bring back former closer Jeurys Familia, this time as an eighth-inning setup guy, and traded for Seattle closer Edwin Diaz, whose 57 saves led the American League in 2018 with 15.2 strikeouts per 9 innings. To say that neither lived up to expectations would be an understatement. They were both terrible. Familia's earned run average in 66 games was 5.70, and Diaz, despite striking out 15.4 batters per 9 innings, gave up 15 home runs in 58 innings, lost seven of the 33 games he was called upon to save, and had a 5.59 ERA.

The Nationals' bullpen earned run average of 5.68 was the second worst. No team gave up as many runs in the final three innings—during which managers routinely turn to their bullpen to protect leads—as Washington, whose ERA those innings was an unsightly 5.58. While the 2019 Mets were done in by their bullpen, relief woes only cost the Nationals the NL Eastern Division title. Having committed $93 million of their payroll to veterans Scherzer, Strasburg, and Corbin, the Nats had little margin for improving their unreliable bullpen either before or during the season even as it became a growing liability. The Nationals nonetheless earned a wild-card berth and then relied on their trio of aces as both starters and relievers to make the World Series for the first time in franchise history. Strasburg pitched three superb innings in relief of Scherzer to win the wild-card game; Scherzer pitched once and Corbin twice in relief as the Nationals took down the league-best Dodgers in their five-game division series; and Corbin pitched once in relief in the Nats' sweep of the Cardinals in the NLCS.

Rookie right-hander Ryne Stanek started 29 games for the Tampa Bay Rays in 2018, second on his team behind Blake Snell, whose 21–5 record and 1.89 earned run average in 31 starts earned him the AL Cy Young Award. Stanek was one of 63 pitchers to make at least 29 starts that year; 36 of them won more than they lost, 23 lost more than they won, and 4 others had an equal number of wins and losses. Even though starting pitchers—even the best of them—were not expected to go the distance anymore, that kind of distribution in won-lost records among regular starters would have been recognized by every past generation of major-league pitchers.

But Stanek in 2018 was an unprecedented outlier. The Rays went 15–14 in the 29 games Stanek started. He was charged with two of the losses. Ryne Stanek was not credited with a single win—not one—even though his team won more than half of his 29 starts and he started the second-most games on the club. All but eight of the 63 pitchers making that many starts officially qualified for the ERA title by pitching at least 162 innings. The indomitable CC Sabathia, who turned 38 that July, pitched 153 innings. Only two pitchers making at least 29 starts threw fewer innings—Philadelphia's Vince Velasquez, who worked 6 fewer innings in 30 starts, and Stanek, who pitched many fewer. Although he was trusted by his manager to make 29 starts, Stanek did not pitch more than 2 innings in any of them. Hence, by rule requiring the starter to throw at least five innings to qualify for a win, he could not win any game he started, even if his team did. In 29 starts he threw only 40 innings. Total. By design. Ryne Stanek was called upon by Tampa Bay to be an opener, not a traditional starting pitcher.

Rays manager Kevin Cash used an opener 55 times in 2018. More than a third (31) of his team's 90 wins were in games started by openers. It was a radical strategy born of necessity. Snell was the only healthy reliable starter the Rays had, and Tampa Bay did not have starting pitcher depth. Rays games started by openers were designed to be "bullpen" games. The opening pitcher in Cash's game plan was always a hard-throwing reliever whose starting mission was to throw for only an inning or two before yielding to a succession of relievers—typically, first a contrasting pitcher with significant movement on his pitches capable of throwing three or four innings, followed by another hard thrower—that would hopefully land the game on the doorstep of the closer to save. It worked for the Rays, with the ironic result that Tampa Bay ended the season with the best starters' ERA in the American League, notwithstanding their averaging fewer than four innings a start, thanks to 55 games started by an opener.

Having an opener to start games that would otherwise be handled by mediocre bottom-tier starting pitchers whose game longevity was likely to be no more than twice through the batting order was a new wrinkle—a perfectly logical corollary to using the closer to secure a victory. The concept rested on the fact that more runs are scored in the first inning than any other. Just as the role of a hard-throwing, dominant closer is to prevent the other team from scoring in the final inning, the role of the opener is to prevent the other team from scoring in the first. As such, the opener's job description also calls for a pitcher with dominant stuff: in this case, specifically to go against the opposing team's best hitters, almost all invariably slotted at the top and middle of the batting order.

Stanek faced just 162 batters in the 29 games he opened in 2018; he blew away one-third on third strikes—53 in 40 innings, and he did not allow a run in 22 of his 29 game openings.

Oakland's Athletics, still in the hunt for the 2018 AL Western Division title, began employing an opener for the final month after two of their core starting pitchers were sidelined by injuries in late August. Liam Hendriks, a hard-throwing right-handed reliever, returned from his own two-month stint on the disabled list to start the first inning eight times in September, typically every three days. He did not allow a run in any of those first innings, and only in his first start did he pitch into the second, giving up two runs. In a September 4 start against the Yankees he retired all three batters he faced before manager Bob Melvin turned the game over to a succession of relievers. That probably contributed to Melvin's gamble to go with Hendriks as his opener against the Yankees in the win-or-go-home wild-card game. This time, however, Hendriks walked the leadoff batter, gave up a two-run homer to Aaron Judge, and escaped the rest of the first inning unscathed. But the Yankees had a lead they never surrendered.

Milwaukee Brewers manager Craig Counsell played a different angle of the opener gambit by using a "decoy" starting pitcher in Game Five of the 2018 NLCS against the Dodgers. 'Twas a move reminiscent of the Deadball Era (and occasionally even later), when prospective starting pitchers were not routinely announced and teams sometimes warmed up two pitchers to keep the other team guessing which would really start. Counsell's decision to start southpaw Wade Miley was unsurprising. Miley was pitching on three days' rest and had yet to allow a run in two starts and $10\frac{1}{3}$ innings so far in the postseason. Counsell's intent, however, was for Dodgers manager Dave Roberts, who platooned at several positions, to commit to a predominantly right-handed batting order against the lefty Miley; Counsell would then bring in right-hander Brandon Woodruff to force Roberts to decide very early in the game whether to swap out some of his righty batters for left-handers. As scripted, Miley walked off the mound after facing just one batter, whom he walked on five pitches. While the decoy worked, the Brewers wound up losing the game. It would be unfair to say the strategy itself failed, because the winning runs scored in the late innings when the game would have been in the hands of Brewers relievers anyway. Miley started the very next game two days later, for real this time, pitching 4⅓ innings to help his team to a Game Six victory. Milwaukee lost the series in seven games.

The Rays' proof of the concept gave the opener gambit traction with other teams the very next year. But while for Tampa Bay using an opener was a deliberate choice in lieu of relying on a five-man rotation, the other teams that relied on bullpen games the most in 2019—the Mariners in 27 games, Blue Jays in 22, Angels in 21, and Yankees in 20—did so principally as an expedient to bridge injuries or ineffective pitchers in their starting rotations. The Jays, Angels, and Mariners were among the 10 major-league teams whose starting pitchers combined for a horrific earned run average over 5.00. The Yankees, faced from the beginning of the season with the injury loss of Luis Severino and persistent questions about the durability of Sabathia, decided in mid-May that the opener-bullpen game gambit was worth trying whenever they did not have a fifth healthy pitcher in their starting rotation. The four teams with the worst records in baseball, however—the Royals with 103 losses, Marlins with 105, Orioles with 108, and Tigers with 114—whose starters' ERAs were also well over 5.00, as well as the Rockies, whose pitchers had the worst starters' ERA in the majors, rarely, if ever, used an opener to alleviate the pressure on their ineffective five-man rotations.

The 2019 ALCS showdown between pitching philosophies—the Astros' den of elite starters versus the Yankees' pen of power relievers—came down to openers and a bullpen game in Game Six for both clubs. One reason that happened was the recent trend of teams forsaking the back end of their starting rotation in the postseason, considering their season-long fourth and fifth starters to not be up to the challenge for the high stakes and stress of short postseason series. The ALCS had returned to Houston, the Astros holding a three-games-to-two lead.

The bullpen game both teams were forced into—an elimination game for New York, a possible advance to the World Series for Houston—seemed to favor the Yankees, one of the teams that used the stratagem the most during the regular season and had success doing so. The Yankees won the first 11 times they used an opener and were 13–7 in their 20 bullpen games. The Astros had started an opener only three times all year, losing all three. Hard-throwing Chad Green was the obvious opener for the Yankees in their must-win bullpen game; during the regular season, the Yankees were 11–4 in his opener starts, in none of which he went more than two innings, and he was the losing pitcher only once. His earned run average in 19⅓ innings as the opener was 3.72, and he struck out 32 of the 84 batters he faced. The Astros went with Brad Peacock, who began the season as their fifth starter until shoulder problems took him out of the rotation and landed him on the injured list at the end of June. He had pitched in only seven games since—including a scoreless inning in Game Five—all in relief.

Green gave up a three-run homer in the first inning. Peacock surrendered a run in the second. Six pitchers followed Green to the mound for the Yankees, and Yankees batters faced six Astros relievers after Peacock—the last of whom was closer Roberto Osuna, who entered in the ninth inning to protect a 4–2 lead to win the pennant. Except the Yankees weren't done yet. Osuna gave up a two-run homer. Aroldis Chapman, their overpowering closer, took over for the Yankees in the bottom of the ninth. He retired the first two Astros. He walked a batter. And then a no-doubt-about-it walk-off home run by Jose Altuve sent Houston to the World Series. It was his last pitch of 2019.

Chapman had been through this ignominy before, in the 2016 World Series, Game Seven. He was the closer for Chicago's Cubs, trying to put an end to 108 years since they last won a World Series. The Cubs held a 6–3 lead over Cleveland when the Indians began to rally in the eighth. A two-out single convinced manager Joe Maddon to call on Chapman and his 100-mile-per-hour fastball to get the final four outs. But this was also the fifth time he was pitching in the World Series, following appearances in eight of the Cubs' 10 previous 2016 postseason games. Chapman gave up a double and a home run to the first two Cleveland batters he faced, blowing the save, before getting the final two outs of the inning. The Cubs, however, got him off the hook—indeed, he got the win—with a 10th-inning rally to end their championship drought. Unlike then, two years later when Chapman walked off the field, it was amidst the Astros' celebration of a pennant.

Aroldis Chapman was only the latest closing ace to perp-walk off the mound having given up a decisive home run that sent his team with championship pretensions home for the winter a loser. Teams' reliance on closers makes the role exceedingly stressful, especially when division titles, pennants, and World Series are at stake. The consequences of failure in baseball's most high-profile games—to which none are immune, not even the greatest of them—has in some cases proven devastating to the confidence and competence of the closer who blew it. The careers of Donnie Moore and Mitch Williams, both considered elite closers at the time, disintegrated after they surrendered home runs that lost the lead they had just been called in to protect—Moore in the 1986 ALCS and Williams in the 1993 World Series—and their teams a pennant (the 1986 Angels) or a World Series (the 1993 Phillies).

Armando Benitez, the Mets closer with 41 saves in 2000, is perhaps best remembered, notwithstanding his 289 career saves, for blowing a ninth-inning lead to the Yankees in Game One of the World Series, greasing the skids for another Yankees championship. The modest major-league career of Byung-Hyun Kim, just the third Korean-born player to make it to the major leagues, is remembered for his failure to protect a two-run Arizona Diamondbacks ninth-inning lead in Game Four that would have given the D-Backs a three games-to-one lead in the 2001 World Series; Tino Martinez hammered him for a home run to tie the score, after which he gave up Derek Jeter's game-winning home run the next inning. The next day he served up a game-tying two-run homer to Scott Brosius that ultimately led to another Yankees win.

While those home runs might forever haunt Kim, the D-backs' young Korean closer was spared from having to live forever with the burden of costing his team the World Series when none other than the great Mariano Rivera had his own blown save and loss in Game Seven. It was his 52nd postseason appearance, during which he pitched 79 innings and faced 299 batters, and only the second time he blew a would-be Yankees win. The first time was Game Four in the 1997 division series when Rivera gave up a game-tying home run to Cleveland's Sandy Alomar in a game that, had the Yankees won, would have sent them into the ALCS. Instead, the Indians finished off the Yankees the next day.

In 1997, Rivera was in only his first year as the Yankees' closer. So too was Dennis Eckersley in his first full season as Oakland's closer in 1988 when he blew the save and took the loss on a game-winning walk-off two-run pinch-hit homer by barely-able-to-walk Kirk Gibson in Game One of the World Series that propelled the Dodgers to a five-game rout of the A's. Their blown saves in turning-point games that cost their teams a critical postseason series could have derailed either pitcher's career as a closer. (It should be remembered that Eckersley had prior long experience as a starting pitcher.) But they were the relatively rare exceptions of closers being able to shrug off the ignominy of giving up series-deciding game-winning runs and continuing to be stellar in their roles, building their case for all-time greatness. Three years after losing Game Seven of the 2001 World Series, Rivera would have his own Byung-Hyun Kim moments in Games Four and Five when his back-to-back blown saves helped pave the way for Boston's epic comeback to win the 2004 American League Championship Series. After that he pitched 26 games in nine more postseason series, giving up only 2 earned runs in 32⅓ innings without blowing another save opportunity.

Notwithstanding the overwhelming importance of high-powered closers, the tension and the stakes of decisive games in the postseason—especially in league championship series and the World Series—are such that managers have not always preferred to close out those games with their closer. In the deciding fifth game of the 2016 division series between Los Angeles and Washington, it was Dodgers starting ace Clayton Kershaw who finished off the Nationals, relieving ordinarily stellar closer Kenley Jansen in the bottom of the ninth after he had walked two batters in a one-run game. Kershaw got the final out on a strikeout. By Game Seven of the 2017 World Series against Los Angeles, Houston manager A. J. Hinch had lost confidence in his closer, Ken Giles, despite his 34 saves and 83 K's in 62⅔ innings during the season, because he had given up 10 runs in 7⅔ innings in five postseason games. Instead of Giles, Hinch allowed Charlie Morton, a starter who averaged 10 strikeouts per 9 innings that year, to pitch the final four innings for the win. And in the Red Sox' five-game takedown of the Dodgers in the 2018 World Series, manager Alex Cora did not turn to All-Star closer Craig Kimbrel, more than half of whose outs in 62⅓ innings during the regular season were strikeouts to secure the final three outs. He turned instead to his number one starter, Chris Sale, who struck out the side.

With the Yankees and their superior corps of relievers watching on TV (if they watched at all), the 2019 World Series was teed up to be a classic matchup of two teams with outstanding starting pitching—the Houston Astros and their trio of aces against the Washington Nationals and theirs. Notwithstanding their collective excellence, the new pitching orthodoxy made it virtually a given that none of the aces would be on the mound at the end of any games, at least not as the starting pitcher. Patrick Corbin was the only Nationals starter to throw a complete game all year, a shutout against woeful Miami in May. Justin Verlander was the only

Astros pitcher to complete a start—he had two, one a 2–1 loss and the other a no-hitter nine days later in Toronto.

The Nationals won in seven games. They won all four of the games started by Max Scherzer and Stephen Strasburg. Their three aces, including Corbin, who lost his only start, surrendered 12 runs in 30⅓ innings. Houston's trio gave up 16 runs in 36 innings. Gerrit Cole lost the opener but was dominant to win Game Five; Verlander lost both his starts, giving up 7 runs in 11 innings; and Zack Greinke did not get a decision in either of his starts, although his 2.45 ERA in 11 innings was the best of the six aces headlining the World Series.

Ironically, but not unexpectedly as many Astros fans in their home ballpark watched with trepidation when it happened, it was the prevailing philosophy of *not* letting a starting pitcher lose a lead after the fifth or sixth innings that might well have cost Houston Game Seven and the World Series. Greinke took the mound in the seventh inning, protecting a 2–0 lead, having given up just one hit and walked a batter. But Anthony Rendon belted a home run with one out. And Greinke walked the next batter. Even though he had thrown just 80 pitches, Greinke had been precise and efficient. Nonetheless, his manager marched to the mound to relieve Greinke, explaining later that he thought his starter had reached his limit for the night.

The Astros' bullpen, however, had a troubling 4.47 earned run average through the first six games of the series. Hinch also had Cole throwing in the pen, on two days of rest following his stellar start in Game Five. Instead of calling on Cole with the tying run on base to get the last two outs of the inning, Hinch went to Will Harris, who had given up a home run the previous day that put Game Six out of reach. Harris did so again on the second pitch to the first batter he faced. And the Nationals had a lead they did not relinquish, thanks in large part to Washington manager Dave Martinez calling on Corbin, one of his trio of aces, to replace a tiring Scherzer in the sixth. Corbin worked three scoreless innings to earn the win before handing the game off to the Nationals' closer in the ninth. Hinch was left to explain that he had *not* brought in Cole to shut down the Nats in the seventh because he was saving him for a ninth-inning save. Alas, Gerrit Cole's Chris Sale moment never came.

16

NOT THE SAME FREE AGENCY, OR BACK TO THE FUTURE

It wasn't supposed to be this way. Two of baseball's brightest young stars, both in their mid-20s, and a handful of top-tier pitchers were on the market in one of the most anticipated free agent classes in recent history. At least one of the bright young stars was expecting a blowout record-setting contract. It didn't happen that way. 'Twas the free-agent class of 2018.

The bright young stars were Bryce Harper and Manny Machado. Both had debuted in 2012. Both had seven years in the big leagues. Both had just turned 26. Until Machado was sent to the Dodgers for prospects before the 2018 trade deadline, they played within 65 miles of each other—one in Baltimore, the other in Washington, DC. Harper had played 927 games for the Nationals, starting 912 in the outfield; Machado had played 926 major-league games, all but 66 for the Orioles, beginning his career at third base before shifting over to shortstop in 2018. Harper was one of the most feared sluggers in the game. Machado was outstanding defensively and formidable offensively, with four straight years of 33 or more homers heading into free agency.

Even though Machado was, objectively speaking, the player with the better career through exactly the same number of seasons and playing almost exactly the same number of games—an average of 5.5 wins above replacement per 650 plate appearances compared to 4.6—Harper was considered the superior talent. He was presumed to be such a godsend to baseball that he was featured on the cover of *Sports Illustrated* as a 16-

year-old high school ballplayer in 2009. He was promoted to the Washington Nationals as a 19-year-old in April 2012 after just a year and 21
games in the minor leagues and promptly won the National League's
Rookie of the Year Award. Three years later, at the age of 22, Harper
banged 42 home runs to lead the league, his .330 batting average was
second, just two hits short of the league leader, he topped the majors in
both on-base and slugging percentages, and he was (unsurprisingly) the
unanimous choice for National League MVP. That, however, was his
only great season.

Fourteen position players accumulated at least 30 wins above replacement in the first seven years of his career, but Bryce Harper was not one
of them, dragged down by three years in which his player value was less
than 2 wins above replacement—the typical standard for an everyday
regular. Machado, whose career total of 34.1 wins above replacement
through 2018 outpaced Harper's 27.5, never had the equal of Harper's
stunning 2015 campaign but was much more consistent. Every year except his MVP season, Harper went through at least one monthlong stretch
where he struggled at the plate. Given his imposing physical presence at
the plate and potential for a home run every time he came to bat, Harper
sometimes had a tendency to start chasing pitches when he was given
nothing in his zone to hit.

If Manny Machado was expecting to break the bank, Bryce Harper
was anticipating becoming the first major-league player to sign a contract
worth at least $400 million, notwithstanding only one truly outstanding
year so far in his career. At the very least, Harper was expecting to exceed
the 13-year, $325 million deal the Miami Marlins gave outfielder Gian-
carlo Stanton, who had just turned 25 with five major-league seasons
behind him, as a contract extension in November 2014. Along with Harper and Machado, Stanton was one of baseball's young power-hitting stars
expected to be an impact player well into the 2020s. His average annual
player value of 5.7 wins above replacement per 650 plate appearances
since 2012, the rookie year for both Harper and Machado, exceeded both
higher-profile stars.

The entire off-season went by without either being signed. Their asking price was too high. Spring training 2019 began and neither had a new
team to report to. Houston lefty Dallas Keuchel, the most accomplished
starting pitcher on the free agent market, didn't either. Neither did Boston's exceptional closer Craig Kimbrel. (Dodgers ace Clayton Kershaw

would have been the best pitcher up for grabs had he not signed a $93 million, three-year extension soon after opting out of his existing contract.) The only top-ranked free agent to get a lucrative long-term deal before the end of December was Arizona Diamondbacks lefty Patrick Corbin, signed by Washington for six years and $140 million to join an already imposing starting rotation including Max Scherzer and Stephen Strasburg.

Kimbrel, one of baseball's elite closers, was expecting a long-term contract comparable to the five years and $86 million the Yankees gave Aroldis Chapman in December 2016 and the five years and $80 million Kenley Jansen got as a free agent in January 2017 to stay with the Dodgers. All three were rookies in 2011. Chapman entered the free agent marketplace in 2016 with 181 saves in 199 opportunities the five previous years, averaging 16 K's per 9 innings by striking out 44 percent of the batters who dared dig in against him. Jansen entered the market that same year on the back of two 40-save seasons in three years and having whiffed 40 percent of the batters he faced, just under 14 strikeouts per 9 innings. Now, two years later, Kimbrel's résumé was equally impressive—332 saves in 366 opportunities, striking out 42 percent of the batters he faced, in the eight years since his rookie season. With the Chapman and Jansen deals as his baseline, Kimbrel wanted a six-year contract worth $100 million.

Keuchel entered free agency in 2018 having won 60 percent of his decisions in 145 starts since 2014 with a 3.28 earned run average. He won the Cy Young Award in 2015, his 20–8 record pacing the Astros from 91 losses the year before to 86 wins and a wild-card berth, then beat the Yankees in the wild-card game. In 2017 he was 14–5, helping the Astros to their first of three straight 100-win seasons. Although he had since been eclipsed on Houston's staff by Justin Verlander and Gerrit Cole, his résumé should have been attractive to many competitive teams looking to shore up their starting pitching, including the Yankees.

Manny Machado finally agreed to a record 10-year contract worth $300 million with the San Diego Padres two weeks after the start of spring training. Ten days later Bryce Harper reached a $330 million, 13-year deal with the Philadelphia Phillies, eclipsing Stanton's record contract. Both were ready for opening day. But there was still no starting rotation for Dallas Keuchel or closer's role for Craig Kimbrel even as the 2019 season got underway, at least not for the minimum terms they and their agents were demanding. Both finally agreed to undervalued contracts in June: Keuchel took a one-year deal to start for the Braves and Kimbrel a three-year deal to close for the Cubs.

Times had certainly changed. Free agents the caliber of Harper, Machado, Keuchel, and Kimbrel would once have been signed and off the market by Christmas. And this was not just happening to free agents at the high end of the performance spectrum. A waiting game had become the norm for accomplished veteran free agents who were not elite players but whose experience would clearly fortify competitive teams and improve the prospects of teams on the threshold of contention. Until now, it had not been unusual for players in their early 30s to get multiyear deals of four or five years that paid well based on recent performance. Now they languished unsigned when teams convened for spring training and remained unsigned as spring training progressed, with many still unsigned when the 2019 season began. Many settled for contracts much less than fair-market value for their performance in recent years and projected performance for the immediate year or two ahead.

And the free agent class of 2018 wasn't the first this was happening to, making it a trend that the players' union found profoundly disturbing. In the previous year's free agent class, Kansas City third baseman Mike Moustakas, having just set career highs in homers and runs batted in, and veteran catcher Jonathan Lucroy, one of the best at his position just a few years before, both wound up signing *one-year* contracts for much less money than they expected a month into spring training just to be able to play baseball in 2018. Confident of securing a lucrative multiyear deal, Moustakas had turned down Kansas City's qualifying offer of $15 million for 2018, but because the qualifying offer meant that the club signing him would forfeit a pick to his former team in the supplemental round of the amateur draft, Moustakas had no takers. He was forced to re-sign with the Royals for one year at $5.5 million—$3.2 million less than he had earned the previous year when he belted his Royals team record 38 home runs.

It was the same story for nonelite veterans in the free-agent class of 2018. Harper's former teammate in Washington, 33-year-old lefty Gio Gonzalez, was unable to leverage his consistency and durability into a contract worthy of his experience and success—a 120–86 record and 3.49 ERA while averaging over 30 starts and 187 innings without any significant injury since 2010. After earning $12 million the three previous years,

Gonzalez had to accept a one-year, $2 million deal with Milwaukee a month into the season. Likewise, Machado's former teammate in Baltimore, 33-year-old Adam Jones—a five-time All-Star, consistent and rarely hurt, averaging 147 games a year since becoming the Orioles' everyday center fielder in 2008—had to settle for a one-year, $3 million deal with Arizona nearly a month into spring training after averaging over $15 million in salary the five previous years. And back as free agents, Moustakas, despite having just hit 28 home runs for the Royals and Brewers in 2018, and Lucroy, notwithstanding his helping Oakland to the wild-card game, again failed to gain traction in the market. Moustakas was forced to re-sign with Milwaukee after no other teams showed interest in giving him an extended contract, and Lucroy quickly signed a one-year deal with the Angels in December for a mere $3.3 million.

Players in the most recent free agent classes were being stiffed in the marketplace, some missing the first critical weeks of spring training with what would be their new teams and forced to accept contracts below market value in duration and compensation, and major-league players and their union were growing angrier at the injustice of it all. What the heck was going on? Was baseball really going back to the future—back to 1994?

In the late 1980s, the players called it "collusion." Baseball's independent arbitrator agreed, and the owner-run institution of Major League Baseball suffered huge financial penalties. Thirty years later, Major League Baseball and the owners called it "good business practices." It may not have been institutional collusion where team owners were directed to back off from big long-term contracts or explain to the commissioner why they chose to spend big on free agents, or where franchises shared information on contracts being negotiated or offered. There was no coordinated conspiracy not to sign other teams' star players. But franchises were mostly playing off the same page of "good business practices" that could hardly be disputed as *not* good practices for running a profitable business enterprise. The three principal factors now affecting the free-agent market—for which the players and their union had no good answers—were the luxury tax, a player's age, and baseball's analytics revolution.

The players and their union had conceded to the concept of a "luxury tax"—the owners' linguistic artifice to get around the ugly words "salary cap"—in the collective bargaining agreement reached after the devastating strike of 1994–1995. During the going-nowhere negotiations that led up to the strike, the union spurned the very idea of a luxury tax as nothing more than a de facto salary cap that would incentivize teams to keep their payrolls below some arbitrary limit to avoid being "taxed." But having stared into the abyss of an existential threat to the game, the union reluctantly agreed to a three-year trial run, beginning with a tax of 35 percent on payrolls over $51 million in 1997—a figure that only the Yankees and Orioles had exceeded the previous year. But once it was agreed to by both sides, there was no going back.

The luxury tax—formally called a "competitive balance tax," another linguistic artifice by Major League Baseball to get around the ugly insinuation that clubs like Steinbrenner's Yankees were being punished for wanting to field the best team they could afford—became permanent in the next collective bargaining agreement, approved in 2002. The baseline payroll threshold, which would increase each year of the five-year deal, began at $117 million. The Yankees were the only franchise exceeding that figure when the agreement was signed, and only the two New York teams—the Mets by less than $200,000—would cross that threshold in 2003. By 2018, the second year of the latest collective bargaining agreement, the threshold was up to $197 million, and the tax penalties were reset to 20 percent for teams exceeding the threshold the first time, 30 percent the second time, and 50 percent every time after that. The 2017–2021 agreement included a 12-percent surcharge on payrolls $20 million-to-$40 million above the threshold, and up to 45 percent on payrolls in excess of $40 million. Teams more than $40 million above the threshold were also penalized with a lower order of selection in baseball's annual amateur draft.

Even though only eight of Major League Baseball's 30 teams had ever paid the competitive balance tax, and only three had done so more than three times—the Yankees, 15 straight years from 2003 to 2017; the Red Sox, eight times; and the Dodgers, five—the escalating ladder of surcharges in the latest collective bargaining agreement was clearly intended by the owners to encourage those teams over the threshold, six in 2016 and five in 2017, to get back under. The bone given to the players was that any time a team dipped below the threshold for being assessed a penalty, its tax rates were reset. And so, when the Yankees and Dodgers both substantially cut their payroll in 2018 to avoid being taxed, the widespread assumption was that baseball's two wealthiest and most profitable franchises were resetting so that they could go after the likes of first-time free agents Harper and Machado, both of whom were expecting to sign long-term deals that would pay them between $30 and $40 million a year. Instead, both clubs exercised unexpected restraint in the 2018 free agent marketplace.

Because of their history of extravagant spending, especially on free agents, the Yankees were the weather vane for how both the players and the owners viewed the salary-suppression implications of the luxury tax. From the union's perspective, the Yankees' willingness to sign baseball's best players to rich multiyear contracts, even in the face of monetary penalties, made the luxury tax tolerable because the top-dollar value of their contracts set the parameters—a trickle-down effect—not only for other free agents, but for outstanding players in their salary arbitration years. In his heyday, George Steinbrenner had made clear that he liked free agency precisely because he could afford to pay the best players more than his rivals. He was the only owner to vote against the luxury tax in baseball's 2002 collective bargaining agreement. When his heirs to the Yankee dynasty, sons Hal and Hank, asked Bud Selig for relief from the Yankees' competitive balance tax and revenue-sharing burdens in 2011, the commissioner bluntly said no and suggested they get below the luxury tax threshold.

But the next-generation-Steinbrenner Yankees, now committed to fiscal restraint, intended to stay under the luxury tax. They were no longer going to pursue the best free agents with record-setting contracts, even to fill positions of relative weakness. This meant the best free-agent players could not leverage a high-priced Yankees offer to try force an ever-upward bidding war for their services between the New York Yankees and other teams, which would have a trickle-down effect on less-coveted free agents. Having trimmed their 2018 payroll to fall below the competitive balance tax line for the first time in 15 years, even after trading for Giancarlo Stanton and the remaining 10 years of the record-setting deal he signed with the Marlins, the Yankees won 100 games—their most since winning the World Series in 2009. More significantly, the Yankees were considered to be one of the favorites for a pennant and World Series bid in 2019 with the team they had, whether or not they added a Harper, a Machado, or a top starting pitcher like Keuchel or Corbin. The old Steinbrenner regime would have chased—and won—any of those four in an effort to lock it up. The new Steinbrenner regime concluded that the playoff payoff for their big spending wasn't worth it.

The Yankees' engagement with the 2018 free agent market was particularly illuminating. When the Yankees methodically adhered to their plan to fall below baseball's luxury tax threshold in 2018 for the first time since 2003, the widespread assumption was that they were setting the stage to sign Bryce Harper. Even with an outfield that included the sluggers Stanton and Aaron Judge, already with 83 home runs in just 294 big-league games, the prospect of Harper giving the Yankees an unprecedented trio of Bronx Bombers seemed too enticing a prospect to pass up, or at least to explore. Moreover, for most of his time in Washington, Nationals fans expected Harper to defect to the Yankees once he became a free agent—if for no other reason than the expected money, not to mention his affections for the "forever" dynasty as a kid in Las Vegas. Manny Machado should have been particularly attractive to the Yankees because shortstop Didi Gregorius was going to miss most, perhaps even all, of the 2019 season recovering from Tommy John surgery. And given the fragility of their starting rotation, the Yankees were assumed certain to go aggressively after Patrick Corbin—a high-profile pitcher on the free agent market—with an advantage over other potential suitors being that Corbin, growing up in Upstate New York, was also a Yankees fan.

There would have been no surprise had the Yankees signed two of the three. There was widespread speculation the two would be Corbin and Machado. The Yankees *were* active in the free agent marketplace, just not for those players. They met with all three but concluded early on that their outfield and power situation was fine—even though Harper would have provided a left-handed slugging counterpoint to Judge and Stanton, both right-handed batters—and backed off from vigorously pursuing Corbin and Machado. Instead, the Yankees spent more than $200 million to sign two of Colorado's free agents, infielder DJ LeMahieu and reliever Adam Ottavino and to retain four of their own players—starting pitchers J. A. Happ and CC Sabathia and reliever Zack Britton, all three of whom were free agents, and center fielder Aaron Hicks, whom they signed to a seven-year, $70 million contract extension. General manager Brian Cashman justified it as the Yankees having other priorities, specifically, ensuring they retained the most imposing pen of shutdown relievers in the game. None of their free agent signings was for more than three years.

The last time the Yankees spent extravagantly on high-profile free agents was committing $438 million to sign Jacoby Ellsbury, Brian McCann, Carlos Beltran, and Japanese pitcher Masahiro Tanaka after missing the postseason in 2013 with their worst record in 21 years. They had an even worse year in 2014, failing for a second year in a row to play beyond the regular season. Except for Tanaka, signed for seven years and $155 million, that foray into the free agent market did not pay the championship dividends the Yankees expected. Beltran, signed for three years, was 37 in his first year with the Yankees, and Ellsbury, whose contract was seven years, and McCann, a catcher signed for five, were both 30 in 2014. The Yankees were especially badly burned by the $153 million they gave Ellsbury, rewarding him for his seven years playing for archrival Boston. When healthy, Ellsbury was an impact player, but he had a disturbing history of injuries that followed him to New York. By 2018, a year Ellsbury missed entirely with hip and foot injuries, the Yankees were done with him, notwithstanding the $63 million they still owed him for the 2018 through 2020 seasons.

To paraphrase Yogi Berra: veteran players were getting older a lot younger than they had in the steroid-fueled days of Barry Bonds and Roger Clemens. To whatever unknown extent they and others had been using performance-enhancing drugs to extend their careers at a high-level of performance, testing was making that a risky gambit for aging players wanting to keep their edge. The dreaded age of 30—the pivot point for players between their peak years and declining performance—had become a line in the sand in teams' willingness to commit to expensive long-term contracts. Harper and Machado, both in their mid-20s, counted on their youth combined with their extraordinary abilities to give them leverage to hold out for the kind of lucrative long-term contract they felt was their due. As for Keuchel and Kimbrel, there was nothing either could do on entering free agency to prevent turning 31 in the first year of whatever new deal they got.

The upshot was that teams were no longer willing to give veteran free agents already in their 30s, still less in their mid-30s, contracts like the 10-year, $275 million the Yankees gave to 32-year-old Alex Rodriguez in November 2007 after he opted out of the three remaining years of his existing $252 million deal; or the 10-year, $240 million contract Albert Pujols signed with the Angels in December 2011, a month before he turned 32; or the eight-year contract extension the Tigers gave to 31-year-old Miguel Cabrera in March 2014 that, added to the two years remaining on his existing deal, would pay him $292 million over the next 10 years. All three were established superstars coming off outstanding seasons and were expected to continue playing at elite levels for at least the majority of the next 10 years of their deals. The A-Rod and Pujols contracts quickly became gilded anchors weighing down their teams. They were cautionary tales that dovetailed with their team owners' continuing focus on bringing down salaries.

Alex Rodriguez, on whom the Yankees lavished such a generous contract anticipating that within 10 years he—as a Bronx Bomber—would break Barry Bonds's steroids-tainted career home run record, soon became enmeshed in steroid scandals of his own, the second of which resulted in a season-long suspension in 2014. The discredited A-Rod—or A-Fraud, as hostile fans in other ballparks would have it—became an embarrassment to the proud tradition of the Yankees. He was also a shell of his former self: getting older, losing mobility, and more prone to injury, including a debilitated hip that cost him most of the 2013 season. With the franchise in rebuilding mode to restore its "forever" dynasty, the money still owed to A-Rod was a major impediment to spending elsewhere to improve the team. The Yankees couldn't wait to be rid of his contract, which finally occurred in 2016 when Rodriguez agreed to retire in August and not play the final year of his deal, after being bought out for 2017.

Albert Pujols had 445 home runs and a .328 career batting average and .420 on-base percentage when he abandoned the St. Louis Cardinals, after they won the 2011 World Series, for the Los Angeles Angels. The only one of his 11 years in St. Louis that he did not hit .300 or drive in at least 100 runs was 2011, when he had 99 RBIs and batted .299. Since he was getting older, being able to take days off from playing first base to be the designated hitter for his new American League team was probably a selling point for the Angels, in addition to the hefty contract he was given that would extend until he was 42 years old. Pujols in Anaheim, however, was not the offensive force he had been in St. Louis. Given his age when the Angels signed him, that should have been predictable. The Angels were in effect rewarding Albert Pujols for his exceptional Hall of Fame–worthy career his first 11 years with the Cardinals.

In contrast to Pujols, a fair argument could be made that the exorbitant long-term commitment Detroit made to Miguel Cabrera in the spring of

2014 was well worth it as a reward for what he had already done for the franchise, even though a significant age-related decline in performance was probable at least for the second half of his deal, since he was already in his 30s. He had just won three consecutive batting titles. He had just hit 44 homers for the second year in a row. He had just won his second straight MVP Award. In 2012 he became the first player since Carl Yastrzemski in 1967 to win the Triple Crown. Cabrera continued terrorizing pitchers for three years after he signed his extension, including winning a fourth batting title in five years in 2015, before age and a spate of injuries—he was now in his mid-30s—began taking their toll. Going into 2019, the Tigers stilled owed $162 million in salary for a declining Cabrera over the next five years. It shouldn't have mattered that he was no longer the Miguel Cabrera of 2008 to 2016, however, because what he had already done for Detroit when he signed his contract extension was worth every penny he was paid going forward.

The nightmare scenario teams were determined to avoid was the seven-year, $161 million contract the Orioles gave Chris Davis, their power-hitting first baseman on the cusp of his 30th birthday, in 2016. Unlike A-Rod, Pujols, and Cabrera, Davis was not an established superstar. He led the majors with 53 home runs in 2013 and 47 in 2015, and hit 159 the four previous years, convincing Baltimore's front office he would be worth the $23 million annual salary they would pay him through 2022. But Davis was also the very definition of an all-or-nothing slugger, striking out in 31 percent of his plate appearances and 35 percent of his official at-bats between 2012 and 2015, while drawing a walk in only 10 percent of his plate appearances. His .256 batting average those four years included a telling .196 average in 2014.

In the first year of his new deal, Davis hit 38 homers but saw his batting average plummet from .262 to .221. He struck out 219 times in 566 at-bats. In 2017 his totals were 26 home runs, a .215 batting average, and 195 strikeouts in 456 at-bats (a 43 percent K ratio), and in 2018 he finished with the worst batting average (.168) ever by a qualifying batter, striking out 192 times in 470 at bats and hitting 16 homers. Davis also ended the season with just one hit in his last 37 at-bats, including carrying a 0-for-21 streak into 2019 that he extended to a new record of futility—no hits in 62 consecutive at-bats, shattering the previous record of 46—which confronted the rebuilding Orioles with the painful dilemma of whether to bench their highest-paid player, to whom they still owed $93 million in salary and deferred payments. Davis played in only 105 games, starting 86, mostly against righties. He batted just .179 with 12 homers in 352 plate appearances, striking out in nearly 40 percent of them.

Before Machado signed for 10 years and Harper for 13 in 2018, the last player to get as many as 10 years as a free agent was Yankees second baseman Robinson Cano, for $228 million beginning in 2014. But he didn't get it from the Yankees, for whom he had batted .314 with 142 home runs and 513 runs batted in the five previous years. Unlike their dad, the sons of Steinbrenner were averse to investing that much money in a 31-year-old—even their best player—for that many years. While Cano, like A-Rod, Pujols, Cabrera, and Davis, was leaving his prime years—he turned 31 less than two months before signing his big deal with Seattle's Mariners—the much younger (by baseball reckoning) Harper and Machado were just entering theirs. Halfway into his contract, Cano was not only in decline but also tested positive for performance-enhancing drugs in 2018, and in November 2020 it was revealed Cano would be suspended for the entire 2021 season for another failed test.

The owners used age as a double-edged sword against the players. On the free agent front, mindful of the luxury tax and no longer under any illusion that players can defy Father Time, teams were no longer willing to give out expensive long-term contracts to veteran players in their 30s no matter how illustrious their career or how well they had played in recent years. And on the front end of players' careers, aside from amateur-draft signing bonuses, teams took advantage of the system to pay players— even those achieving instant stardom—at or close to the major-league minimum for as long as they could.

Not only that, but teams were routinely manipulating players' service time by bringing up outstanding prospects after the season had begun in order to push back their eligibility years for salary arbitration and free agency. By not putting outstanding rookie Bryce Harper on their Opening Day roster in 2012 and instead calling him up 21 games into the season at the end of April, the Washington Nationals had him for seven years instead of six before he could enter the free agent marketplace. It was the same thing with Manny Machado, although perhaps somewhat less egregiously since the Orioles did not bring him to Baltimore until their 112th game in August 2012.

The players were caught in a catch-22. The owners justified paying even outstanding players in the beginning years of their careers far below fair-market value because they were young and must prove themselves over multiple seasons, and they justified paying experienced, proven players below fair-market value because they were aging out of their peak years. Feeding into this dichotomy was the owners' newfound approach to shaping rosters that diminished the importance of proven veterans the likes of Mike Moustakas, Adam Jones, or Gio Gonzalez, who were no longer or never were top-tier players, to bolster their lineup, bench, or pitching staff—at least not for the length and cost of contracts that might have been given in the recent past. Instead, especially in an era where every team routinely shuttled major-league-capable "replacement players" back and forth between their minor-league affiliates and big-league club, they were prepared to rely on the significantly cheaper alternative of younger players still under franchise control for the necessary ballast to solidify their rosters.

From the owners' perspective, these were good business practices enabling franchises to control expenses, especially with regard to high-value players. From the players' perspective, it was a breach of an implicit compact that had prevailed since the devastation of the 1994 strike. Until now, players understood they would be underpaid—the best players, grossly underpaid—at the beginning of their careers until they became eligible for salary arbitration. And they accepted that big boosts in pay in their arbitration years were likely to be below fair-market value as well. But that was in expectation of securing high-priced long-term contracts, relative to their level of performance, once they hit free agency. The trade-off for players was being rewarded for having proven their worth when they were under team control.

The players had no answer to the owners' "good business practices" argument because modern metrics seemed to agree. The emphasis on analytics was weaponized by front office executives against even the best of baseball's free agents. Whereas once upon a time a free agent's pending big payday was contingent on his recent history of performance and base statistics projected forward, now the player was ruthlessly dissected, supposedly objectively—his stats by advanced data-driven analysis of metrics, and his physical performance by measurements captured forever on digital video. In the free agent class of 2017, Moustakas was undermined by advanced metrics indicating that, for all his home runs, his value was closer to that of a marginal starting position player than to a highly productive one. And Jonathan Lucroy's case for a well-paid multi-year deal was undermined less by his declining offensive production than digital video–based analysis showing that, now in his early 30s, he had become much less adept at framing pitches to secure called strikes from umpires. Would a contending team trade for either in the middle of a pennant race? Yes. Sign either to a premium contract he might once have commanded to bolster a team's prospects to compete before the season begins? Nope.

Far more accomplished than either Lucroy or Moustakas in the free agent the class of 2018, why was elite closer Craig Kimbrel still unsigned as the 2019 season got underway? The three previous years in Boston he had saved 108 Red Sox wins, allowed fewer than a batter an inning to reach base in the 184⅓ innings he pitched in 187 games, and struck out 305 of the 721 batters he faced. Those were impressive numbers, argu-ably worth the six years and $100 million he hoped for. But super high-speed, high-definition digital video comparing his 2018 season with the previous year showed that Kimbrel's fastball velocity and the relative rate of spin on his high hard one—the faster the ball spins on its way to the plate, the more difficult it is to hit—had declined appreciably and that he was missing his intended pitch location much more than before. Since he was about to turn 31, he was unlikely to be the same Craig Kimbrel in the years he wanted out of his new deal.

In fact, one didn't need the latest technology and algorithms to tell you that. In nine postseason games as the Red Sox closer in 2018, Kimbrel had walked 8 batters, gave up 9 hits, and surrendered 7 runs in the 10⅔ innings he pitched. Rather than being the shutdown closer of his reputa-tion, Kimbrel caused many moments of high anxiety for his manager and the fans of Red Sox Nation. He was scored upon in his first four closing assignments in the division and league championship series and in one of his four appearances in the World Series. It was Red Sox starting ace Chris Sale, not closer Craig Kimbrel, to whom manager Alex Cora turned to secure the final three outs of the 2018 World Series.

Perhaps the biggest baseball news in the opening days of the 2019 season was the Atlanta Braves signing two of their exceptional young stars, 21-year-old outfielder Ronald Acuna Jr. and 22-year-old second baseman Ozzie Albies, to long-term contracts that would carry them through their arbitration years and into the first year of free agency eligibility. Acuna, the NL Rookie of the Year in 2018 and a projected superstar, was given an eight-year, $100 million deal after just 111 major-league games. Albies, about to enter his third season with just 215 games on his big-league résumé, was signed for $35 million and five years. Having won the NL East in 2018 for their first postseason in five years and looking to fortify their foundation for competitive success into the mid-2020s, the Braves were locking up their young—very young—talent early. The deals Acuna and Albies signed would almost certainly pay them well below fair-market value in their arbitration-eligible and free agency years if they performed according to expectations.

Although rarely for players so early in their careers, it had become more common for teams to sign outstanding young players to multiyear contracts extending into their would-be free agency years since the Tampa Bay Rays signed rookie Evan Longoria to a six-year deal in 2008. The gambit allowed teams to control their player payroll by avoiding the vagaries of arbitration, where salaries awarded to top-tier players were increasing disproportionately to Major League Baseball's revenue growth. Contract extensions were particularly insidious from the players' perspective because they were an end-run around free agency. Preying on young players still uncertain about their career prospects and longevity to in effect rein in the future value of contracts offered to all but the very best players in arbitration and free agency, they were a way for owners to suppress salary escalation while artificially lowering salary comps.

While paying Acuna and Albies much more than they would have had to in the first half of those contracts, because they would have been under team control, the back end of those contracts, after both players could have entered the free agent market, were likely to be a bargain. Including a team option for two more years in both contracts, they promised to be an extraordinary bargain for the Braves if their young stars stayed on the elite-players track. For Acuna and Albies, agreeing to team-favorable contracts was a way to secure their financial future without having to fret that serious injury or a prolonged ill-timed slump would greatly diminish their value once they were finally eligible for free agency.

The Yankees were not similarly inclined toward their rising superstar slugger, Aaron Judge. Earning slightly more than the $535,000 minimum as a rookie in 2017, Judge led the league with 52 homers, won Rookie of the Year honors, finished second in the MVP voting, and was the best position player in the major leagues based on wins above replacement—for which the Yankees saw fit to pay him just over $622,000 in 2018 when the minimum had gone up to $545,000. Playing in just 112 games in 2018 because of injury, Judge nonetheless blasted 27 home runs and was the most dangerous hitter in the Yankees lineup—which earned him a mere $42,000 raise for 2019, putting him just $130,000 above the minimum salary. He would turn 27 in 2019, a year older than Harper and Machado; would be 28 in 2020 when he reached arbitration eligibility; and by the time he qualified for free agency in 2023, assuming he did not first reach a long-term deal with the Yankees, Judge would be on the other side of 30.

Taking into account his 83 home runs in his first 294 major league games, his popularity with Yankees fans, and his playing in the lucrative New York media market, no other player in baseball was financially more valuable than Aaron Judge. According to one economic estimate, Judge was worth $71 million to the Yankees' business enterprise in 2018. But Yankees executives were not budging from the position that, at least until he was eligible for salary arbitration, they were content to be cheap with their most valuable player—because they could. Judge had no leverage. General Manager Brian Cashman explained that the strength of the Yankees' "formula" for determining the salaries of pre-arbitration-eligible players was "built on its consistency." It didn't matter what Judge had already done for the franchise, both competitively and for the bottom line, that was the formula and "we've stayed disciplined to it."

That didn't mean the Yankees would not offer him a lucrative long-term deal to try to head off the possibility of their headline Bronx Bomber opting for free agency as he approached eligibility—just not until they were convinced Judge's prodigious power swing wouldn't morph into Chris Davis–like futility (Judge had whiffed in nearly 40 percent of his at-bats going into the 2019 season), and even then, perhaps not any sooner than they had to. The Colorado Rockies kept Nolan Arenado, their outstanding 27-year-old third baseman, from becoming the most high-profile player on the 2019 free agent market by signing him before the season began to a new eight-year, $260 million contract that gave him the highest average-annual salary of any position player, including Harper and Machado after their free-agent deals. The Yankees' gamble with Judge was that, to the extent he channeled Ruth and DiMaggio and Mantle and Jeter as the indispensable Yankee, the longer they waited to offer him at least an Arenado-type extension, the more likely their superstar slugger would follow Harper in holding out for a record-setting contract, either from the Yankees or as a free agent.

Bryce Harper did not become baseball's first $400-million-man in 2019, as he had hoped. Los Angeles Angels center fielder Mike Trout did. The two were rivals for bragging rights as to who was the bigger star. At least based on his career up till free agency, Nevada-born Harper was arguably overhyped at the start of his professional journey—making the cover of *Sports Illustrated* in 2009 while still in high school presaged his being the first pick the next year in the amateur draft. Instead, it was less-heralded New Jersey-born Trout—a year older and only the 25th first-round pick in the 2009 amateur draft (and not even the first of the Angels' consecutive picks that year) and fellow 2012 Rookie of the Year (in the American League)—who emerged as the superstar of superstars in the 2010s. Trout's 2012 rookie season was perhaps the best by any player ever. He batted .326, had a .399 on-base percentage, led the league with 129 runs and 49 stolen bases in 54 attempts, belted 30 home runs, and drove in 83 runs as the Angels' leadoff batter. His 10.5 wins above replacement was the best in the majors and the best by any rookie since the end of the nineteenth century.

He never looked back. Not only was he much better in his first seven years than Joe DiMaggio—the patron saint of sustained excellence from the beginning of a major-league career—but Mike Trout was having the best run of consecutive years since Willie Mays in the 1960s. From 2012 to 2018, Trout belted 235 home runs, scored 773 and drove in 632 runs, batted .310, had an on-base plus slugging percentage of exactly 1.000, and was successful in 185 of 219 stolen base attempts. Harper's stats line was 184 homers, 610 runs and 521 RBIs, a .279 batting average and .900 on-base plus slugging percentage in 98 fewer games. More significantly, Trout averaged 9.2 wins above replacement those seven years, compared to Harper's much more modest 3.9.

In spring training 2014, about to enter his third full season at $1 million—double what he had been paid the two previous years—and not eligible for salary arbitration until 2015, Trout signed a 6-year contract extension to take effect in 2015 (through 2020) that would pay him $144.5 million. *Sports Illustrated* called it the "deal of the century" for the Angels because it would delay his free agency by three years. *SI* estimated at the time the Angels were getting anywhere from an $86 million to $175 million bargain on what Trout's actual worth was likely to be. Just before the start of the 2019 season, not taking any chances knowing that Trout would be by far baseball's most coveted free agent in two years and was likely to get a record-shattering contract, the Angels signed him to a 12-year, $430 million deal that superseded the last two years of his 6-year deal. Trout's average annual salary would be close to $36 million, far eclipsing Arenado's deal. It was considered a bargain for the Los Angeles Angels.

The record-setting contracts signed in rapid succession by Machado, Arenado, Harper (disappointed though he may have been by his fate in the free agent market), and Trout were evidence allowing baseball officials to claim that, rather than any collusion or conspiracy against the players, the industry's market was working exactly as it should. "I think it's important to remember that the Major League Baseball Players Association has always wanted a market-based system," Commissioner Rob Manfred asserted in spring training as players griped about the slow pace of the 2018 free agent market; about Harper, Machado, Keuchel, and Kimbrel still being unsigned; about star players not getting what they deserved; and about veteran players being shortchanged and even ignored—effectively discarded on the trash heap despite still being productive. As the 2019 season was about to kick off, Dan Halem, Selig's point man in negotiations with the players' union, clarified that in a market-based system it was entirely reasonable for teams to compensate for high-priced top free agents and for higher salaries being awarded in arbitration hearings (which were becoming fewer) by offering minimalist contracts to the lower and middle class of free agents and relying more on up-and-coming prospects in order to control player payroll.

The players and their union considered it market manipulation. Baseball's revenues continued to grow while player payrolls stagnated. The argument about teams having to be financially responsible to be competitive seemed disingenuous when so many teams were adopting barely concealed strategies of *not* being in it to win. It did not go unnoticed that these teams, and many marginally competitive clubs in the middle, were relying on the cheap labor of young, inexperienced players instead of the stable of available veterans with a proven track record. Nor did it go unnoticed that the five franchises valued by *Forbes* at over $3 billion— the Yankees, Dodgers, Red Sox, Cubs, and Giants—were noticeably inactive when it came to the top echelon of 2018 free agents.

The players' union had been in a defensive crouch since the early 2000s when Bud Selig began leveraging the union's opposition to steroids testing to turn the tables in collective bargaining negotiations. But consecutive years of slow movement in the free agent market was raising the stakes for the next collective bargaining agreement in 2022. The union was particularly alarmed by the number of players having to settle for low-value one- or two-year deals. Player salaries had stagnated—in fact, they declined in 2018—while Major League Baseball's revenues continued to grow. The Yankees not spending big to sign Machado or Corbin or Keuchel to bolster their few positions of weakness was an ominous sign about the future of free agency.

Surveying the scene, players were no longer reticent to utter the one word that had thrust the game into arguably the biggest crisis of its history—bigger even than the Black Sox scandal—in 1994. "Maybe we have to go on strike, to be honest with you" Dodgers closer Kenley Jansen had said when the market was slow to develop for the free agent class of 2017, the year after he signed an $80 million-for-five-years deal as a free agent. By the spring of 2019, that sentiment was being expressed more pointedly. "Unless something changes," said Cardinals pitcher Adam Wainwright, "there's going to be a strike. One hundred percent."

17

BASEBALL'S YEAR OF DISCONTENT

From Astros Cheatskates to the Coronavirus Pandemic

Not only did the Houston Astros lose the 2019 World Series to the wild-card Washington Nationals, a seven-game drama in which the home team *lost* every game, but within weeks of the final out they awoke to an article in the *Athletic* alleging that their 2017 World Series championship was tainted by an elaborate sign-stealing scheme in home games at Minute Maid Park.

The primary source of this revelation was former 2017 Astros right-hander Mike Fiers, now pitching for division rival Oakland, who claimed Houston players in the video replay review room behind the dugout used a real-time video feed from a center field camera to decipher catchers' signs and banged a trash can once or twice to alert the batter as to whether the pitch was a breaking ball or changeup; no bang meant a fastball. The article resonated because Houston's postseason opponents in 2019—the Red Sox in their division series, the Yankees in the ALCS, and the Nationals—were convinced (some might have said, excessively paranoid) that the Astros were cheating, to the point that all three clubs provided their pitchers and catchers cards with multiple sign sequences, any one of which they could switch to at a moment's notice. This bombshell story obligated Commissioner Rob Manfred to investigate the allegation.

It was all true, the commissioner concluded after his investigation was completed. Based on extensive interviews with Houston's players, coaching staff, front office personnel, and other employees, the scheme was, as

Manfred described it, "player-driven," without the authorization or approval of manager A. J. Hinch or general manager Jeff Luhnow. Hinch, however, was at least aware of the sign-stealing enterprise—he twice damaged the video monitor—but did nothing to stop it, and Luhnow should have known it was happening. The Astros began incorporating the trash can "approximately two months into the 2017 season," and "for the postseason" relied on a "portable monitor" that could be quickly taken down if league officials or other prying eyes were nearby: "At some point during the 2018 season, the Astros stopped using the replay review room to decode signs because the players no longer believed it was effective."

Stealing and deciphering signs from the dugout and by players on the field has always been an accepted part of gamesmanship in major-league baseball. Doing so from beyond the perimeter of the ballfield, especially using technological or mechanical aids, is not. That, of course, doesn't mean many teams haven't tried it throughout baseball history. In the final month of the 1948 season, the Cleveland Indians spied on opposing catchers' signs from beyond the center field fence using a naval gunsight that Bob Feller, their ace, brought back from his service in World War II. Trailing by 4½ games with 23 remaining, Cleveland won 16 of their final 20 home games, including three walk-off wins, to end the season tied for first, then won a playoff to decide the American League pennant on the road in Boston.

Much more famously, although not revealed until half a century after the fact in an article by Joshua Prager for the *Wall Street Journal*, New York's 1951 Giants placed their regular third-base coach in the manager's office of their clubhouse beyond center field at the Polo Grounds with a powerful telescope and an intricate buzzer system to tip off Giants batters as to what pitch was coming. They won 23 of their final 28 home games, roaring back from a deficit that reached 13½ games on August 11 to end the regular schedule tied with Brooklyn's Dodgers for first place, forcing a three-game playoff for the pennant. The implication of this revelation is that Bobby Thomson might not have hit his famous pennant-winning home run off Ralph Branca without benefit of his team's center field spy.

By 2017, the sophisticated technology that helped fuel baseball's now-insatiable demand for ever more information to assist players and managers was there to be used in real time, if teams were so inclined to cheat. (And it *was* cheating.) Houston GM Luhnow had taken baseball's "analytics revolution" beyond the sophisticated stats analysis pioneered by Billy Beane to include the use of advanced technology—including motion-capture video—to assist in player development. The temptation for Astros players to use it for in-game advantage proved too great to resist. Houston already had a dedicated camera beyond center field that the commissioner later acknowledged "was allowed under MLB rules at the time" when used for player-development purposes. The Astros were not caught, but late that season the commissioner's office investigated the Red Sox for stealing catchers' signs from the team's video replay review room and relaying them to dugout personnel wearing smart watches, and the Yankees for improperly using the phone to the dugout from their replay review room. Both clubs—intense rivals battling it out for the division title in the AL East—were fined, and Manfred issued a memorandum in September putting "all Clubs on notice . . . that any use of electronic equipment to steal signs would be dealt with *more severely* [italics mine] by my office."

In the case of the 1948 Indians and 1951 Giants, if their out-of-bounds sign-stealing scheme allowed either team to win even just one game before the end of their regular-season schedule, it made a decisive difference in the outcome of the pennant race—because if either team had one loss more, neither would have forced a playoff for the pennant. The irony for the Astros, division winners by a whopping 21 games in 2017, was that they did not need such an advantage. They were a genuinely great team. But just because it didn't make a difference in the outcome of their division race does not mean the Astros' spying enterprise was not effective. Manfred wrote, "I am neither in a position to evaluate whether the scheme helped Astros hitters (who were unquestionably a very talented group), nor whether it helped the Astros win any games." The best evidence that Houston batters benefited was the difference in their batting strikeouts—a full strikeout less per game at home (6.2) compared to on the road (7.2), which was much better than the major-league average; and in strikeouts per game at Minute Maid Park from 6.5 in the 30 home games they played in April and May, compared to just 6.0 in their remaining 51 home games after June.

During the regular season, the 2017 Astros hit more home runs on the road (123) than at home (115), but Minute Maid Park was more favorable to pitchers and not a homer haven. In the postseason, however, the Astros blasted 18 home runs in 9 games played at Minute Maid Park, compared to 9 homers in 11 games at Fenway Park, Yankee Stadium, and Dodger Stadium. Six of the eight homers they hit against Boston in their division series were at home, including three in the opening game by Astros star Jose Altuve; all four of the homers they hit against the Yankees in the ALCS were in the four games played in Houston, two of them by Altuve; and 8 of the 15 home runs they blasted in the World Series against the Dodgers were in the middle three games at Minute Maid, including another by Altuve. In their back-and-forth slugfest with the Dodgers in Game Five at Houston, the Astros smashed five home runs, accounting for 10 runs in their 10-inning 13–12 victory. Three of those homers tied the score and a fourth gave the Astros a lead. The game was finally won on a walk-off single off Dodgers closer Kenley Jansen. Six of the seven postseason home runs hit by Altuve, who would be the near-unanimous selection for American League MVP, were in Houston. During the regular season, only 9 of his 24 homers were at Minute Maid Park. Altuve was one of the Astros players who "didn't use it [the trash can] at all," at least according to his teammate, Carlos Correa.

Despite emphasizing that the sign-stealing, trash can–banging cheating was player driven, Manfred chose not to penalize any Astros players. "Assessing discipline," he wrote, "is both difficult and impractical" because, while "virtually all of the Astros' players had some involvement or knowledge of the scheme," he could not "determine with any degree of certainty every player who should be held accountable, or their relative degree of culpability." Instead, the Astros as a team were fined and stripped of their first- and second-round selections in the June amateur draft, and manager Hinch and general manager Luhnow were suspended for a year for failing to ensure "that the players both understand the rules" against technology-based cheating, which were explicitly stated by Manfred in his September 2017 memo, "and adhere to them."

Besides Hinch, Houston's manager since 2015, the cheating scandal cost two other managers their jobs: Alex Cora, Hinch's bench coach at the time, and Carlos Beltran, the elder statesman on the Astros in his final big-league season as a player in 2017, with a presumption of strong consideration in Hall of Fame balloting once he was eligible. Cora had gone from the World Series champion Astros to take command of the Red Sox in 2018, and it was his team that kept Houston from a next-year return to the World Series. Beltran had just been hired to manage the Mets in 2020. Cora's intimate involvement in the conspiracy to cheat laid out in Manfred's investigation—he "arranged for a video room technician to install" the monitor—made his continued tenure as Boston's manager untenable. Beltran, as the only player singled out by the commissioner and portrayed as a ringleader for his involvement in orchestrating the scheme, was also in an untenable situation. While Cora, brought back by the Red Sox, and Hinch, hired by Detroit, resumed their managerial careers in 2021, Beltran has yet to manage a game.

Although he lost his job in 2020, the commissioner deferred any punishment until after Major League Baseball completed its investigation of allegations, in another article in the *Athletic*, that his 2018 Red Sox engaged in video sign stealing of their own. The scheme outlined in this article, and confirmed for the most part by the commissioner in April 2020, was "unlike the Astros' 2017 conduct," Manfred wrote, in that it "was far more limited in scope and impact." Rather than being real-time, it was more about a staffer frequently checking the video feed to see if catchers' sign sequences had changed and passing that information to the dugout. Furthermore, rather than any signal such as banging trash cans to inform Red Sox batters about the pitch, it was up to any runner on second base to use the information on sign sequences signaled from the bench to alert the batter.

Major League Baseball's investigation concluded that the employee in the video replay review room was a self-appointed spy, that most of the players had no idea of the scheme, and that it was done without the knowledge of Cora the manager or any of his coaches. Moreover, in the aftermath of the Red Sox being called out in the 2017 incident and Manfred's memo warning against technology-aided sign stealing, "the evidence demonstrates that in both 2018 and 2019, the Red Sox' front office consistently communicated MLB's sign-stealing rules to non-player staff and made commendable efforts toward instilling a culture of compliance in their organization." The only penalties Manfred chose to impose were taking away Boston's second-round pick in the June draft and suspending the video room employee for the 2020 season. Cora, no longer the manager, was also suspended for the 2020 season, but for his role in the 2017 Astros' sign-stealing caper, not for approving or even being aware of what was happening in Boston's replay review room.

One Astros player who did not have to answer for what happened in 2017 was Gerrit Cole, one of their three aces in 2019. He did not pitch for

Houston in their championship season, and he was now with the Yankees, having signed a nine-year, $324 million free agent contract in December. After consecutive years in which the free agent market was slow to develop for even top-tier players and many solid veteran players were forced to accept undervalued contracts or were not signed at all—the "integrity of the entire free-agent system" was at stake, Tony Clark, the head of the players union and a former major-league first baseman, warned in November—the market moved quickly and proved lucrative for the best players in the free agent class of 2019. The three most coveted players on the market—Cole, Nationals third baseman Anthony Rendon, and Nationals pitcher Stephen Strasburg—were not there for long. Strasburg re-signed with Washington for seven years and $245 million on December 9; four days later, Rendon also accepted a seven-year, $245 million deal, from the Angels; and Cole signed with the Yankees five days after that.

Except for third baseman Josh Donaldson, all the top free agents in 2019 were signed to multiyear contracts by January, and Donaldson may have waited till late January before signing with Minnesota for four years only because teams were waiting to see whether the Rockies would trade Nolan Arenado, their outstanding third baseman, just a year after giving him an eight-year, $260 million contract. (They didn't.) Back on the free agent market a year after having to wait till June 2019 before signing an undervalued one-year deal with Atlanta, Dallas Keuchel accepted a three-year $55.5 million contract from the Chicago White Sox at the end of December. A month earlier, the White Sox signed veteran catcher Yasmani Grandal, also back on the market after having to accept a one-year deal for 2019, to four years and $73 million. The two signings clearly signaled the White Sox' intention to compete in the AL Central Division in 2020. And in his third consecutive year as a free agent, third baseman Mike Moustakas finally got a multiyear contract for four years and $64 million from the Cincinnati Reds.

But if Major League Baseball hoped that teams committing more than $1 billion before January to top players in the free agent class of 2019 took the issue of "club coordination"—as Clark described it—to suppress salaries off the table, the players and their union remained skeptical of the owners' intentions. The issue rising to the forefront was the owners' manipulation of service time, especially for top minor-league prospects, to delay players' eligibility for both arbitration and free agency. Cubs star Kris Bryant, claiming he should be a free agent after the 2020 season rather than in 2021, took his case to arbitration. After all, in his 2015 rookie season, Bryant was on the Cubs' roster virtually the entire season, playing in 151 of their 162 games. But he didn't make the Cubs' Opening Day roster, despite his .425 batting average, 9 home runs, and 15 RBIs in spring training. Major League Baseball defines one year of service as 172 days, but because the Cubs deliberately kept him in the minor leagues until April 17, 2015, Bryant would have only five years and 171 days of service time by the end of the 2020 season—one day short of the six years required to be eligible for free agency. Bryant lost his case, but the players were determined to press the issue of service time manipulation in negotiations for the new collective bargaining agreement to take effect in 2022.

Major League Baseball was entering the 2020 season with the conundrum that, while annual revenues continued to reach new highs—particularly from high-priced broadcast rights for regional sports networks and sponsorships—attendance at games had been in a decadelong decline. The aftermath of the 2008–2009 recession, high ticket prices, and the growing number of teams in any given year that were not competitive were significant contributors. But baseball also had an image problem—specifically that it was a slow, lazy game in which nothing much happened very often. The game was boring, perhaps best suited to listening on the radio or watching on television at home while doing other things. To keep young and even middle-aged fans engaged at the ballpark, teams bombarded them with constant high-volume entertainment on massive jumbotrons between innings and during pitching changes—a much different environment than the organ music their parents or grandparents heard at major-league stadiums in what now seems like the ancient past.

Pace of play was a big problem. Fifty years before, in 1969, the average major-league game was a little more than two and a half hours. Ten years before, in 2009, the time of game was just under three hours. By 2015 it was over three hours. A big reason why was the time required for video replay review by umpires monitoring all games from New York whenever a manager challenged an umpire's call on the field. Replay review of contested boundary calls (foul or fair, over the fence or off the fence, fan interference), safe or out calls, base-running calls (interference by the runner or fielder and illegal slides), and whether or not a batter was hit by a pitch—but not balls and strikes—have been in effect since September 2008. Because most plays challenged are close calls that could have gone either way depending on how the umpire saw it, the average time for a review to uphold or overturn the umpire's call on the field was nearly a minute and a half, according to 2017 data.

Rather than imposing stringent limits on the decision time for replay review—for example, by defaulting to the human element of an umpire's decision on the field of play if it takes longer than, say, 45 seconds to determine whether his call was incorrect—Major League Baseball has adopted pace-of-play rules on the game itself. After the average length of game increased to a record three hours and five minutes in 2016, hitters were no longer allowed to step out of the batter's box between pitches to take a long breather and attend to any number of personal rituals, as had become routine, without the umpire's permission. In 2018, new rules limited the number of mound visits by coaches and players to consult with the pitcher before requiring a pitching change, and time limits between innings and during pitching changes were clock-enforced.

While those changes reduced the average game to three hours in 2018, it was back over three hours and five minutes in 2019—the major reason being that teams were averaging nearly three and a half pitching changes in games that the starting pitcher did not complete, which was less than 1 percent. That prompted a new rule for 2020 that all pitchers—both starters and relievers—had to face at least three batters, or pitch until the end of the inning he was brought in if there were outs on the board, before they could come out of the game. With highly specialized bullpens, including situational relievers brought in specifically to get one batter out and then his day was done, the rule change was notable for deliberately limiting managers' options for shutting down a rally or strategically navigating through the late innings in a close game until it was closing time.

It turned out 2020 was closing time for baseball instead. When spring training began in February, a virulent coronavirus—COVID-19—was silently positioning itself to become a disruptive global pandemic. It surfaced in China in December 2019, but there was no immediate outbreak of cases elsewhere. Despite warnings by epidemiologists that it was only a matter of time in a globalized world before the United States would be hit—and hit hard—by the virus, the threat seemed remote. There was no reason for teams not to begin spring training, and for spring training games not to be played before thousands in Florida and Arizona, including elderly fans who were the most vulnerable to lethal consequences should they catch COVID-19. At the beginning of February, there were only eight cases in the United States, according to the US Centers for Disease Control and Prevention. The number was up to about 15 by the time spring training games began. And then it escalated.

On March 12, two weeks before opening day, Major League Baseball announced that the start of the season would be delayed at least two weeks. The number of cases was now more than 1,600 in the United States. Two weeks almost instantly became two months as the federal government warned against gatherings larger than 50 people and then recommended social distancing as a means to contain the spread of the virus. On what would have been Opening Day, the number of confirmed COVID-19 cases in the United States exceeded 80,000, overtaking China. More than a thousand Americans had died. The US government was widely perceived as fumbling its response. As COVID-19 cases soared and the death toll escalated alarmingly, state governors and mayors across the country imposed social distancing guidelines that shut down large segments of the economy. And it soon became clear that if the 2020 season was played, at least at first it would be before television, radio, and streaming audiences only, without fans in the stands, because of federal and state government guidelines inveighing against spectator crowds.

By mid-May, more than 36 million Americans had been laid off or furloughed from their jobs. Economists projected the US unemployment rate might reach as high as at the worst of the Great Depression. Epidemiologists warned of the high likelihood of a second wave in the fall and winter, especially if social distancing guidelines were relaxed before achieving a significant drop in new cases. And medical scientists were warning it might be years before a safe vaccine was available to protect against COVID-19.

Major League Baseball had endured two world wars and the Great Depression without being shut down. The only reason Major League Baseball had ever shut down, and never for a full year, was because of labor disputes between owners and players—the player lockout by the owners in 1972, the two-month players' strike in the middle of the 1981 season, and the devastating players' strike in 1994 that cost the postseason and extended into 1995 before a federal judge ordered the strike be ended. But this was different. Baseball had never before had to grapple with a virulently infectious pandemic.

The last global influenza pandemic of such severity to sweep the United States was in 1918–1919. It ultimately claimed 50 million lives worldwide, 675,000 in the United States. And it started when America was fully mobilizing for World War I, which was furiously being fought in the trenches of Europe. Surfacing in March 1918, it spread unevenly across the country, at first without claiming many lives. The baseball season was unaffected by the pandemic. It was, however, greatly affected by World War I, including many star players called to serve or working in defense industries. The 1918 pandemic returned with a vengeance in September—the very month the baseball season came to a premature end because of the war. The second wave of the 1918 pandemic was far more severe; 195,000 Americans died in October alone.

The only active major-league personage to die in the pandemic was American League umpire Silk O'Loughlin in December 1918. Only four *former* major leaguers died from the flu, none of whom had success in the big leagues and all of whom were serving in the armed forces. According to Gary Bedingfield's excellent "baseball in wartime" website, eight active minor-league players serving in the armed forces during the war succumbed to the disease, six of them at military bases in the United States. Indeed, the pandemic was particularly lethal in spreading through packed barracks in stateside bases where soldiers were training for war in Europe. In the seven and a half months from April 1918 to November 11, 1918, when World War I finally came to an end, the US armed forces had increased from 378,000 soldiers to more than 4.7 million. More than half of the 4.7 million Americans trained for war did not deploy to fight in Europe before it ended. A third wave of the pandemic that hit the United States in January 1919 petered out by spring and had no effect on the major-league schedule.

During two world wars and the Great Depression, and even just a week after the 9/11 terrorist attacks on New York City and Washington, DC, going ahead with major-league baseball was seen as a palliative to the shared crisis Americans were enduring. It was a bonding experience, a pretense at normality in fearful and uncertain times. And even as America reeled from the new reality of the pandemic, playing the major-league season was held out as a panacea. "We will be part of the recovery, the healing of the country," said the commissioner. "Baseball has stepped up in troubled times to be a leader," said Yankees team president Randy Levine. Perhaps exercising the "forever" dynasty's grandiosity, he called the Yankees' players "patriots." Dr. Anthony Fauci, the US government's leading immunologist (and a big baseball fan), suggested that playing baseball would benefit the mental well-being of Americans—precisely the rationale presidents Woodrow Wilson and Franklin D. Roosevelt gave for continuing baseball during World Wars I and II.

But for all the talk of games shown only on TV helping to bring the country together in a time of crisis, playing in stadiums without fans would be an empty experience. In baseball's return from two world wars and in the games after 9/11, the US raid that got bin Laden, and the Boston Marathon bombing, it was fans crowding into ballparks sitting shoulder to shoulder that made coming together as a country at a baseball game a communal experience. Social distancing at home, watching on television, would not be the same. The last time a major-league game had been played without any fans in attendance at the ballpark—indeed, the only time in memory—was on April 29, 2015, in Baltimore's Oriole Park at Camden Yards. The reason then was massive citywide protests resulting from the death of Freddie Gray, a 25-year-old Black man, given a rough ride while in police custody. It was a surreal experience, listening to a game on radio or watching on television played in an empty baseball stadium. Instead of raucous cheering when the Orioles scored six runs in the first inning on their way to an 8–2 victory, there were sounds of silence from the stands—except for the foul balls banging around seats and off concrete steps and concourses.

The timing of the COVID-19 pandemic couldn't have been worse for Major League Baseball. Not only did it explode in America during spring training, jeopardizing the entire season, but it exposed the fault line between the owners and the players' union in the year before baseball's existing collective bargaining agreement would expire. In March, when it seemed possible the major-league shutdown because of COVID-19 would not be too long, the players and the owners had agreed to prorated salaries based on length of schedule. But they also agreed to "discuss in good faith the economic feasibility of playing games in the absence of spectators." Since at least a third of its revenues—Major League Baseball claimed as much as 40 percent—came from fans attending games in person, the reality of playing with no fans in the stands in 2020 on top of four straight years of declining attendance was presented by the institution of Major League Baseball as an existential threat. The owners and the commissioner were now insisting that players agree to a sliding salary scale—in effect, a pay cut—for the coronavirus season. They also wanted to make up for lost revenues with an expanded postseason involving four additional teams beyond the six division winners and four wild cards, which would increase their earnings from lucrative postseason broadcast rights.

The players' union was not at all receptive. Having come to the conclusion that their existing collective bargaining agreement had enabled the owners' incessant maneuvering to suppress player salaries, the union was adamantly opposed to any sliding scale of salaries that would necessarily diminish the per-game earnings of players with top-tier and even middle-tier contracts. The players fully expected that if they conceded on that point for *just* the unique circumstance of the 2020 coronavirus season, the owners would try to leverage it as a "given" they would not surrender in 2021's negotiations for the next collective bargaining agreement. In June, Commissioner Manfred threatened to cancel the season if an agreement with the players was not reached, and a few days later he claimed the league and the players' union had developed a framework on how to proceed with the season. The union said it had not. The commissioner announced he would unilaterally impose a short schedule. The union retained its right to file a grievance against Major League Baseball for not negotiating in good faith.

On June 23, 2020, Major League Baseball announced a 60-game season for the year, to begin on July 23. (The major leagues had not had such a short schedule since the National League, still in its infancy, played 60-game seasons in 1877 and 1878.) The season would end on September 27, as originally scheduled. The postseason would begin on schedule. The union ultimately agreed to an expanded postseason that would involve 16 of the major leagues' 30 teams—the first- and second-place teams in each division and the two other teams in each league with the best record. There would be no real-person attendance at major-league games. Because of the shortened 60-game schedule, and to limit travel-exposure to the virus, teams would play games only within their division and against teams in the corresponding division of the other league. And because there would be no minor-league baseball, teams were allowed an "active" reserve of 24 players not on the major-league roster who could be called upon when needed.

Strict health protocols would be in place to protect the players. New rule changes for 2020 included the designated-hitter being imposed on the National League, every half-inning of extra-inning-games beginning with a runner already on second base, and seven-inning games in any doubleheaders that might need to be played. The players' union would have to agree if any of those rules were to become permanent after 2020. And it was understood it could all come undone should COVID-19 infect more than a mere smattering of players on major-league teams—or worse, escalate into an even bigger problem in America than it already was.

And in fact, even though new Covid-19 cases had plateaued at a lower level since mid-May, and notwithstanding that every state lifted economic shutdowns to some degree, the coronavirus pandemic was far from over. Again, Major League Baseball's timing couldn't be worse. On the very day the season go-ahead was announced, the number of new cases in the United States was the highest since April 24, and the third highest of any day since the pandemic began. The number of Americans killed by the virus was more than 121,000. Within the previous week alone, players on several teams working out in spring training facilities had tested positive for COVID-19. Because the pandemic was skyrocketing in Florida and Arizona—the two states on June 23 combined for one-fifth of the country's new cases—the spring training home base for all major-league clubs, most teams were going to resume training in their home-city stadiums.

By the time players reported for preseason "summer training" on July 3, there had been nearly 400,000 new cases the previous nine days in America, and deaths now exceeded 129,000. Thirty-one players from 19 major-league clubs had tested positive for the coronavirus. The pandemic was so dire in the United States—widespread, gaining momentum in new cases and new places—that Americans were no longer welcome in most of Europe and elsewhere in the world unless they were first quarantined. This included Canada, which meant major-league teams, and the Blue Jays themselves, could not travel from any big-league city in the United States to Toronto for games. The Blue Jays' home for 2020 would be Buffalo, New York.

On July 23, the 2020 season finally got under way: the Yankees at the Nationals, with no fans in Washington's ballpark. Dr. Fauci, who grew up a Yankees fan and was now a Nats fan, threw out the first pitch of the season. More than 4 million Americans had been infected with COVID-19. More than 144,000 had died. The seven-day average of new cases was more than double what it had been a month earlier when Major League Baseball announced there would be a season. Both teams had a star player on the injured list for having tested positive for COVID-19: for the Yankees, elite closer Aroldis Chapman; for Washington, superb young outfielder Juan Soto, whose positive test was confirmed just hours before game time.

In only a matter of days, baseball's ad hoc season was in jeopardy. By the fifth day of the season, nearly half the players on the Miami Marlins' roster tested positive for COVID-19 during their opening series in Philadelphia. That potentially compromised the Phillies. Not only did the Marlins and Phillies not play for an entire week, the Nationals did not play the next weekend because they were supposed to be in Miami, and the Cardinals-Brewers weekend series in Milwaukee was also postponed because players on the St. Louis roster became infected somewhere, somehow. It would be 9 days before the Marlins played another game. The Cardinals were out of action for 16 days.

A summary investigation by Major League Baseball concluded the Marlins' outbreak may have happened when their players went out in Atlanta, where they played "summer-camp" tune-up games just before the season began. Commissioner Manfred suggested the players were at fault—a position that drew criticism from a public health expert who faulted Major League Baseball's health protocols for failing to address what to do in the event of an outbreak and criticized the commissioner for putting "the burden of all this on the players." Marlins CEO Derek Jeter said his team's players were unfairly maligned: "This is a health crisis that we're all dealing with." Left-hander David Price, one of 16 players who as of August 1 had decided to sit out the season, said he did so because Major League Baseball—for all 113 pages of its health manual for the season—wasn't putting players' health first.

Indisputably, as so many—including Dr. Fauci—surmised, being able to watch and listen to baseball, if only from the comfort of home or your car, was a palliative for so many Americans at a time of an unprecedented (at least since 1918) health crisis. Perhaps playing ball was "patriotic," in the words of the Yankees' team president, in this time of crisis, as it had been during World Wars I and II. But epidemiologists had been warning that even without fans in the stands, playing team sports like baseball outside of an enforced prophylactic bubble—nobody in, nobody out—that involved travel and hotel stays was an open invitation to contagion, especially at a time when the coronavirus was spreading unconstrained, mitigated only by stringent adherence to social distancing practices.

Just as Major League Baseball did not *really* face an existential threat from the 1919 Black Sox scandal or even when the long players' strike of 1994–1995 canceled an entire postseason, World Series included, because baseball is so ingrained in the fiber of America, it would not have faced an existential crisis in 2020 even had there been no attempt to play the season. For all the blessed diversion sports provide for moments like this, there were many who wondered whether Major League Baseball, and the NFL for that matter, were insensitive to the magnitude of the health crisis America faced—the death toll, the economic toll—especially if the coronavirus played havoc with teams, the schedule, and the season, and compromised the health of many players and their families. Rather than baseball's traditional role as a beacon of comfort and coming together as a nation as during two world wars, the Depression, and even the singular event of 9/11, the worst-case scenario then might have been Major League Baseball being shown as feckless in the face of adversity and hardly the master of its own destiny. But perhaps a year without baseball in the year of the coronavirus global pandemic would have brought the game back stronger than ever when the rhythms of life returned to something closer to what we remember—maybe even causing the players and the owners to be less contentious in their approach to player relations in the great game of baseball.

As it happened, the worst-case scenario did not come to pass. It may have been only 60 games instead of 162, but an official 2020 Major League Baseball season was played, complete with a postseason—even though, on September 27, the day the regular season ended, more than 7 million Americans had contracted the coronavirus, of whom 205,000 had died. But Major League Baseball's gamble paid off. Except for fans not being able to go *see* a game at the ballpark, particularly for those listening on the radio, where empty stands could not be seen (as they were on TV) and ambient crowd noise between pitches and crowd reactions to plays were teched-up for broadcasts, it felt like a real season. The only problem was, it was too short.

QUOTES AND NOTES

BASEBALL IN RECOVERY

Reinsdorf explained, "It doesn't mean I like the system." (Jon Pessah, *The Game: Inside the Secret Game of Major League Baseball's Power Brok*ers, 2015.) (p. 9)

Williams called Steinbrenner, asking for "the kind of offer you make to free agents from other teams that have never done anything for the Yankees." (Bill Madden, *Steinbrenner: The Last Lion of Baseball*, 2010.) (p. 10)

"CHICKS DIG THE LONG BALL"

Rumblings of steroid use by some sluggers, including a *Los Angeles Times* exposé in 1995. (Bob Nightengale, "Steroids Become an Issue," *Los Angeles Times*, July 15, 1995.) (p. 30)

SELIG'S GROWTH LEGACY

"This search for a commissioner is a charade," Steinbrenner told the *New York Times* in February 1998. (Jon Pessah, *The Game: Inside the Secret World of Major League Baseball's Power Brokers*, 2015.) (p. 35)

35,000 "baffled English spectators." (Frank Deford, *The Old Ball Game: How John McGraw, Christy Mathewson, and the New York Giants Created Modern Baseball*, 2005.) (p. 45)

"Your game is very interesting," said the king. (Joseph Durso, *The Days of Mr. McGraw: The Wild, Wacky, Wooly Era of John J. McGraw and his Baseball Giants*, 1969.) (p. 45)

BASEBALL'S ASIAN-PACIFIC TIDE

Seattle Mariners stars Ken Griffey Jr. and Randy Johnson said so specifically to Hideo Nomo. (Robert Whiting, *The Meaning of Ichiro*, 2004.) (p. 55)

New York Mets manager Bobby Valentine called Suzuki one of the five best baseball players in the world. (Tim Kurkjian, "Kaz Matsui Is 'Next,'" *ESPN The Magazine*, December 22, 2003.) (p. 58)

The Mets' signing of Kazuo was heralded by his being the cover story for *ESPN The Magazine*. (Kurkjian, "Kaz Matsui.") (p. 63)

Sixty-three Japanese have left Nippon Professional Baseball to play in the major leagues; [and] 23 South Koreans and 16 born in Taiwan have played in the major leagues. (Does not include players born in those countries to US servicemen, or those who went to high school or college in the United States and were subject to baseball's annual amateur draft. All data on major-league players born in Asian countries from "Place of Birth Report" link in baseball-reference.com.) (pp. 64–65)

The Dodgers considered Park to be one of the best amateur pitchers in the world based on having seen him pitch in international competition. (UPI, "Dodgers Sign Korean Pitcher Park," January 11, 2014.) (p. 66)

BASEBALL'S FINEST HOURS

Mayor Giuliani called the Yankees to ask if they could "help with morale." (Jon Pessah, *The Game: The Inside Secret Game of Major League Baseball's Power Brokers*, 2015.) (p. 70)

"You needed to be reminded that life goes on," said America's mayor, "and baseball reminds you of that." (Buster Olney, *The Last Night of the Yankee Dynasty: The Game, The Team, and The Cost of Greatness*, 2004.) (p. 70)

"We're not playing for ourselves," said Mets reliever John Franco. (Pessah, *The Game*.) (p. 70)

Chipper Jones, had to admit that if he wasn't playing for Atlanta, he'd be "rooting for the Mets." (Pessah, *The Game*.) (p. 71)

"Ladies and gentlemen, your attention please. You will be happy to know that Apollo 11 has landed safely on the moon." (Scott Allen, "For Apollo 11's Moon Landing, Baseball Came to a Standstill," *Washington Post*, July 18, 2019.) (p. 72)

On Memorial Day 2019, a Triple-A affiliate of the Washington Nationals stepped out of bounds in pregame ceremonies. (Thomas Boswell, "Nats Must Make Sure Someone Is Fired for Hateful Video," *Washington Post*, May 30, 2019.) (p. 76)

David Ortiz said: "This jersey that we wear today, it doesn't say 'Red Sox.' It says 'Boston.'" (Scott Lauder, "David Ortiz's Finest Moment with the Red Sox Wasn't at the Plate," ESPN, April 10, 2016, https://www.espn.com/mlb/story/_/id/15175959/david-ortiz-finest-moment-red-sox-plate.) (p. 77)

SMALL MARKETS ON THE BRINK

Selig quoted as saying that Major League Baseball "will continue to evaluate our weakest franchises to determine how much contraction is warranted." (Murray Chass, "Baseball Won't Drop Teams in 2002," *New York Times*, February 6, 2002.) (p. 83)

FROM A'S TO THE RAYS

Beane saw great potential in Youkilis being the "Greek god of walks." (Michael Lewis, *Moneyball: The Art of Winning an Unfair Game*, 2003.) (p. 96)

"We realized there was a lot more going on in this game than met the eye," Yankees historian Marty Appel quotes Cashman as saying.

(Appel, *Pinstripe Empire: The New York Yankees from before the Babe to after the Boss*, 2012.) (p. 97)

A financial analysis showed that Crawford's actual value to Tampa Bay those six years was nearly $110 million. (R. J. Anderson, "Updated 2010 Tampa Bay Rays Payroll and Carl Crawford's Contract," DRaysBay, January 4, 2010, https://www.draysbay.com/2010/1/4/1230024/updated-2010-tampa-bay-rays.) (p. 99)

"None of it," said Maddon, "is done by the seat of our pants." (Hunter Atkins, "Rays' Joe Maddon: The King of Shifts," *New York Times*, May 7, 2012.) (p. 103)

BASEBALL'S DIVERSITY SCORECARD

African Americans topped 10 percent of major-league players in 1962 and 15 percent in 1971. (Data in this chapter on the percentage of white, Black, Latino, and Asian players, unless otherwise specified, was compiled in a study by Mark L. Armour and Daniel R. Levitt, "Baseball Demographics, 1947–2016," for the Society for American Baseball Research.) (p. 110)

Kansas City's general manager later said firing McRae was his worst mistake. (*The New Bill James Historical Baseball Abstract*, 2001.) (p. 113)

Gaston was brought back 11 years after the Blue Jays fired him for not being able to respond "to the challenges of the American League East." (Blue Jays' GM Gordon Ash, as quoted in "Blue Jays Fire Gaston," *New York Times*, September 25, 1997.) (p. 116)

Minorities and women accounted for 20 percent of front office positions in Major League Baseball in 2013, up from 3 percent in 1999. (Richard Justice, "Selig Rule First of Its Kind in Sports," MLB.com, August 26, 2013, https://www.mlb.com/news/richard-justice-selig-rule-first-of-its-kind-in-sports/c-58500104.) (p. 116)

Dusty Baker thought institutional discrimination abounded in baseball. (Bob Nightengale, "MLB's Minority Hiring Woes Continue as Job Candidates Shut Out Again," *USA Today*, December 4, 2019.) (p. 117)

Commissioner Manfred explained that front offices "hire who they feel to be the most qualified person for the job." (Michael Powell, "With Managers, Major League Baseball Is Forward in Thinking but Backward in Hiring," *New York Times*, October 26, 2015.) (p. 118)

42 percent of the players on major-league rosters were nonwhite, according to Major League Baseball's own data for 2016. (Richard Lapchick, founder and director of the Institute for Diversity and Ethics in Sport, "MLB Race and Gender Report Card Shows Progress Still Needed," ESPN, April 18, 2017, https://www.espn.com/mlb/story/_/id/19185242/mlb-race-gender-report-card-shows-progress-needed.) (p. 118)

This time (October 2017) Manfred's explanation was that the game had evolved to be "much more focused on analytics." (Tyler Kepner, "Baseball's Minority Managing Problem," *New York Times*, October 29, 2018.) (p. 118)

"I've made no secrets about my desire to manage," Randolph said years later. (Brendan Kuty, "Yankees Great Willie Randolph: I'd Still Make 'Really Good' Manager," NJ.com, April 10, 2017, https://www.nj.com/yankees/2017/04/yankees_great_willie_ranoldph_id_still_make_really.html.) (p. 119)

Blacks accounted for only 7.7 percent of major-league teams' Opening Day rosters in 2019. (Billy Witz, "Even Black Colleges Struggle to Draw in Black Ballplayers," *New York Times*, May 13, 2019.) (p. 120)

Pitcher Steve Blass said, "We were white and we felt the same way." (John Florio and Ousie Shapiro, "When King Died, Major League Baseball Struck Out," *The Undefeated*, April 4, 2018, https://theundefeated.com/features/when-martin-luther-king-died-major-league-baseball-struck-out/.) (p. 122)

THE LATIN TSUNAMI

The large numbers of players from the Caribbean on major-league rosters is a relatively recent development. (All data on major-league players born in Caribbean countries from "Place of Birth Report" link in baseball-reference.com.) (p. 123)

As many as 500 Dominican teens were signed to attend a baseball academy in any given year. (Enrique Rojas, "Baseball Academies Thrive in the Dominican Republic," ESPN, July 1, 2015, https://www.espn.com/blog/onenacion/post/_/id/710/baseball-academies-thrive-in-the-dominican-republic.) (p. 125)

According to a 2013 investigative report in *Mother Jones* magazine. (Ian Gordon, "Inside Major League Baseball's Dominican Sweatshop System," *Mother Jones*, March 2013, https://www.motherjones.com/politics/2013/03/baseball-dominican-system-yewri-guillen/.) (p. 125)

"It wasn't a raft," according to the boat's owner. (Jon Wertheim and Don Yaeger, "Fantastic Voyage: Three Fellow Refugees Say the Tale of Yankees Ace Orlando (El Duque) Hernandez's Escape from Cuba Doesn't Hold Water," *Sports Illustrated*, November 30, 1998.) (p. 132)

Major-league scouts assessed the Cuban league's competitiveness to be no better than Double-A. (Michael S. Schmidt, "Baseball Looks to Create a Possible Portal to Cuba," *New York Times*, April 26, 2007.) (p. 133)

"A payment to the Cuban Baseball Federation is a payment to the Cuban government," the Trump administration explained to Major League Baseball in April 2019. (David Waldstein and Michael Tackett, "Citing Trade Laws, Trump Cancels Deal Between MLB and Cuban Federation," *New York Times*, April 9, 2019.) (p. 136)

THE DARK (STEROIDS) SIDE OF RECOVERY

"People say, 'Why didn't you know Barry was taking steroids?'" (John Shea, "The Man Who Went to Bat for Ballpark Shares Credit," *San Francisco Chronicle*, May 14, 2016.) (p. 137)

McGwire said, "Everybody that I know in the game uses the same stuff that I do." (Howard Bryant, *Juicing the Game*, 2006.) (p. 138)

Tom Verducci of *Sports Illustrated* put it all into perspective with a damning article entitled "Totally Juiced." ("Totally Juiced: Confessions of a Former MVP," *Sports Illustrated*, June 3, 2002.) (p. 140)

Bill James called it "one of the top fluke seasons of all time." (*The New Bill James Baseball Historical Abstract*, 2001.) (p. 141)

Giants' manager Dusty Baker attributed [Bonds's injury] to "20 years of throwing." (Murray Chass, "Bonds Joins the Long List of Stars Who Are Injured," *New York Times*, April 21, 1999.) (p. 145)

In December 2004 the *San Francisco Chronicle* published an investigative report by Mark Fainaru-Wada and Lance Williams on grand jury testimony by Bonds. ("What Bonds Told Grand Jury," *San Francisco Chronicle*, December 3, 2004. Fainaru-Wada and Williams had been reporting on the federal investigation of BALCO since the summer.) (p. 147)

Giambi told the BALCO grand jury he started injecting steroids in 2001. (Fainaru-Wada and Williams, "Giambi Admits Taking Steroids," *San Francisco Chronicle*, December 2, 2004.) (pp. 147–148)

Featured witnesses included a handful of prominent current and former major-league stars, as well as Commissioner Selig and Donald Fehr, his counterpart as head of the players union. (Quotes from testimony are from news coverage by the *New York Times* and the *Washington Post*, as well as from Bryant's book *Juicing the Game*.) (p. 149)

Saying that Rocket Roger was *in fact* "in the twilight of his career." (Boston GM Dan Duquette, quoted by Howard Bryant in *Shut Out: A Story of Race and Baseball in Boston*, 2002.) (p. 152)

The weekly alternative newspaper *Miami New Times* published a detailed investigative report on Biogenesis. (Tim Elfrink, "A Miami Clinic Supplies Drugs to Sports' Biggest Names," *Miami New Times*, January 31, 2013.) (p. 158)

A-Rod qualified that by saying, "I'm guilty for being negligent." (Transcript of Alex Rodriguez interview with Peter Gammons, ESPN, February 9, 2009, https://www.espn.com/mlb/news/story?id=3895281.) (p. 158)

SHOW ME THE MONEY

The city's economic development corporation warned the mayor that failure to provide tax-free financing would result in "the loss of the New York Yankees," [and] Yankees team president said the franchise would have left town. (Richard Sandomir, "Yankees Say

They Would Have Left Bronx if Pushed," *New York Times*, October 24, 2008.) (p. 167)

WHERE LOSING WAS A WINNING PROPOSITION

According to *Baseball America*'s farm system ratings, by 2008 Houston's was the second worst of the 30 major-league franchises. (Evan Drellich, "Ex-GM Wade Believes His Efforts Now Bearing Fruit for Astros," *Houston Chronicle*, June 14, 2014.) (p. 181)

The 2019 Astros, whose potent lineup, hammering out 288 home runs, were compared to the historic 1927 Yankees' Murderers' Row. (Chris Perry, "The 2019 Houston Astros Have the Best Offense Since in the '27 Yankees," The Crawfish Boxes, September 21, 2019, https://www.crawfishboxes.com/2019/9/21/20876611/the-2019-houston-astros-have-the-best-offense-since-the-27-yankees; Travis Sawchik, "The Astros Are Hitting Like the 1927 Yankees," FiveThirtyEight, October 29, 2019, https://fivethirtyeight.com/features/the-astros-are-hitting-like-the-1927-yankees/.) (p. 183)

Data-driven insight "helped show guys what they do well," as Verlander put it. (Tyler Kepner, "The Happiest Place on Earth Might Be in Houston," *New York Times*, August 18, 2019.) (p. 184)

Baltimore's farm system ranked in 2018 among baseball's worst. (Joel Reuter, "MLB Farm System Rankings: Pre-2018 Spring Training Edition," *Bleacher Report*, February 13, 2018, https://bleacherreport.com/articles/2759103-mlb-farm-system-rankings-pre-2018-spring-training-edition.) (p. 186)

BASEBALL'S POWER DYNAMIC

But most pitchers, including Verlander, blamed the baseball. (James Wagner, "Suddenly Losing Their Grip," *New York Times*, August 6, 2019.) (p. 193)

Commissioner Rob Manfred insisted that Major League Baseball had done nothing to change the baseball. (Tyler Kepner, "Pitchers Blame MLB for All Those Dingers," *New York Times*, July 10, 2019.) (p. 193)

The commissioner's interview on Fox Sports Radio. (*The Dan Patrick Show*, June 24, 2019, https://foxsportsradio.iheart.com/content/2019-06-24-mlb-officially-acknowledges-the-baseballs-are-different-this-season/.) (p. 193)

More than a third of swing-and-miss strikes were outside the strike zone, according to data on pitch-location. (Joe Lemire, "Strikeouts Are Up, Strikes Are Not," *New York Times*, July 17, 2019.) (p. 198)

STRATEGIZING PITCHING

The Pirates would have traded Cole to New York in January 2018 for either Gleyber Torres or Miguel Andujar. (Ken Davidoff, "The Trade That Fell Apart Is Burning the Yankees Now," *New York Post*, October 13, 2018.) (p. 201)

There was criticism over the Yankees' decision *not* to strengthen their corps of starting pitchers for the postseason. (Bob Klapisch, "Justin Verlander Shows Yankees What They're Missing on the Mound," *New York Times*, June 23, 2019.) (p. 201)

The argument is made, including by Gossage in the role of cranky old fireman, that closers have the easier job. (James Wagner, "The Power and the Questioned Glory of Baseball's Save State," *New York Times*, April 30, 2017.) (p. 206)

Counsell's intent was for Dodgers manager Dave Roberts, who platooned at several positions, to commit to a predominantly right-handed batting order. (James Wagner, "After Brewers' Misdirection, Wade Miley Will Pitch Game 6, for Real This Time," *New York Times*, October 18, 2018.) (p. 210)

Hinch was left to explain why he had *not* brought in Cole. (David Waldstein and Benjamin Hoffman, "Nationals Win Their First World Series with One Last Rally," *New York Times*, October 30, 2019.) (p. 215)

NOT THE SAME FREE AGENCY

Bryce Harper was presumed to be such a godsend to baseball that he
was featured on the cover of *Sport Illustrated* as a 16-year-old high
school ballplayer. (Tom Verducci, "Baseball's LeBron," *Sports Illustrated*, June 8, 2009.) (pp. 217–218)

According to one economic estimate by Block Six Analytics, Judge
was worth $71 million to the Yankees' business enterprise in 2018.
(James Wagner, "The Yankees' Underpaid Superstar," *New York
Times*, March 28, 2019.) (p. 232)

General Manager Brian Cashman explained that the strength of the
Yankees' "formula" for determining the salaries of pre-arbitration-
eligible players was "built on its consistency." (Wagner, "Yankees.") (p. 232)

Sports Illustrated called it the "deal of the century" for the Angels
because it would delay his free agency by three years. (Cliff Corcoran, "Deal of the Century: Angels Delay Mike Trout's Free Agency
with Six-Year Extension," *Sports Illustrated*, March 29, 2014.) (p.
233)

"I think it's important to remember that the Major League Baseball
Players Association has always wanted a market-based system,"
Commissioner Rob Manfred asserted in spring training. (Tyler
Kepner, "A Free Agency Crisis? The Commissioner Scoffs," *New
York Times*, February 18, 2019.) (p. 234)

Dan Halem, Selig's point-man in negotiations with the players union,
clarified baseball's market-based system. (Wagner, "Yankees.") (p.
234)

"Maybe we have to go on strike, to be honest with you," Dodgers
closer Kenley Jansen had said. (Michael Powell, "Lonely at the
Top of the Free Agent Market," *New York Times*, January 30,
2019.) (p. 235)

"Unless something changes," said Cardinals pitcher Adam Wainwright, "there's going to be a strike." (Kepner, "Free Agency Crisis?") (p. 235)

BASEBALL'S YEAR OF DISCONTENT

Article in the *Athletic* alleging that Houston's 2017 World Series
championship was tainted. (Ken Rosenthal and Evan Drellich.
"The Astros Stole Signs Electronically in 2017—Part of a Much
Broader Issue for Major League Baseball," *Athletic*, November 12,
2019.) (p. 237)

Altuve was one of the Astros players who "didn't use it [the trash can]
at all," at least according to his teammate, Carlos Correa. (Chandler
Rome, "Carlos Correa's Fiery Interview in Defense of Teammates," *Houston Chronicle*, February 15, 2020.) (p. 240)

Another article in the *Athletic*, that the 2018 Red Sox engaged in video
sign stealing of their own. (Ken Rosenthal and Evan Drellich,
"MLB's Sign-Stealing Controversy Broadens: Sources Says the
Red Sox Used Video Replay Room Illegally in 2018," *Athletic*,
January 7, 2020.) (p. 241)

"The integrity of the entire free-agent system" was at stake, Tony
Clark, the executive director of the players union, warned. (Barry
M. Bloom, "Tony Clark and MLB Union Clearly Not Happy with
State of Free Agency as GM Meetings Begin," *Forbes*, November
11, 2019.) (p. 242)

The average time for a review to uphold or overturn the umpire's call
on the field was nearly a minute and a half, according to 2017 data.
(Maury Brown, "Early Numbers Show How MLB Pace of Play Is
Trending," *Forbes*, April 9, 2018. (pp. 243–244)

The global influenza pandemic of 1918–1919 ultimately claimed 50
million lives worldwide, 675,000 in the United States. (Centers for
Disease Control and Prevention. "1918 Pandemic Influenza Historic Timeline," March 20, 2018, https://www.cdc.gov/flu/pandemic-
resources/1918-commemoration/pandemic-timeline-1918.htm.) (p.
246)

"We will be part of the recovery, the healing of the country," said the
commissioner. (Jeff Passan, "Rob Manfred Says 'Nothing off Table' Regarding MLB's Return," ESPN, March 25, 2020, https://
www.espn.com/mlb/story/_/id/28955618/rob-manfred-says-table-
regarding-mlb-return.) (p. 246)

"Baseball has stepped up in troubled times to be a leader," said Yankees team president Levine. (James Wagner, "Can Sports Help

Heal the Country? Some Have Second Opinions," *New York Times*, May 17, 2020.) (p. 246–247)

Anthony Fauci suggested that playing baseball would benefit the mental well-being of Americans. (Scott Boras, "We Have to Bring Baseball Back," *New York Times*, May 5, 2020.) (p. 247)

Commissioner Manfred suggested the players were at fault [and] Price comment on why he decided to sit out the season. (James Wagner, "Commissioner's Optimistic Tone Fails to Reassure the Players," *New York Times*, August 3, 2020.) (p. 250)

Marlins CEO Derek Jeter said his team's players were unfairly maligned. (Tyler Kepner, "As the Virus Spreads through MLB, So Does the Frustration, *New York Times*, August 4, 2020.) (p. 250)

BIBLIOGRAPHY

STATISTICAL SOURCES

This book relies on the indispensable website baseball-reference.com for player and team statistics. The site includes multiple data aggregations, including batter and pitcher splits, game logs, complete play-by-play, player transactions and salaries, and teams' player payrolls. This book also uses the baseball-reference.com version of wins above replacement (WAR), an advanced metric that measures the totality of a player's contributions in terms of how many additional wins that player contributed to his team over what a replacement player from the highest minor-league level would have contributed instead.

RECOMMENDED READING

Documents

1997–2001 Basic Agreement. December 7, 1996. (http://roadsidephotos.sabr.org/baseball/cba9701.pdf)

2003–2006 Basic Agreement between the 30 Major League Clubs and Major League Baseball Players Association. September 30, 2002. (https://digitalcommons.ilr.cornell.edu/cgi/viewcontent.cgi?referer=https://www.google.com/&httpsredir=1&article=1598&context=blscontracts)

2012–2016 Basic Agreement between the 30 Major League Clubs and Major League Baseball Players Association. Summary, December 2011. (http://www.mlb.com/2011_CBA.pdf)

2017–2021 Basic Agreement between the 30 Major League Clubs and Major League Baseball Players Association. December 1, 2016. (http://www.mlbplayers.com/cba)

Major League Baseball Update to the Report of the Independent Members of the Commissioner's Blue Ribbon Panel on Baseball Economics. Major League Baseball, December 2001. (http://roadsidephotos.sabr.org/baseball/BRPanelupd.htm)

Official Press Release Announcing 2020 Regular Season. Major League Baseball, June 23, 2020. (https://www.mlb.com/press-release/press-release-mlb-announces-2020-regular-season?t=mlb-press-releases)

Levin, Richard C., George J. Mitchell, Paul A. Volcker, George F. Will. *The Report of the Independent Members of the Commissioner's Blue Ribbon Panel on Baseball Economics.* Major League Baseball, July 2000. (http://roadsidephotos.sabr.org/baseball/2000blueribbonreport.pdf)

Manfred, Robert D. Jr. *Decisions and Findings of the Commissioner in the Red Sox Investigation,* April 22, 2020. (https://img.mlbstatic.com/mlb-images/image/upload/mlb/scn5xwigcottcbte7siw.pdf)

———. *Statement of the Commissioner (re Houston Astros Decision),* January 13, 2020. (https://img.mlbstatic.com/mlb-images/image/upload/mlb/cglrhmlrwwbkacty27l7.pdf)

Mitchell, George J. *Report to the Commissioner of Baseball of an Independent Investigation into the Illegal Use of Steroids and Other Performance Enhancing Substances by Players in Major League Baseball,* December 13, 2007. (https://files.mlb.com/mitchrpt.pdf)

Books

Appel, Martin. *Pinstripe Empire: The New York Yankees from before the Babe to after the Boss.* New York: Bloomsbury, 2012.

Armour, Mark L., and Daniel R. Levitt. *In Pursuit of Pennants: Baseball Operations from Deadball to Moneyball.* Lincoln: University of Nebraska Press, 2018.

Bjarkman, Peter C. *Cuba's Baseball Defectors: The Inside Story.* Lanham, MD: Rowman & Littlefield, 2016.

———. *A History of Cuban Baseball, 1864–2006.* Jefferson, NC: McFarland, 2017.

Bjarkman, Peter C., and Bill Nowlin, eds. *Cuban Baseball Legends: Baseball's Alternate Universe.* Phoenix, AZ: Society for American Baseball Research, 2016.

Bradbury, J. C. *The Baseball Economist: The Real Game Exposed.* New York: Plume, 2007.

Bryant, Howard. *Juicing the Game: Drugs, Power, and the Fight for the Soul of Major League Baseball.* New York: Plume, 2006.

———. *Shut Out: A Story of Race and Baseball in Boston.* Boston: Beacon Press, 2002.

Canseco, Jose. *Juiced: Wild Times, Rampant 'Roids, Smash Hits, and How Baseball Got Big.* New York: Regan Books, 2005.

Carleton, Russell A. *The Shift: The Next Evolution in Baseball Thinking.* Chicago: Triumph Books, 2018.

Dominguez, Eddie, with Christian Red and Teri Thompson. *Baseball Cop: The Dark Side of America's National Pastime.* New York: Hachette Books, 2018.

Elfrink, Tim, and Gus Garcia-Roberts. *Alex Rodriguez, Biogenesis, and the Quest to End Baseball's Steroid Era.* New York: Dutton, 2014.

Fainaru, Steve, and Ray Sanchez. *The Duke of Havana: Baseball, Cuba, and the Search for the American Dream.* New York: Villard Books, 2001.

Fainaru-Wada, Mark, and Lance Williams. *Game of Shadows: Barry Bonds, BALCO, and the Steroids Scandal That Rocked Professional Sports.* New York: Gotham Books, 2006.

Francona, Terry, and Dan Shaughnessy. *Francona: The Red Sox Years.* New York: Mariner Books, 2014.

Goldberger, Paul. *Ballpark: Baseball in the American City.* New York: Alfred A. Knopf, 2019.

Jaffe, Chris. *Evaluating Baseball's Managers: A History and Analysis of Performance in the Major Leagues, 1876–2008.* Jefferson, NC: McFarland, 2010.

James, Bill. *The New Bill James Baseball Historical Abstract.* New York: Free Press, 2001.

Keri, Jonah. *The Extra 2%: How Wall Street Strategies Took a Major League Baseball Team from Worst to First.* New York: Ballantine Books, 2011.

————. *Up, Up, & Away: The Kid, The Hawk, Rock, Vladi, Pedro, Le Grand Orange, Youppi!, the Crazy Business of Baseball, & the Ill-Fated but Unforgettable Montreal Expos*. Toronto: Vintage Canada, 2014.

Klapisch, Bob, and Paul Sulotaroff, *Inside the Empire: The True Power behind the New York Yankees*. New York: Houghton Mifflin Harcourt, 2019.

Knight, Molly. *The Best Team Money Can Buy: The Los Angeles Dodgers' Wild Struggle to Build a Baseball Powerhouse*. New York: Simon & Schuster, 2015.

Lewis, Michael. *Moneyball: The Art of Winning an Unfair Game*. New York: Norton, 2003.

Madden, Bill. *1954: The Year Willie Mays and the First Generation of Black Superstars Changes the Game Forever*. Boston: Da Capo Press, 2014.

————. *Steinbrenner: The Last Lion of Baseball*. New York: Harper, 2010.

O'Connor, Ian. *The Captain: The Journey of Derek Jeter*. Boston: Mariner Books, 2012.

Olney, Buster. *The Last Night of the Yankee Dynasty: The Game, the Team, and the Cost of Greatness*. New York: Ecco, 2005.

Pessah, Jon. *The Game: Inside the Secret World of Major League Baseball's Power Brokers*. New York: Back Bay Books, 2015.

Ruck, Rob. *Raceball: How the Major Leagues Colonized the Black and Latin Game*. Boston: Beacon Press, 2011.

Schiavone, Michael. *The Dodgers: 60 Years in Los Angeles*. New York: Sports Publishing, 2018.

Soderholm-Difatte, Bryan. *The Golden Era of Major League Baseball: A Time of Transition and Integration*. Lanham, MD: Rowman & Littlefield, 2015.

Torre, Joe, and Tom Verducci. *The Yankee Years*. New York: Anchor Books, 2009.

Verducci, Tom. *The Cubs Way: The Zen of Building the Best Team in Baseball and Breaking the Curse*. New York: Crown Archetype, 2017.

Weaver, Earl, with Terry Pluto. *Weaver on Strategy: A Guide for Armchair Managers by Baseball's Master Tactician*. Revised edition. Dulles, VA: Potomac Books, 2002.

Whiting, Robert. *The Meaning of Ichiro: The New Wave from Japan and the Transformation of Our National Pastime*. New York: Warner Books, 2004.

Selected Articles

Forbes (forbes.com)

Bloom, Barry M. "Tony Clark and MLB Union Clearly Not Happy with State of Free Agency as GM Meetings Begin," November 11, 2019.

Brown, Maury. "Breaking Down MLB's New 2017–21 Collective Bargaining Agreement," November, 30, 2016.

————. "Breaking Down over $400 Million in MLB Luxury Tax Penalties Since 2003," December 3, 2015.

————. "Early Numbers Show How MLB Pace of Play Is Trending," April 9, 2018.

————. "From Terrible Teams to Rising Costs: Why MLB Attendance Is Down over 7% since 2015," October 4, 2019.

————. "Inside the Details of Giancarlo Stanton's Mega-Contract with Marlins," November 24, 2014.

————. "MLB Players Reject Offer; Manfred on Cusp of Imposing 60-Game Schedule," June 22, 2020.

————. "MLB Sees Record Revenues for 2015," December 4, 2015.

————. "MLB Sees Record Revenues of $10.3 Billion for 2018," January 7, 2019.

————. "Something to Consider in MLB Labor Talks: What If There's New Deal but No Strike or Lockout, Either," December 31, 2019.

Kaplan, Ari. "The MLB Deal with Cuba: Measuring the Value of Cuban Players," December 23, 2018.

Ozanian, Mike. "Murdoch Buys Control of New York Yankees Channel for $3.9 Billion," January 24, 2014.

———. "New York Yankees Buy Back YES Network for $3.47 Billion," March 8, 2019.

Ozanian, Mike, and Kurt Badenhausen, "Baseball Team Values 2019," April 10, 2019.

Schlossberg, Dan. "Player Service Time Tops Agenda of Baseball Labor-Management Talks," March 20, 2020.

Smith, Chris. "Texas Rangers Make $108 Million Gamble with Yu Darvish," January 20, 2012.

Witrado, Anthony. "Mike Trout Signs Record-Breaking Extension with the Angels," March 19, 2019.

Wyllys, Jared. "The Cubs Are a Mess, and Tom Ricketts Isn't Helping," February 19, 2019.

Sports Illustrated (si.com)

Apstein, Stephanie. "Why Baseball Is Losing Black America," July 17, 2020.

Chen, Albert. "The Secret of Yankees Ace Wang," April 15, 2008.

Corcoran, Cliff. "Deal of the Century: Angels Delay Mike Trout's Free Agency with Six-Year Extension," March 29, 2014.

Drottar, Casey. "Indians Lookback: The Strange Saga of the Man One Called Fausto Carmona," April 6, 2020.

Jaffe, Jay. "Rays' Exhibition Game in Cuba Brings Two Countries Closer," March 22, 2016.

Jones, Kaelen. "Angels, Mike Trout Finalizing 12-Year, $430+ Million Extension for Largest Contract in Pro Sports," March 19, 2019.

McCann, Michael. "Do Yankees Have Legal Right to Deny A-Rod Bonus Money for 660th Home Run?," May 5, 2015.

Noden, Merrell. "Happy Days in Havana: Host Cuba Powered Its Way to the Gold Medal in Pan Am Games Baseball," August 26, 1991.

Reilly, Rick. "Heaven Help Marge Schott: Cincinnati's Owner Is a Red Menace," May 20, 1996.

Roberts, Selena. "Confronting A-Rod," February 16, 2009.

Shapiro, Michael. "Nolan Arenado Agrees to Eight-Year, $260 Million Extension with Rockies," February 26, 2019.

Tayler, Jon. "The Luxury Tax Won't Bankrupt Your Favorite Team," December 18, 2018.

Verducci, Tom. "Baseball's LeBron," June 8, 2009.

———. "Home Economics: The Inside Story of the Deal That Sent Ken Griffey Jr. Back to Cincinnati at a Bargain Price," February 21, 2000.

———. "Powerball: Alex Rodriguez Hit the Jackpot," December 18, 2000.

———. "Totally Juiced: Confessions of a Former MVP," June 3, 2002.

Wertheim, Jon, and Carl Prine. "The Evidence That Persuaded US Department of Justice to Investigate MLB Recruitment of Foreign Players," October 2, 2018.

Wertheim, L. Jon, and Don Yaeger. "Fantastic Voyage: Three Fellow Refugees Say the Tale of Yankees Ace Orlando (El Duque) Hernandez's Escape from Cuba Doesn't Hold Water," November 30, 1998.

Other Selected Publications Articles

Cramer, Michael J., and James W. Swiatko Jr. "Did Major League Baseball Balk? Why Didn't MLB Bargain to Impasse and Impose Stricter Testing for Performance Enhancing Substances?" *Marquette Sports Law Review* (fall 2006).

Daniels, John, Sara Andrasik, and David Hooley. "The Specialized Bullpen: History, Analysis, and Strategic Models for Success." *Baseball Research Journal* (fall 2018).

Frankel, Matthew J. "Major League Problems: Baseball's Broken System of Cuban Defection." *Boston College Third World Law Journal* 25, no 2 (May 2005).

Gatto, Tom. "Complete List of MLB Players Opting Out of 2020 Season." *Sporting News*, July 31, 2020, https://www.sportingnews.com/us/mlb/news/mlb-players-opting-out-2020-season/1m10laov5in4y11vn0ojmi8srw.

Gordon, Ian. "Inside Major League Baseball's Dominican Sweatshop System." *Mother Jones*, March 2013, https://www.motherjones.com/politics/2013/03/baseball-dominican-system-yewri-guillen/.

Katz, Jesse. "Escape from Cuba: Yasiel Puig's Untold Journey to the Dodgers." *Los Angeles Magazine*, April 14, 2014.

Kurkjian, Tim. "Kaz Matsui Is 'Next.'" *ESPN The Magazine*, December 22, 2003.

Manuel, John. "The History and Future of the Amateur Draft." *Baseball Research Journal* (summer 2010).

Martinen, Abbygale Sarah. "Baseball and the US-Cuban Diplomatic Relationship: Why Did Baseball Serve as an Ineffective Diplomatic Tool for the United States and Cuba?" *University of New Hampshire Scholars' Repository* (spring 2017).

McKenna, Thomas. "The Path to the Sugar Mill or the Path to Millions: MLB Baseball Academies' Effect on the Dominican Republic." *Baseball Research Journal* (spring 2017).

Memmott, Mark. "Kidnapping of MLB's Wilson Ramos Part of Trend in Venezuela." *The Two-Way*, National Public Radio, November 20, 2011, https://www.npr.org/sections/thetwo-way/2011/11/10/142215717/kidnapping-of-mlbs-wilson-ramos-part-of-trend-in-venezuela.

Otis, John. "As Venezuelan Crisis Deepens, US Baseball Teams Close Academies." *Parallels*, National Public Radio, February 24, 2016, https://www.npr.org/sections/parallels/2016/02/24/467914426/as-venezuela-crisis-deepens-u-s-baseball-teams-close-academies.

Pou, Jackeline. "Dominican Teams Keep Baseball Hopes Alive, but Not without Risks." NBC News, October 9, 2019, https://www.nbcnews.com/news/latino/dominican-teens-keep-baseball-hopes-alive-not-without-risks-n1062061.

Reinsdorf, Jonathan M. "The Powers of the Commissioner in Baseball." *Marquette Sports Law Review* (fall 1996).

Rios, Edwin. "The Color Line Baseball Doesn't Want to Talk About." *Mother Jones*, October 28, 2015, https://www.motherjones.com/media/2015/10/baseball-color-line-black-latino-managers/.

Rosenthal, Ken, and Evan Drellich. "The Astros Stole Signs Electronically in 2017—Part of a Much Broader Issue for Major League Baseball." *Athletic*, November 12, 2019.

———. "MLB's Sign-Stealing Controversy Broadens: Sources Says the Red Sox Used Video Replay Room Illegally in 2018." *Athletic*, January 7, 2020.

Wasserman, Howard. "The Mitchell Report on Steroids in Major League Baseball: Historical Accounting, Future Recommendations, and What Lies Ahead for Our National Pastime." FindLaw, December 21, 2007, https://supreme.findlaw.com/legal-commentary/the-mitchell-report-on-steroids-in-major-league-baseball.html

Newspapers

The following newspapers were consulted in researching this book:

Baltimore Sun (http://www.baltimoresun.com)
Boston Globe (http://www.bostonglobe.com)
Boston Herald (http://www.bostonherald.com)
Chicago Tribune (http://www.chicagotribune.com)
Dallas Morning News (http://www.dallasnews.com)
Houston Chronicle (http://www.chron.com)
[Minneapolis] *Star Tribune* (http://www.startribune.com)
Los Angeles Times (http://www.latimes.com)
New York Daily News (http://www.nydailynews.com)
New York Post (http://www.nypost.com)
New York Times (http://www.nytimes.com)

Newsday (http://www.newsday.com)
Philadelphia Inquirer (http://www.inquirer.com)
Pittsburgh Post-Gazette (http://www.post-gazette.com)
San Francisco Chronicle (http://www.sfchronicle.com)
Seattle Times (http://www.seattletimes.com)
South Florida Sun Sentinel (http://www.sun-sentinel.com)
St. Louis Post-Dispatch (http://www.stltoday.com)
USA Today (http://www.usatoday.com)
Wall Street Journal (http://www.wsj.com)
Washington Post (http://www.washingtonpost.com)

Selected Newspaper Articles

Chicago Tribune

Gonzales, Mark. "Kris Bryant Loses His Service Time Dispute with Cubs, Keeping Him under Contract through 2021," January 29, 2020.
Hopkins, Jared S. "Jose Abreu of White Sox Paid $5.8 Million to Agents after Cuban Defection: Court Papers," April 25, 2016.

Houston Chronicle

Barron, David. "CSN Houston's Collapse a Cautionary Tale for Regional Sports Networks," October 5, 2014.
Rome, Chandler. "Carlos Correa's Fiery Interview in Defense of Teammates," February 15, 2020.

Los Angeles Times

James, Meg. "Yankees Fans Strike Out as YES Network-Comcast Battle Heats Up," March 9, 2016.
Moura, Pedro. "Shohei Ohtani Agrees to Sign with Angels," December. 8, 2017.
Nightengale, Bob. "Steroids Become an Issue," July 15, 1995.
Shaikin, Bill. "Dodgers, Time Warner Cable Announce New Channel: SportsNet LA," January 28, 2013.
———. "For the Sixth Year in a Row, Most Dodgers Fans Can't Watch Their Team on Television," March 8, 2019.

New York Times

Allentuck, Danielle, and Kevin Draper. "Baseball Saw a Million More Empty Seats: Does It Matter?" September 29, 2019.
Araton, Harvey. "The News Is Out: Popeye Is Spiking His Spinach," August 23, 1998.
Archibold, Randal C. "This Cuban Defector Changed Baseball. Nobody Remembers," March 18, 2016.
Atkins, Hunter. "Rays' Joe Maddon: The King of Shifts," May 7, 2012.
Augustin, Ed. "Cuba Learns to Live without Its Stars," December 30, 2018.
Bagli, Charles V. "As Stadiums Rise, So Do Costs to Taxpayers," November 4, 2008.
Chass, Murray. "For Cuban Players, Teams Try to Count Runs, Hits and Birthdays," April 27, 1997.
———. "League Presidents out as Baseball Centralizes," September 16, 1999.
———. "Twins Avoid Contraction for 2003 Season," May 30, 2002.
Coleman, Nancy. "Let's Just Say It: God Bless Irving Berlin," July 4, 2019.

Drape, Joe, Ken Belson, and Billy Witz. "Sports Yearning for a Comeback Despite the Risk," April 20, 2020.

Greenhouse, Steven. "Clinton Signs Order Easing Travel, Aid, and Money Transfers between US and Cuba," October 6, 1995.

Jenkins, Lee. "In Choosing Experience, Dodgers Forgo a Chance at History," November 17, 2005.

———. "Randolph Is Named to Lead the Mets," November 4, 2004.

Kepner, Tyler. "Always Be Closing: Brewers See Nine Save Situations a Game," March 7, 2019.

———. "As the Virus Spreads through MLB, So Does the Frustration," August 4, 2020.

———. "Baseball Had Scheduled Its Earliest Opening Day Ever. No Longer," March 13, 2020.

———. "Baseball's Minority Managing Problem," October 29, 2018.

———. "Baseball's Nightmare: One Team, 14 Infections," July 28, 2020.

———. "Bursting at the Seams," March 28, 2019.

———. "A Free Agency Crisis? The Commissioner Scoffs," February 18, 2019.

———. "A Joyous Return to MLB's Ballparks, with a Dose of Wariness," July 3, 2020.

———. "Labor Spat Could Sink Season Just as It's about to Start," May 16, 2020.

———. "Matsui and Yankees Agree to a Deal," December 20, 2002.

———. "MLB Proposes 82-Game Season Starting in July with No Fans," May 12, 2020.

———. "Pitchers Blame MLB for All Those Dingers," July 10, 2019.

———. "The Rays Embrace Their Weirdness, and Success Follows," May 17, 2019.

———. "Rays Win a Wild-Card Matchup of Overachievers," October 3, 2019.

———. "The Silence Breaks: Baseball Must Make Sure Fans' Trust Doesn't," November 15, 2019.

———. "Trying to Build a Better Pitcher," April 7, 2019.

———. "Uncertainty as Far as the Eye Can See," June 29, 2020.

———. "What Could Stop the Season? For One Thing, Money," April 19, 2020.

———. "Yankees May Pay Rodriguez for Home Run Record," November 16, 2007.

Kepner, Tyler, and James Wagner. "Union Chief's Second Chance to Fix the Labor Landscape," July 9, 2019.

Lemire, Joe. "Strikeouts Are Up, Strikes Are Not," July 17, 2019.

———. "Using 'Opener,' Yankees Beat Rays at Their Own Game," May 20, 2019.

Macur, Juliet. "In Testimony, Pettitte Says Clemens Spoke of Drug Use," May 1, 2012.

Powell, Michael. "Astros Crossed the Line from Quaint Con to High-Tech High Crime," January 15, 2020.

———. "Lonely at the Top of the Free Agent Market," January 30, 2019.

———. "Where Are Baseball's Minority Managers," October 27, 2016.

———. "With Managers, Major League Baseball Is Forward in Thinking but Backward in Hiring," October 26, 2015.

Schmidt, Michael S. "Baseball Looks to Create a Possible Portal to Cuba," April 26, 2007.

———. "Drug Test Results from 2003 Could Soon Be in Evidence," May 18, 2008.

———. "Ortiz and Ramirez Said to Be on '03 Doping List," July 30, 2009.

———. "Sosa Is Said to Have Tested Positive in 2003," June 16, 2009.

Shpigel, Ben. "Randolph Says He Is 'Stunned' by Mets Firing," June 18, 2008.

Strauss, Ben. "Stream of Talent Continues to Flow from Cuba, with or without Permission," August 25, 2013.

Wagner, James. "Can Sports Help Heal the Country? Some Have Second Opinions," May 17, 2020.

———. "How the Yankees Became the Hardest-Hitting Team," October 5, 2019.

———. "On Opening Day, a Rarity for MLB: Support for Black Lives Matter," July 23, 2020.

———. "The Power and the Questioned Glory of Baseball's Save State," April 30, 2017.

———. "A Shortened Baseball Season in Trouble before It Even Starts," June 24, 2020.

———. "A Yankee Does His Homework and Now He's at the Top of the Class," August 17, 2019.

———. "The Yankees' Underpaid Superstar," March 28, 2019.

Waldstein, David. "Alex Rodriguez to Retire and Join Yankees as an Adviser," August 7, 2016.
———. "When MLB Broke the Ice with a Game in Havana," March 20, 2016.
———. "Sold on Yankees, Masahiro Tanaka Gets $155 Million," January 22, 2014.
Waldstein, David, and Katie Rogers. "Deal to Give Cuban Players an Easy Path to MLB Meets Government Resistance," December 19, 2019.
Waldstein, David, and Michael Tackett. "Citing Trade Laws, Trump Cancels Deal between MLB and Cuban Federation," April 9, 2019.
Wilson, Duff. "Congress Calls on Clemens and 4 Others to Testify," January 5, 2008.
———. "McGwire Offers No Denials at Steroid Hearings," March 18, 2005.
Witz, Billy. "Even Black Colleges Struggle to Draw Black Ballplayers," May 13, 2019.
Wong, Edward. "Astros' Ballpark No Longer Enron Field," February 28, 2002.

Wall Street Journal

Costa, Brian. "The Cubs Prove That Tanking Works," November 4, 2016.
Diamond, Jared, and Kejal Vyas. "MLB Prohibits Its Players from Participating in Venezuela's Winter League," August 22, 2019.
Rhoads, Christopher. "Baseball Scout's Ordeal: 13 Years in Cuban Prison," April 24, 2010.

Washington Post

Justice, Richard. "Orioles Leave Cuba with a Win," March 29, 1999.
Sheinin, Dave. "Hot Stove, Cold Shoulder," January 22, 2019.
Svrluga, Barry. "Scherzer's Return Aids Bullpen Even When He's Not Pitching," August 22, 2019.

USA Today

Nightengale, Bob. "It's a Baseball Problem: MLB Redoubles Its Efforts as Sport's Black Population Remains Low," April 16, 2019.
———. "It's Just Getting Worse: MLB's 'Disgusting' Minority Hiring Woes Continue as Job Candidates Shut Out Again," December 4, 2019.
———. "In Firing Dusty Baker, Nationals' Gutless Arrogance on Display," October 20, 2017.
———. "MLB Players Are Furious, Willing to Strike over Economic System: 'We're United,'" July 10, 2019.

Other Newspaper articles

Davidoff, Ken. "MLB's Tanking Culture Can Trace Its Roots to 2011 Rule Changes," *New York Post*, February 6, 2019.
Divish, Ryan. "Mariners' ·Contingent of Black Players Will Make Sure Their Voices Are Heard," *Seattle Times*, July 5, 2020.
Elfrink, Tim. "A Miami Clinic Supplies Drugs to Sports' Biggest Names," *Miami New Times*, January 31, 2013.
Grant, Evan. "Changing the Game: Ron Washington and Dusty Baker, Two of Only Three African-American Managers in MLB, Continue to Find Success," *Dallas Morning News*, June 28, 2013.
Healey, Tim. "Marlins Sale Finalized as Derek Jeter Group Officially Takes Over for Jeffrey Loria," *Sun-Sentinel*, October 2, 2017.
Hochman, Benjamin. "Cuban Players Owe Gratitude to Arocha," *St. Louis Post-Dispatch*, April 5, 2016.
Hoornstra, J. P. "Joe Maddon, Angels Innovators of Infield Shifts," *Los Angeles Daily News*, May 18, 2014.

Lennon, David. "The Infield Shift Has Brought MLB's Offensive Numbers Down," *Newsday*, July 5, 2014.

O'Connor, Ian. "Clueless Joe: Torre Has No Idea What He's Getting Into," *New York Daily News*, November 3, 1995.

Ramirez, Deborah. "Special Agent in Charge," *South Florida Sun Sentinel*, March 29, 1998.

Sherman, Joel. "Cheating Black Eye Could Bring MLB and Union Together," *New York Post*, March 7, 2020.

Zielonka, Adam, and David Driver. "Baseball Vexed by Longer Games, Shrinking Attendance," *Washington Times*, May 22, 2019.

Blogs

Bleacher Report (http://www.bleacherreport.com)

Chiari, Mike. "Wilson Ramos Kidnapped: MLB Should Prevent Players from Playing Winter Ball," November 11, 2011.

Grant, Ethan. "Boston Red Sox Pay Tribute to Marathon Victims with Touching Ceremony," April 20, 2013.

Kasabian, Paul. "Craig Kimbrel Seeking 6-Year Contract Worth More than $100 Million," December 12, 2018.

Reuter, Joel. "MLB Farm System Rankings: Pre-2018 Spring Training Edition," February 13, 2018.

Rymer, Zachary D. "Andrew Friedman's Baseball Genius, Dodgers Resources Are Dangerous MLB Marriage," October 14, 2014.

Shafer, Jacob. "MLB Free Agents Who May Be Screwed in Search for Big Paydays," January 3, 2018.

Business Insider (http://www.businessinsider.com)

Gaines, Cork. "George Steinbrenner Purchase of the Yankees Paid Off Big Time for His Family," March 25, 2015.

"There's a Revolution Going on in How Baseball Teams Play Defense," May 25, 2012.

ESPN (http://www.espn.com)

"Beisbol Is Booming in Venezuela, but as MLB Teams Flee the Country, Will Its Pro Pipeline Run Dry?" June 30, 2015.

Lapchick, Richard. "MLB Race and Gender Report Card Shows Progress Still Needed," April 18, 2017.

Law, Keith. "2019 MLB Baseball Free Agent Tracker," 2020. (updated regularly)

Rojas, Enrique. "Robinson Opened the Door for Black Hispanics," April 14, 2007.

Fan Graphs (http://www.fangraphs.com)

Edwards, Craig. "Estimated TV Revenues for All 30 MLB Teams," April 25, 2016.

Thurm, Wendy. "Dodgers Send Shock Waves through Local TV Landscape," November 27, 2012.

FiveThirtyEight (http://www.fivethirtyeight.com)

Paine, Neil. "Why Baseball Revived a 60-Year-Old Strategy Designed to Stop Ted Williams," October 13, 2016.

———. "Would the Expos Have Won the 1994 World Series?" October 25, 2019.

Sawchik, Travis. "Don't Worry MLB: Hitters Are Killing the Shift on Their Own," January 17, 2019.

———. "For Decades, Relievers Pitched Better Than Starters. Not Any More," August 22, 2019.

———. "Home Runs Are Soaring; Could Declining Backspin Be a Factor?" September 12, 2019.

———. "Is a 40-Homer Season a Big Deal Anymore?" August 21, 2019.

———. "What's behind MLB's Bizarre Spike in Contract Extensions," April 12, 2019.

MLB.com (http://www.mlb.com)

Adler, David. "Here's Why the Kimbrel Market Has Been So Slow," February 27, 2019.
Berra, Lindsay. "Lat Muscle Injuries in Baseball," May 16, 2017.
Feinsand, Mark. "Play Ball: MLB Announces 2020 Regular Season (Rules and Regulations)," June 24, 2020.
Justice, Richard. "'Selig Rule' First of Its Kind in Sports," August 26, 2013.
Kelly, Matt. "The 10 Largest Contracts in MLB History," March 19, 2019.
Petriello, Mike. "Rays Are Shifting in Ways You've Rarely Seen," May 2, 2019.
Toribio, Juan. "How Arrojo Fulfilled 'Impossible' Dream with Rays," January 14, 2020.

Other Blog Articles

Badler, Ben. "How Will Baseball Handle Big Changes with Cuba?" *Baseball America*, December 18, 2014, https://www.baseballamerica.com/stories/how-will-mlb-handle-big-changes-with-cuba/.
Clavin, Jim. "The Inside Story of Baseball's Grand Tour of 1914." *Smithsonian*, March 21, 2014, https://www.smithsonianmag.com/history/inside-story-baseballs-grand-world-tour-1914-180950228/.
Gough, Christina. "New York Yankees Franchise Value from 2002 to 2019." Statista, April 29, 2020, https://www.statista.com/statistics/194628/mlb-franchise-value-of-the-new-york-yankees-since-2006/.
Hildebrand, Jeff. "Interleague Play: An Attendance Study." *Baseball Prospectus*, December 28, 2004, https://www.baseballprospectus.com/news/article/3689/interleague-play-an-atten-dance-study/.
Hunzinger, Erica. "Major League Baseball Is Trying to Bring More Women into Front Offices and Fields." *All Things Considered*, April 8, 2019, https://www.npr.org/2019/04/08/711169787/major-league-baseball-is-trying-to-bring-more-women-into-game-related-roles.
James, Frank. "Court Rules Law Enforcement Went Too Far in Baseball Steroid Probe." *The Two-Way*, National Public Radio, August 27, 2009, https://www.npr.org/sections/thetwo-way/2009/08/court_rules_fed_cops_went_too.html.
Koichi [Jaered Koichi Croes]. "A History of Japanese Baseball: From Pre-War to Post-War." *Tofugu*, March 26, 2013, https://www.tofugu.com/japan/japanese-baseball-history/.
Lindbergh, Ben. "The Five Trends That Could Define Baseball's Future." *Ringer*, July 19, 2019, https://www.theringer.com/mlb/2019/7/19/20700250/baseball-rarities-become-common-fastball-shift.
Miller, Randy. "Yankees Paying Luxury Tax Again: How It Could Affect Hal Steinbrenner's Spending Moving Forward." NJ.com, November 12, 2019, https://www.nj.com/yankees/2019/11/yankees-paying-luxury-tax-again-what-it-means.html.
Neyer, Rob. "Are Rays' Shifts Redefining Infield Defense," *SBNation*, April 10, 2012, https://www.sbnation.com/2012/4/10/2939078/tampa-bay-rays-joe-maddon-infield-shifts-shifting.
Rothenberg, Matt. "Team Tours of Japan Bridged Cultural Gap following World War II." National Baseball Hall of Fame, https://baseballhall.org/discover-more/stories/short-stops/team-tours-of-japan-bridged-cultural-gap.

Taylor, Brett. "Per Forbes, the Chicago Cubs Are Now Worth $3.1 *BILLION*." *Bleacher Nation*, April 11, 2019, https://www.bleachernation.com/cubs/2019/04/11/per-forbes-the-chicago-cubs-are-now-worth-3-1-billion/.
Tusa, Alfonso. "What Remains of the Venezuelan League." *Hardball Times*, December 4, 2019, https://tht.fangraphs.com/what-remains-of-the-venezuelan-league/.

Other Websites

http://www.ballparksofbaseball.com
http://www.baseball-almanac.com ("Steroid Suspensions in Major League Baseball")
http://www.baseball-reference.com (including the Society for American Baseball Research "Bio Project" and "Team Ownership Histories Project")
http://www.baseballinwartime.com (players who died in military service during World War I)
http://www.mlbplayers.com (website of Major League Baseball Players Association. "MLBPA History")
http://www.mlbtraderumors.com (includes average annual salaries of free agents signed since 2014.)

INDEX

ABOUT THE AUTHOR

Bryan Soderholm-Difatte is the author of *The Golden Era of Major League Baseball: A Time of Transition and Integration* (2015), *America's Game: A History of Major League Baseball through World War II* (2018), *Tumultuous Times in America's Game: From Jackie Robinson's Breakthrough to the War over Free Agency* (2019), and *America's Game in the Wild-Card Era: From Strike to Pandemic* (2021).